SPECIAL PLACES TO STAY

£14.99/$19.95

£14.99/$19.95

£9.99/$14.95

£13.99/$19.95

Credit card orders (free p&p) 01275 464891
www.specialplacestostay.com

In US: credit card orders (800) 243-0495, 9am-5pm EST,
24-hour fax (800) 820-2329 www.globepequot.com

Sixth edition

Published in November 2004
Alastair Sawday Publishing Co. Ltd
The Home Farm Stables,
Barrow Gurney, Bristol BS48 3RW
Tel: +44 (0)1275 464891
Fax: +44 (0)1275 464887
E-mail: info@specialplacestostay.com
Web: www.specialplacestostay.com

The Globe Pequot Press
P.O. Box 480, Guilford,
Connecticut 06437, USA
Tel: +1 203 458 4500
Fax: +1 203 458 4601
E-mail: info@globepequot.com
Web: www.globepequot.com

Design:
Caroline King

Maps & Mapping:
Bartholomew Mapping, a division of
HarperCollins, Glasgow

Printing:
Pims, UK

UK Distribution:
Penguin UK, 80 Strand, London

US Distribution:
The Globe Pequot Press, Guilford,
Connecticut

A catalogue record for this book is available from the British Library.

ISBN 1-901970-47-7

Printed in UK on Revive Silk: 75% de-inked post-consumer waste, 25% mill broke and virgin fibres.

ALASTAIR SAWDAY'S
SPECIAL PLACES TO STAY

BRITISH
HOTELS, INNS
& OTHER PLACES

Contents

Guide entries

Back

Alastair Sawday Publishing

We began by chance, in 1993, seeking a job for a friend. On my desk was a file: a miscellany of handsome old houses in France, some that could provide a bed, and some a meal, to strangers.

I ran a small travel company at the time, taking people off the beaten track; these places were our 'finds'. No chain hotels for us, no tourist restaurants if we could possibly visit old manor houses, farms and châteaux whose owners would breathe new life into our enthusiasm for France.

So Jane set off with a file under her arm and began to turn it into a book. We were then innocent enough to ignore advice and print 'far too many' – 10,000. We sold them all, in six months – and a publishing company was born.

We exhorted readers to enjoy a 'warm welcome, wooden beams, stone walls, good coffee' and nailed our colours firmly to the mast: 'We are not impressed by TVs, mini-bars and trouser-presses'. We urged people to enjoy simplicity and authenticity and railed against the iniquities of corporate travel. Little has changed.

Although there are now more than 25 of us working out here in our rural idyll, publishing about 20 books, we are holding tightly to our original ethos and gradually developing it. Our first priority is to publish the best books in our field and to nourish a reputation for integrity. It is critically important that readers trust our judgement.

Our next priority is to sell them – fortunately they sell themselves, too, such is their reputation for reliability and for providing travellers with memorable experiences and friendships.

However, publishing and selling books is not enough. It raises other questions: what is our impact on the world around us? How do we treat ourselves and other people? Is not a company just people working together with a shared focus? So we have begun to consider our responses to those questions and thus have generated our Ethical Policy.

There is little intrinsically ethical about publishing travel guides, but there are ways in which we can improve. Firstly, we use recycled paper and seek the most eco-friendly printing methods. Secondly, we are promoting local economies and encouraging good work. We seek beauty and are providing an alternative to the corporate culture that has done so much damage. Thirdly, we celebrate the use of locally-sourced and organic food among our owners and have launched a pilot Fine Breakfast scheme in our British B&B guide.

But the way we function as a company matters too. We treat each other with respect and affection. An easy-going but demanding office atmosphere seems to work for us. But for these things to survive we need to engage all the staff, so we are split into three teams: the Green team, the Better Business team and the Charitable Trust team.

Each team meets monthly to advise the company. The Green team uses our annual Environmental Audit as a text and monitors progress. The Better Business team ponders ethical issues such as flexible working, time off in lieu/overtime, and other matters that need a deep airing before decisions are made. The Trust team allocates the small sum that the company gives each year to charities, and raises extra money.

A few examples of our approach to company life: we compost our waste, recycle the recyclable, run a shared car to work, run a car on LPG and another on a mix of recycled cooking oil and diesel, operate a communal organic food ordering system, use organic or local food for our own events, take part in Bike to Work day, use a 'green' electricity supplier, partially bank with Triodos (the ethical bank in Bristol), have a health insurance scheme that encourages alternative therapies, and sequester our carbon emissions.

Especially exciting for us is an imminent move to our own eco offices; they will conserve energy and use little of it. But I have left to the end any mention of our most tangible effort in the ethical field: our Fragile Earth series of books. There are The Little Food Book, The Little Earth Book and The Little Money Book – hugely respected and selling solidly – look out for new titles in the Fragile Earth series.

Perhaps the most vital element in our growing Ethical Policy is the sense of engagement that we all have. It is not only stimulating to be trying to do the right thing, but it is an important perspective for us all at work. And that can only help us to continue to produce beautiful books.

Alastair Sawday

Photo Paul Groom

Acknowledgements

If this book were a tombstone, upon it would be written 'Nicola Crosse fecit'. She has laboured mightily to bring this edition together, for the qualities required are immense and wide-ranging: tact, chutzpah, guile, energy, writing, reading, good taste, kindness, wisdom and 'brio'. Hoteliers are often too busy to bother with a mere guide book, though their livelihood may depend on it. Nicola has charmed and chatted her way to the hearts of many owners – and they were right to be seduced.

In full support has been an Amazon army: Jackie for emotional support, Jo for careful research and a way with words, Ro for logistical help, Julia for general nurturing, Laura for tidying her desk and everybody else for enjoying her peculiarities.

Your job, dear reader, is now to sally forth and brandish this book as you use it.

Alastair Sawday

Series Editor
Alastair Sawday

Editor
Nicola Crosse

Editorial Director
Annie Shillito

Managing Editor
Jackie King

Production Manager
Julia Richardson

Web & IT
Russell Wilkinson, Matt Kenefick

Production
Rachel Coe, Paul Groom, Allys Williams, Ezra Chambers

Copy Editor Jo Boissevain

Editorial
Roanne Finch, Jonathan Mann, Philippa Rogers, Danielle Williams

Sales & Marketing & PR
Siobhan Flynn, Paula Brown, Sarah Bolton

Accounts
Sheila Clifton, Bridget Bishop, Christine Buxton, Jenny Purdy, Sandra Hasell

Writing
Nicola Crosse, Tom Bell, Jo Boissevain, Jackie King

Inspections
Jan Adam, David Ashby, Tom Bell, Gillian Charlton-Meyrick, Nicola Crosse, Jackie King, Vickie MacIver, Aideen Reid, Toby Sawday,

And many thanks to those people who did just a few inspections.

A word from Alastair Sawday

We've reached the English islands at last: the Scillies are here, in the shape of Hell Bay, and so is the inimitable Burgh Island Hotel with its chuntering 'tractor' device to get you there across the tide. (We've long been in the Scottish isles, as you can see from a quick look at the maps.) Our tentacles are reaching into the crevices of British hotellery, where some of the best places are to be found. We have found more special places in London, and have even tracked down a few splendid spa hotels.

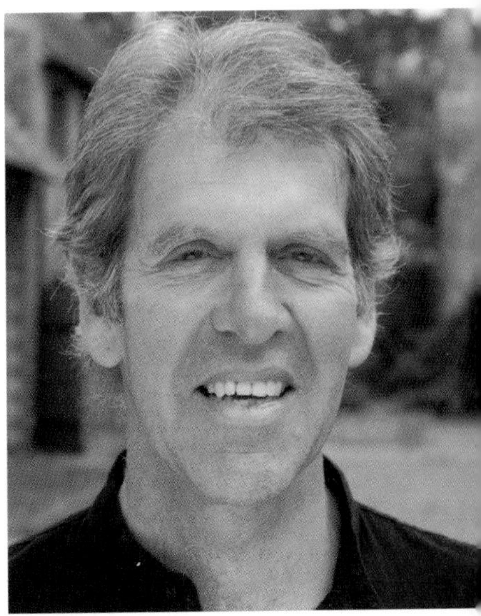

I marvel at the survival of the 'hotel' in its old-fashioned guises, for so many of the assumptions behind them are Edwardian, such as the notion that we all want to be served in our rooms and have uniformed porters opening doors for us. Such phenomena are alien to most of us. However, self esteem is ever in need of service so these hotels continue to flourish, even at huge prices. The chintz has now nearly all gone, but where it is still to be found it is nurtured with devotion and, even, panache.

We began this series determined to be eclectic – and we are still succeeding. There is something for everyone here, except for those seeking food that is a farce and bedrooms that are a tragedy. We look for style, authenticity, fun and imagination in great quantities. And, above all, we revel in introducing you to some fine people, for whom a hotel is a means of giving pleasure and expressing ideas. We also revel in lifting the cover from some wonderful food, more and more frequently home-grown and organic. Bad food is going out of fashion and we will gaily give it a little kick as it makes an exit.

The grim corporate hotels that seemed to threaten our cultural landscape are still out there, but they have inspired a flurry of imaginative and highly individual attempts to provide an alternative. The sheer enterprise of it all is exhilarating.

Alastair Sawday

Photo Paul Groom

Introduction

WE LIKE THE FACT THAT PEOPLE ARE DIFFERENT AND THEY DON'T ALWAYS WANT THE SAME EXPERIENCE

I like hotels. I mean I like staying in them, or having afternoon tea in them, or just sitting downstairs in them watching people come and go. And, if I've chosen wisely, I enjoy shutting the door on whoever has ushered me to my room, knowing that I am the absolute owner of a beautiful space for a while. Running a huge bath filled with every smelly to hand, putting on very loud music, hurling myself into the white goose-down pillows on the bed, opening a bottle of ridiculously priced champagne at tea-time and ringing room service for some nibbles to help it down are all part of the fun for me. I like bath towels to be white, bigger than me and preferably left on the floor, and I like to look at glossy magazines full of impossibly thin and beautiful people just before I have dinner. This is probably why Alastair calls me a sybarite.

He, on the contrary, is proud to be deeply hardy – spurning luxury even – and is well able to cope with flannel-sized towels and very little in the way of soft-furnishing shenanigans. In fact he positively prefers a spartan style. That is his way. And there are others who like the old-fashioned comfort of chintzy bedspreads and a room kettle, some who relish stark minimalism, and a few, mainly men, who don't actually notice their surroundings at all – poor dears.

Then there are children who don't care about the beds as long as they're good for bouncing, dogs who don't want to be left at home, granny who needs a room next to you and young couples who loathe being near any of the above. Business folk will need computer access and a bit of peace and quiet, lustful lovers will not want to leave their room much; yompers with a laminated map will.

Nor do our own needs and wants remain forever static. We know that

Photo Strattons, entry 129
Photo opposite The Lugger Hotel, entry 30

food, where it is sourced, and what it is sprayed with are of deep concern to many these days, but that doesn't mean we want menus to be entirely 'healthy' or to scrap the ketchup entirely from our shopping list. Those of us who are normally happy to slosh down a bottle of 'house' can, given the right dining-room, become wine bores in a trice.

In short, not only are we not the same, we can't even be trusted to stay like that. Which makes choosing somewhere to stay for a night or a weekend a tricky business. For most, time away is hard-earned and expectations are at cloud height so even the slightest setback seems impossibly unfair (and is usually blamed on the person who did the choosing).

This book, used properly, will remove some – if not all – of that risk. It is unashamedly multifarious, happily lacking in brochure speak and entirely unaffected by diamonds or stars. We like it that way because people are different and don't always want the same experience or have the same budget. In these pages you will find swish hotels, cosy inns, restaurants with rooms and some places that refuse to be labelled. Hotels can vary from huge, humming and slick to those with only a few rooms, run by the owners, at their pace. So you may not get room or laundry service or have your bags carried in and out. If these things are important to you then do check when you book: a simple question or two can avoid lamentable misunderstandings.

In some smaller hotels there may be a fixed menu for dinner with very little choice, so if you have any favourite foods or dishes that leave you cold, it's important to say so if you book for dinner. If you decide to stay in a pub do remember that it is likely to be noisy, especially at weekends, and in some remote country places chucking out time can be very late indeed. If you like to be snuggled up in bed early, these are not the places to choose.

Photo above Seaview Hotel and Restaurant, entry 104
Photo opposite Tresanton Hotel, entry 27

Introduction

All these places are special in one way or another. All have been visited and then written about honestly so that you can take what you like and leave the rest.

That old chestnut about not being able to please everybody all the time is only a cliché because it's true. And many hotel guides are as bland as blancmange simply because they ignore this and impose a blanket standard on their readers – a standard that they have devised through a tick-box method of inspection. They then describe the 'winners' with the same hackneyed phrases. Those of you who swear by Sawday books trust our write-ups because we recognise those differences and celebrate them. We include places because we like them – not because of how many H's for hygiene or helipads they score, nor for the amount of 'facilities' flaunted and norms conformed to.

Photo The Felin Fach Griffin, entry 257

Our books are people-led, not standard-fed. This makes for the most eclectic mix between our pages: our owners are artists, designers, cooks, gardeners, photographers, ex-city folk, marketing professionals, furniture restorers, young and enthusiastic, older and more experienced, gay, straight, horsey and happy to shoot anything for the pot, or fiercely urban and politically correct. Oh, and everything in between. All human life is here. There are places in this book that, frankly, I would not choose to stay in. But I know that my mother, who adores huge cabbage roses on chintzy thick curtains, my child, who really appreciates a flat-screen TV and a mountain of video games, or my friend, who happens to be obsessed with art deco, will probably relish the experience. And so we write it like that. Do read between the lines; what we don't say can speak volumes.

Quick Reference Indices

At the back of the book are quick reference indices showing those places that you can stay in for under £100 a night, those that have a garden, places that offer deals during the week or at the weekend, or that are in a particularly peaceful area. So if you are looking for a particularly cheap weekend, in a quiet, leafy, place – look no further.

Maps

Each property is plotted on the map and flagged by an entry number in the section at the beginning of the book. Don't use the maps as anything other than a general guide and a good starting point for planning your trip; use a decent road map for real navigation. Most places will send you detailed instructions once you have booked your stay.

Photo Kingston House, entry 65

Bedrooms

Bedrooms are described as double, twin, suite or single. A double may contain a bed which is anything from 135cm wide to 180cm wide, so check when you book if you cannot bear to sleep pressed up against your beloved. A twin will contain two single beds (usually 90cm wide). A suite is assumed to have either a separate sitting room or a large sitting space in the room. Family rooms can vary in size and quantity of beds so do ask.

Bathrooms

All bedrooms have their own bathrooms unless we say that they don't. If you have your own bathroom but you have to leave the room to get to it we describe it as 'private'. There are very few places in the book that have shared bathrooms and they usually will only be shared between members of the same party – but do check. Or don't check if you like the idea of meeting the person of your dreams in a dash along a corridor.

Prices

We quote the lowest price for a double room in low season to the highest, high season price.

If you are travelling singly but want to 'do a starfish' in a double bed, we quote the price after the double room price.

Half board
The price quoted is per person per night and includes a three-course dinner. A minimum length of stay often applies, so do check.

Meals
Breakfast is included in the room price unless we state otherwise. It will usually be the full monty but sometimes it will be 'continental'. If you are fond of bacon and eggs and prefer to leave a breakfast table with buckled legs and a straining belt then check when booking. Dinner is a fixed price for three, or four, courses without wine and à la carte gives an average price without wine. Occasionally, seating is at one communal table so if you loathe making small talk with strangers eschew these places. (Alastair relishes a shared table because they restore his faith in human nature.)

Closed
When given in months this means the whole of the month.

Symbols
See inside back cover for full list.

Children
Our symbol shows places which are happy to accept children of all ages. This does not, however, mean that they will necessarily have all the equipment that children of today appear to need, or toys or cots, so check when booking. The European habit of breeding quiet, late-eating children seems to work well in France (where they beat their children into behaving well) and Spain and Italy (where they kiss them into behaving well). In England it is different; we tend to dither with any method, preferring in our modest way to spend time perusing self-help parenting books. Which is confusing for the children, the onlookers, and, frankly, the parents. If you dislike the combination of food and children then dinner is going to be a nightmare in a place with a child symbol.

Pets
Our symbol shows places which are happy to accept pets of any age too! It means they can sleep in the bedroom with you, but not on the bed. If you cannot warm to dogs and the delicious aroma of freshly-rolled-in badger muck they can leave on the air, be warned. And this applies also to owners who keep animals, who are marked with a cat symbol (even though it could refer to a parrot, goldfish or a horse).

Payment
Those places that do not accept credit or debit cards are marked with a cash/cheque symbol.

Photo Lake Vyrnwy Hotel, entry 252

Smoking

Oh dear. An emotional subject. Smokers want to smoke, non-smokers want them to stop. It's a stand-off. I wish I could say that I was a virtuous non-smoker. In fact, when I wrote the first draft of this I was, and boy, was I smug! Since then I've had a 'slip' which has become a landslide and now I'm back in the hinterland of knowing I must set another date to stop and adoring every feeble drag I can get in before that time.

Smoking is, to normal people, completely unacceptable, and smelly. Our symbol shows those places where smoking is not allowed anywhere, so proper smokers can avoid them – or stay in them and have frequent tours of the garden with their baccy and a king-sized packet of polo mints.

Photo above The Big Sleep Hotel, entry 244
Photo opposite Hell Bay Hotel, entry 26

Disabled/wheelchair access

The limited mobility symbol shows those places where at least one bedroom and bathroom is available without using stairs. The wheelchair access symbol means there are full and approved wheelchair facilities.

Booking and cancellation

Most places ask for a deposit at the time of booking, either by cheque or credit/debit card. If you cancel – depending on how much notice you give – you can lose all or part of this deposit and sometimes have to pay for rooms not used. Check the exact terms when you book.

Arrivals and departures

Usually your room will be ready by about mid-afternoon and you will have to wave goodbye to it somewhere between 10 and 11am. If you are truly ensconced and cannot bear to be levered out of the room then do say so; sometimes one can pay to linger.

Subscriptions

Owners pay to appear in this guide. Their fee goes towards the high costs of inspecting and producing an all-colour book. We only include places that we like and find special for one reason or another, so it is not possible to buy – or bribe! – your way in.

Regulations

We are not like the tourist board. We do not check such things as fire alarms, swimming pool security or any other regulation with which owners of properties receiving paying guests should comply. This is the responsibility of the owners.

Feedback

We cannot be everywhere at once and things are mercurial in the world of hotels and inns. Do let us know whether your stay has been a roaring success, a miserable failure or anything in between. We do value your comments and always act on them. The accuracy of the book depends on what you, and our inspectors, tell us. So do tell us about new places you have found too.

Photo The Samling, entry 44

Disclaimer

We make no claims to pure objectivity in choosing these places. They are here simply because we like them. We try our utmost to get our facts right but we apologise unreservedly if any errors have sneaked in.

Internet

www.specialplacestostay.com has online pages for all the special places featured here and from all our other lovely books – around 4,500 places to stay in total. There's a searchable database, a snippet of the write-up and colour photos. New kid on the block is our dedicated uk holiday home web site, www.special-escapes.co.uk

And finally

This book is a tribute to all the hard work put in by the managers and owners. They get up early and stay up late and are courteous in between. Some have very few staff to help and others have to manage a huge workforce. I take my hat off to them and hope you enjoy reading about, and staying in, some of these special places.

Nicola Crosse

General Map

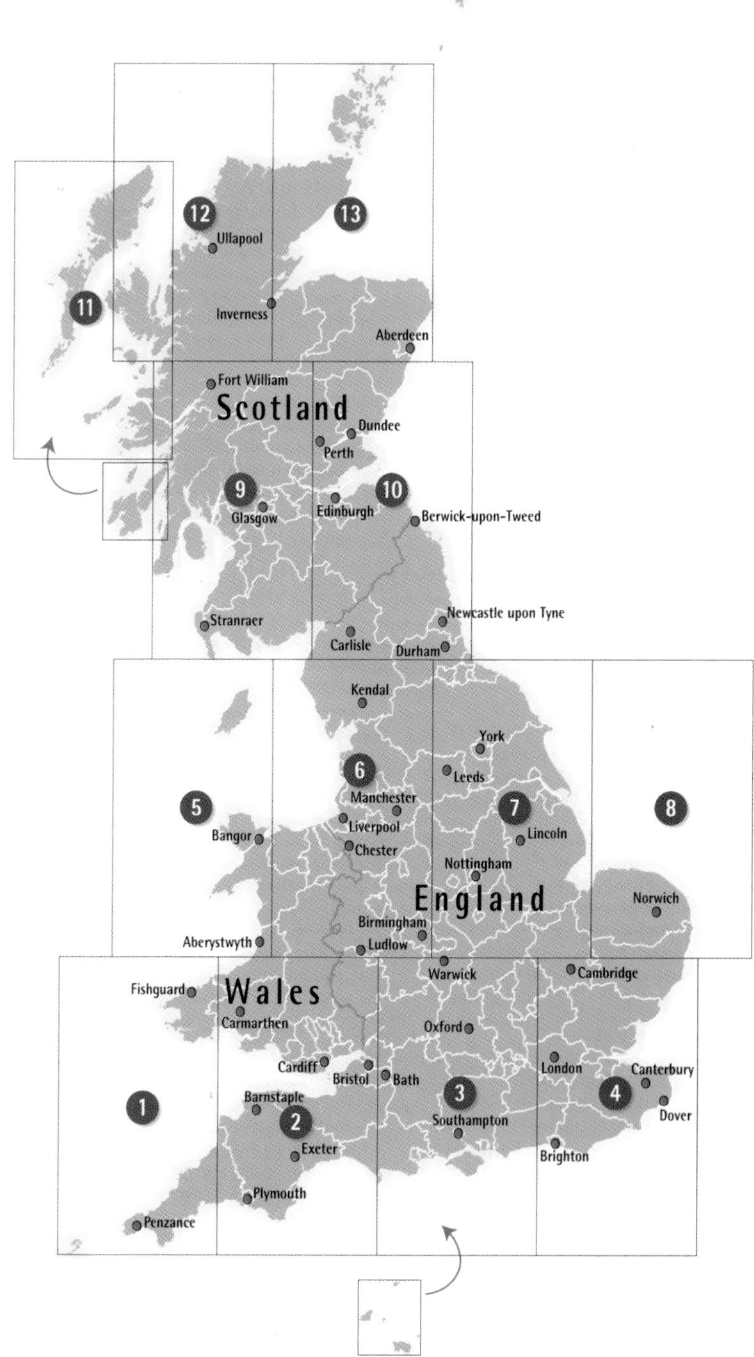
12
13
Ullapool
11
Inverness
Aberdeen
Fort William
Scotland
Dundee
Perth
9
10
Glasgow
Edinburgh
Berwick-upon-Tweed
Stranraer
Newcastle upon Tyne
Carlisle
Durham
Kendal
York
6
Leeds
5
Manchester
7
8
Bangor
Liverpool
Lincoln
Chester
Nottingham
England
Norwich
Birmingham
Aberystwyth
Ludlow
Warwick
Cambridge
Fishguard
Wales
Carmarthen
Oxford
Cardiff
Bristol
Bath
London
Canterbury
3
4
1
Barnstaple
Dover
2
Southampton
Exeter
Brighton
Plymouth
Penzance

Map 1

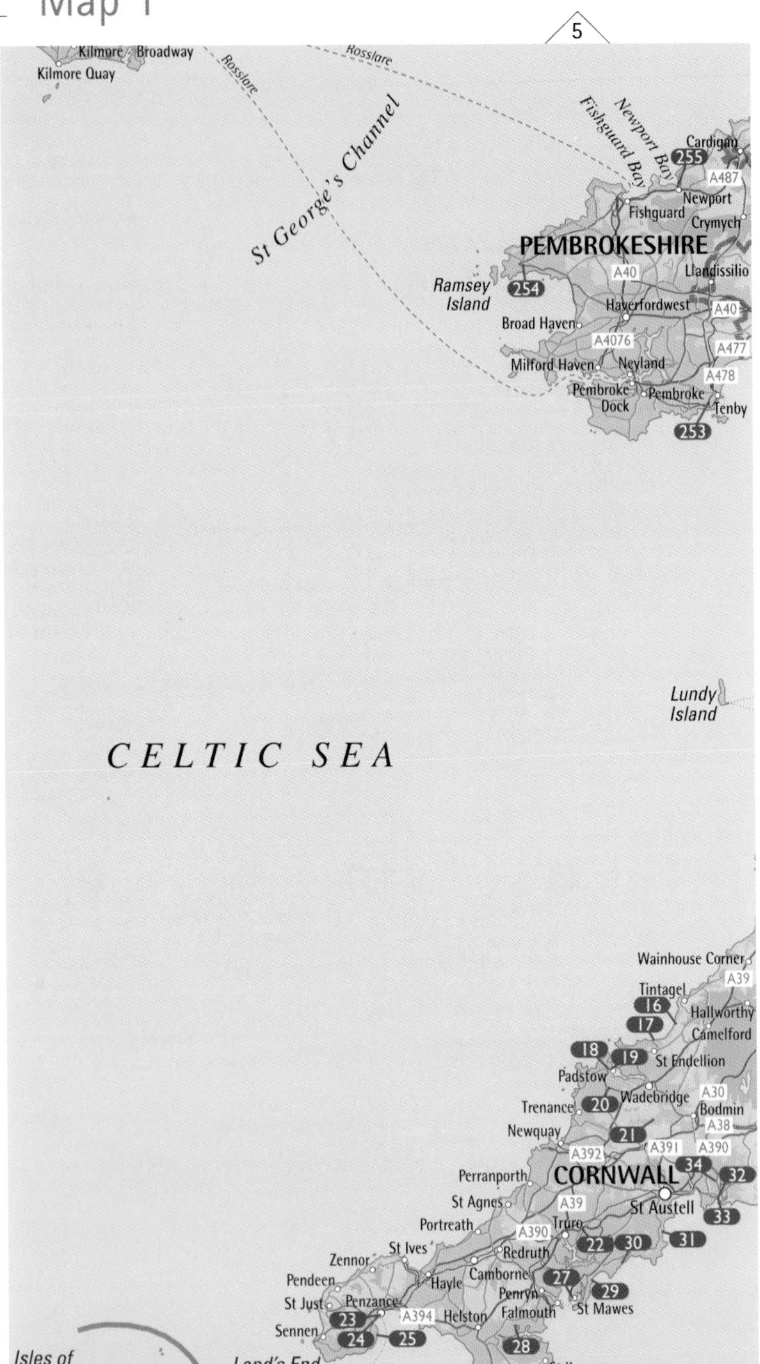

5
Kilmore
Broadway
Kilmore Quay
Rosslare
Rosslare
St George's Channel
Newport Bay
Fishguard Bay
Cardigan
255
A487
Newport
Fishguard
Crymych
PEMBROKESHIRE
A40
Llandissilio
Ramsey Island
254
Haverfordwest
A40
Broad Haven
A4076
A477
Milford Haven
Neyland
A478
Pembroke Dock
Pembroke
Tenby
253
Lundy Island
CELTIC SEA
Wainhouse Corner
A39
Tintagel
16
Hallworthy
17
Camelford
18
19
St Endellion
Padstow
Trenance
20
Wadebridge
A30
Bodmin
A38
Newquay
21
A392
A391
A390
Perranporth
CORNWALL
34
32
St Agnes
A39
St Austell
33
Portreath
Truro
A390
22
30
31
St Ives
Redruth
Zennor
Pendeen
Hayle
Camborne
27
Penryn
29
St Just
Penzance
St Mawes
23
A394
Helston
Falmouth
Sennen
24
25
28
Land's End
St Keverne
Isles of Scilly
26
ISLES OF SCILLY
Hugh Town
Lizard Point
Lizard

Scale 1: 1,400,000

Map 2

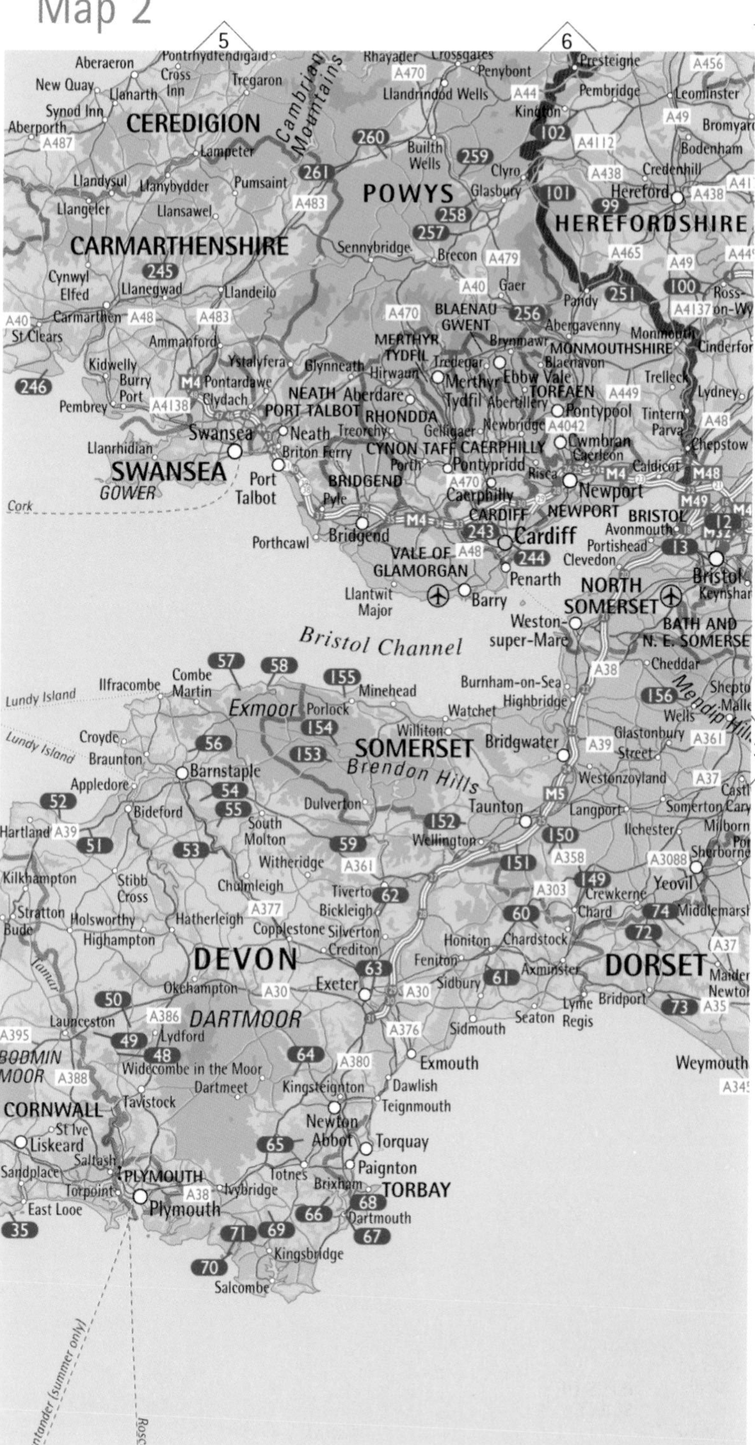

CEREDIGION
POWYS
HEREFORDSHIRE
CARMARTHENSHIRE
SWANSEA
GOWER
Bristol Channel
Exmoor
SOMERSET
Brendon Hills
DEVON
DARTMOOR
DORSET
CORNWALL
TORBAY
Cardiff
Swansea
Bristol
Exeter
Plymouth
Taunton
Barnstaple
Newport

Map 3

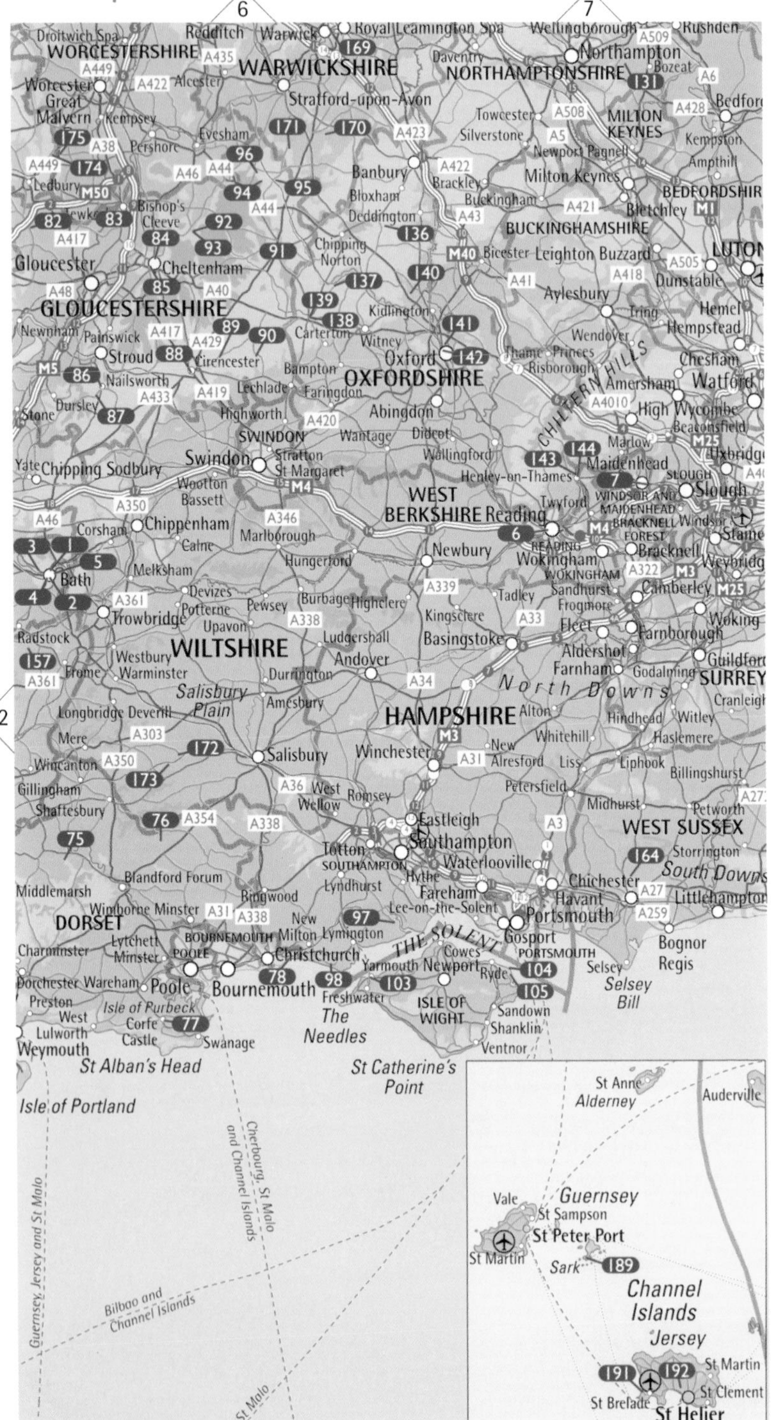
WORCESTERSHIRE
WARWICKSHIRE
NORTHAMPTONSHIRE
MILTON KEYNES
BEDFORDSHIRE
BUCKINGHAMSHIRE
GLOUCESTERSHIRE
OXFORDSHIRE
SWINDON
WEST BERKSHIRE
WILTSHIRE
HAMPSHIRE
SURREY
WEST SUSSEX
DORSET
ISLE OF WIGHT
Worcester
Gloucester
Cheltenham
Stroud
Swindon
Oxford
Banbury
Northampton
Milton Keynes
Aylesbury
Reading
Newbury
Basingstoke
Bath
Trowbridge
Chippenham
Salisbury
Andover
Winchester
Southampton
Portsmouth
Chichester
Bournemouth
Poole
Weymouth
Christchurch
Guildford
Slough
Watford
Luton
Salisbury Plain
North Downs
South Downs
Chiltern Hills
The Solent
The Needles
St Alban's Head
St Catherine's Point
Isle of Portland
Selsey Bill
Guernsey
Alderney
Sark
Jersey
St Peter Port
St Helier
Channel Islands
Cherbourg, St Malo and Channel Islands
Bilbao and Channel Islands
Guernsey, Jersey and St Malo
St Malo

Map 4

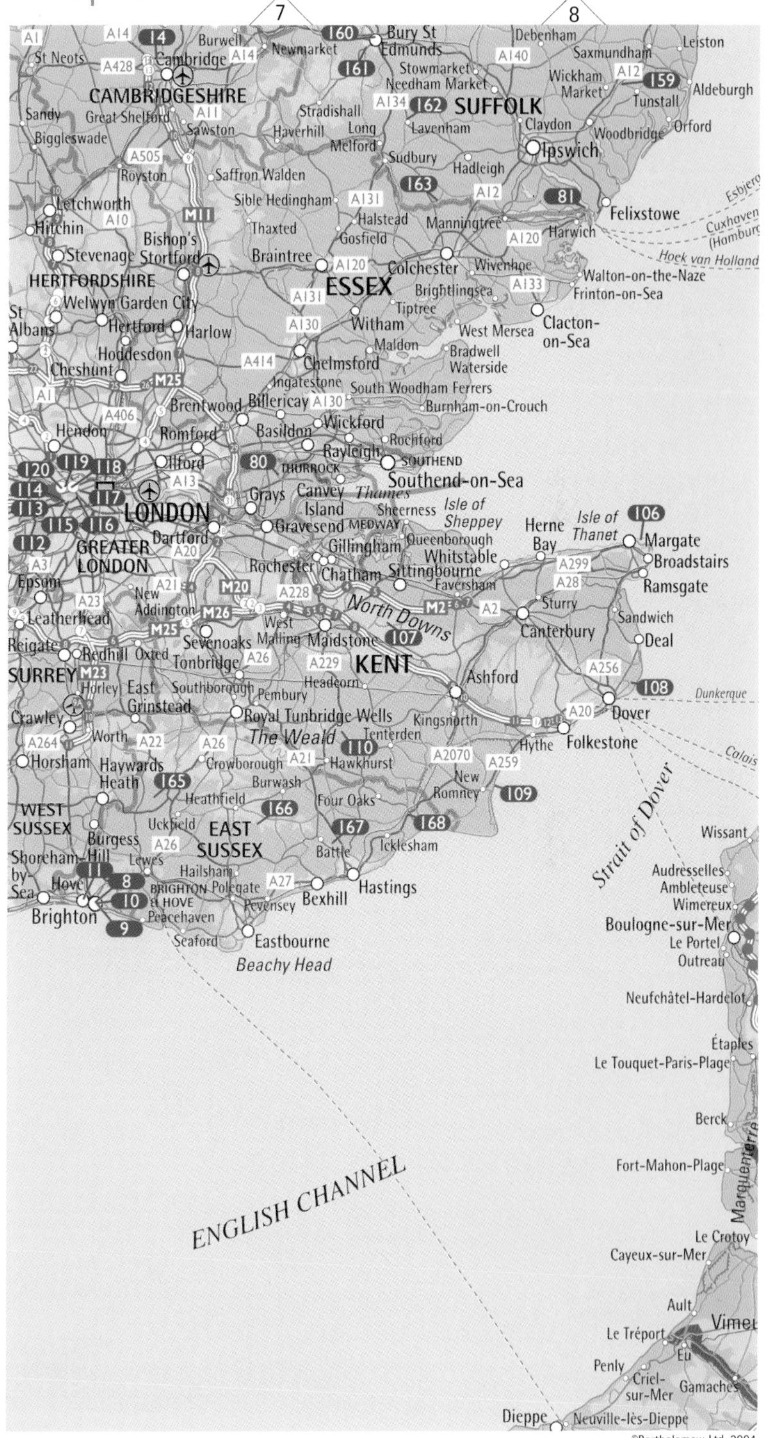

7
8
CAMBRIDGESHIRE
SUFFOLK
HERTFORDSHIRE
ESSEX
LONDON
GREATER LONDON
KENT
SURREY
WEST SUSSEX
EAST SUSSEX
Cambridge
Ipswich
Felixstowe
Harwich
Colchester
Chelmsford
Southend-on-Sea
Canterbury
Dover
Folkestone
Hastings
Eastbourne
Brighton
Beachy Head
ENGLISH CHANNEL
Strait of Dover
Boulogne-sur-Mer
Dieppe

Map 5

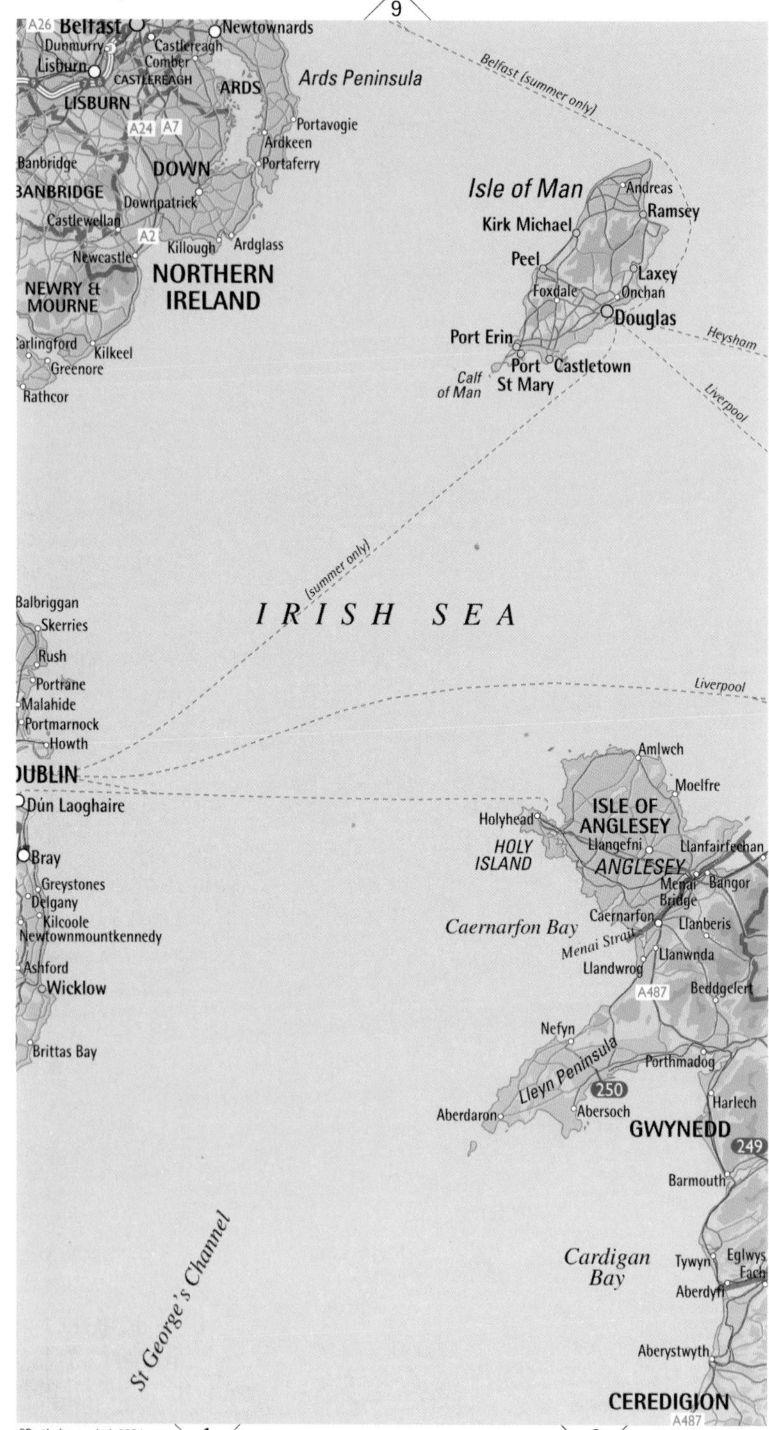
9
Belfast
Newtownards
Dunmurry
Castlereagh
Lisburn
Comber
CASTLEREAGH
ARDS
Ards Peninsula
LISBURN
Belfast (summer only)
A24 A7
Portavogie
Ardkeen
Portaferry
Banbridge
DOWN
BANBRIDGE
Isle of Man
Andreas
Downpatrick
Castlewellan
Ramsey
Kirk Michael
A2
Killough
Ardglass
Newcastle
Peel
NORTHERN
IRELAND
NEWRY &
MOURNE
Laxey
Foxdale
Onchan
Douglas
Heysham
Carlingford
Kilkeel
Port Erin
Greenore
Port
Castletown
Calf of Man
St Mary
Liverpool
Rathcor
(summer only)
Balbriggan
Skerries
IRISH SEA
Rush
Portrane
Liverpool
Malahide
Portmarnock
Howth
Amlwch
DUBLIN
Moelfre
Dún Laoghaire
ISLE OF
Holyhead
ANGLESEY
HOLY
ISLAND
Llangefni
Llanfairfechan
Bray
ANGLESEY
Menai Bridge
Bangor
Greystones
Delgany
Caernarfon
Kilcoole
Caernarfon Bay
Llanberis
Newtownmountkennedy
Menai Strait
Llanwnda
Ashford
Llandwrog
Wicklow
A487
Beddgelert
Nefyn
Brittas Bay
Lleyn Peninsula
Porthmadog
250
Harlech
Aberdaron
Abersoch
GWYNEDD
249
Barmouth
St George's Channel
Cardigan
Bay
Tywyn
Eglwys
Fach
Aberdyfi
Aberystwyth
CEREDIGION
A487
1
2

Map 6

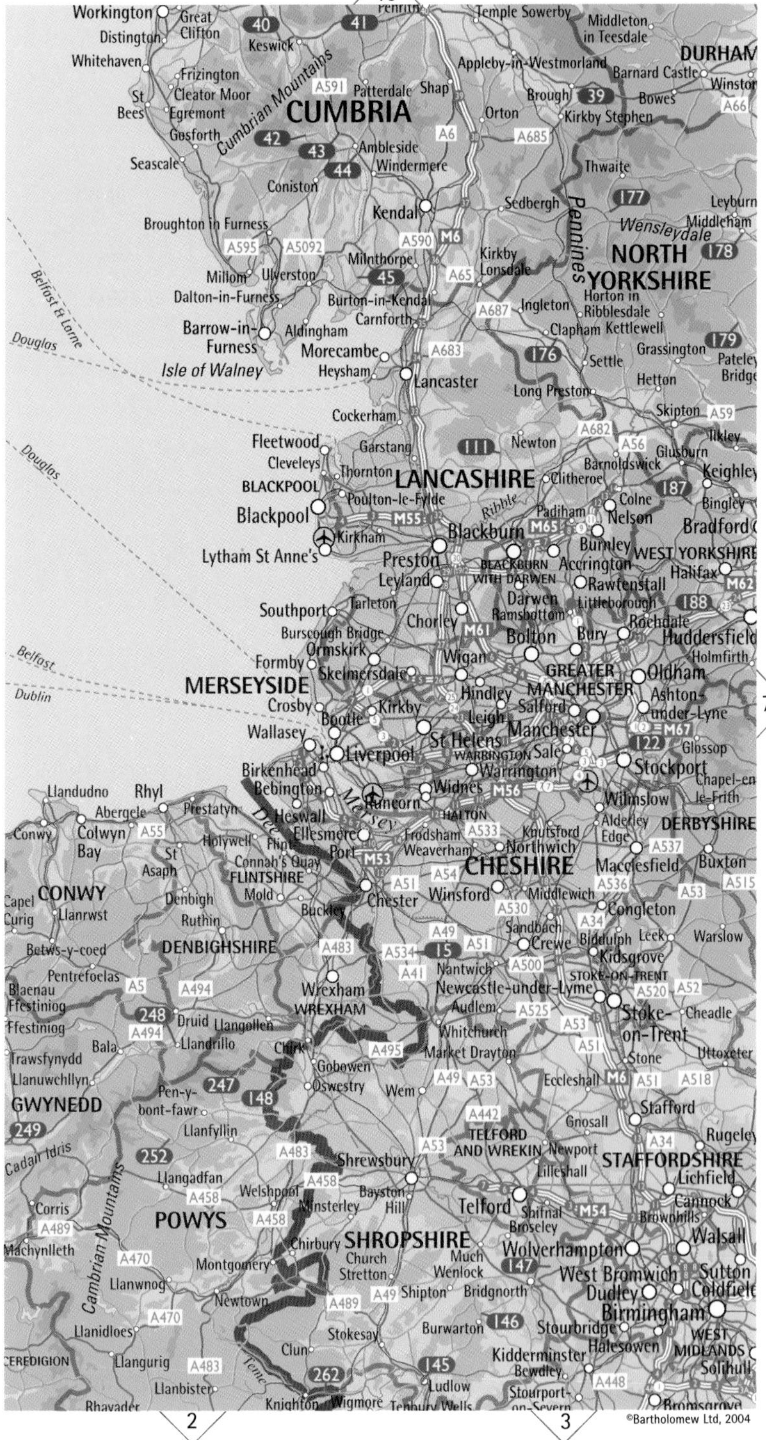
10
Workington
Great Clifton
Distington
Whitehaven
Keswick
Cumbrian Mountains
Frizington
Cleator Moor
St Bees
Egremont
Gosforth
CUMBRIA
Patterdale
Shap
Penrith
Temple Sowerby
Middleton in Teesdale
DURHAM
Appleby-in-Westmorland
Barnard Castle
Winston
Brough
Bowes
Orton
Kirkby Stephen
Ambleside
Windermere
Seascale
Coniston
Thwaite
Kendal
Sedbergh
Pennines
Leyburn
Middleham
Wensleydale
Broughton in Furness
NORTH YORKSHIRE
Milnthorpe
Kirkby Lonsdale
Millom
Ulverston
Dalton-in-Furness
Burton-in-Kendal
Ingleton
Horton in Ribblesdale
Carnforth
Clapham
Kettlewell
Barrow-in-Furness
Aldingham
Belfast & Larne
Douglas
Morecambe
Grassington
Pateley Bridge
Settle
Isle of Walney
Heysham
Lancaster
Hetton
Long Preston
Skipton
Cockerham
Ilkley
Fleetwood
Garstang
Newton
Glusburn
Cleveleys
Thornton
Barnoldswick
Keighley
BLACKPOOL
LANCASHIRE
Clitheroe
Colne
Bingley
Poulton-le-Fylde
Ribble
Padiham
Nelson
Blackpool
Bradford
Kirkham
Blackburn
Burnley
Lytham St Anne's
Preston
BLACKBURN WITH DARWEN
Accrington
WEST YORKSHIRE
Halifax
Leyland
Rawtenstall
Darwen
Southport
Tarleton
Ramsbottom
Littleborough
Burscough Bridge
Chorley
Rochdale
Ormskirk
Bolton
Bury
Huddersfield
Formby
Wigan
Holmfirth
Belfast
Skelmersdale
GREATER MANCHESTER
Oldham
Dublin
MERSEYSIDE
Hindley
Ashton-under-Lyne
Crosby
Kirkby
Salford
7
Bootle
Leigh
Manchester
Wallasey
St Helens
Glossop
Liverpool
WARRINGTON
Sale
Birkenhead
Warrington
Stockport
Chapel-en-le-Frith
Bebington
Widnes
Llandudno
Rhyl
Mersey
Wilmslow
Abergele
Prestatyn
Runcorn
HALTON
Heswall
Dee
Alderley Edge
DERBYSHIRE
Conwy
Colwyn Bay
Holywell
Flint
Ellesmere Port
Frodsham
Knutsford
Northwich
St Asaph
Connah's Quay
Weaverham
CHESHIRE
Macclesfield
Buxton
FLINTSHIRE
Capel Curig
CONWY
Llanrwst
Denbigh
Mold
Chester
Winsford
Middlewich
Ruthin
Buckley
Congleton
Betws-y-coed
DENBIGHSHIRE
Sandbach
Crewe
Biddulph
Leek
Warslow
Pentrefoelas
Nantwich
Kidsgrove
Blaenau Ffestiniog
Wrexham
STOKE-ON-TRENT
Ffestiniog
Druid
Llangollen
WREXHAM
Newcastle-under-Lyme
Audlem
Stoke-on-Trent
Cheadle
Bala
Llandrillo
Whitchurch
Trawsfynydd
Chirk
Market Drayton
Stone
Uttoxeter
Gobowen
Llanuwchllyn
Oswestry
Wem
Eccleshall
GWYNEDD
Pen-y-bont-fawr
Stafford
Llanfyllin
Gnosall
Rugeley
Cadair Idris
TELFORD AND WREKIN
Newport
Shrewsbury
STAFFORDSHIRE
Llangadfan
Lilleshall
Lichfield
Welshpool
Bayston Hill
Corris
Cambrian Mountains
POWYS
Minsterley
Telford
Shifnal
Cannock
Brownhills
Broseley
Machynlleth
Chirbury
SHROPSHIRE
Walsall
Church Stretton
Much Wenlock
Wolverhampton
Montgomery
West Bromwich
Sutton Coldfield
Llanwnog
Shipton
Bridgnorth
Dudley
Newtown
Birmingham
Stokesay
Burwarton
Stourbridge
Llanidloes
Halesowen
WEST MIDLANDS
Clun
Kidderminster
CEREDIGION
Llangurig
Teme
Bewdley
Solihull
Llanbister
Ludlow
Stourport-on-Severn
Rhayader
Knighton
Wigmore
Tenbury Wells
Bromsgrove
2
3
©Bartholomew Ltd, 2004

Map 7

10

6

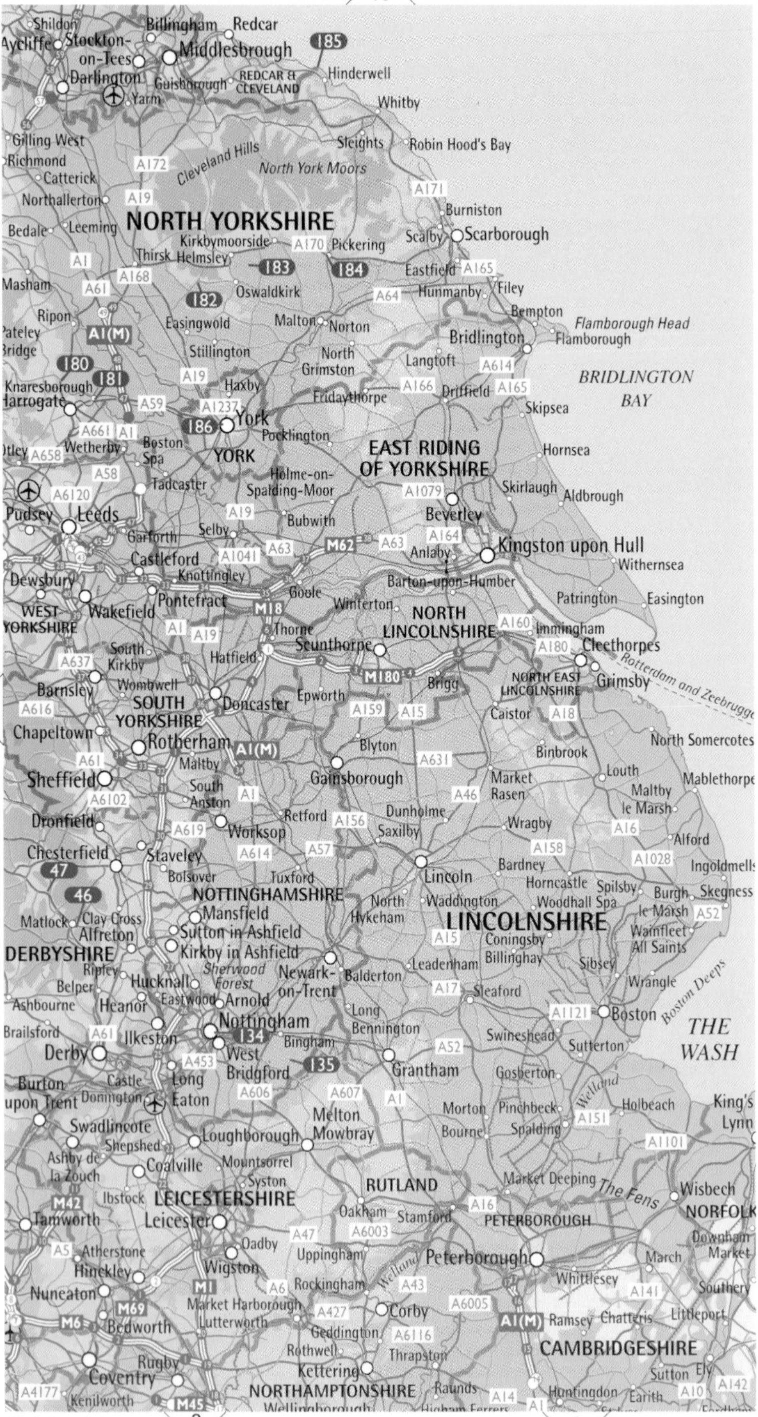

3

4

Map 8

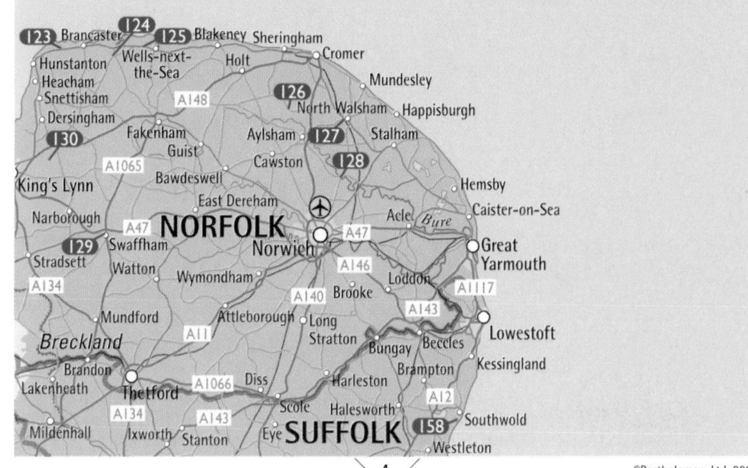

123
Brancaster
124
125
Blakeney
Sheringham
Cromer
Hunstanton
Wells-next-the-Sea
Holt
Heacham
Mundesley
Snettisham
A148
126
North Walsham
Happisburgh
Dersingham
130
Fakenham
Aylsham
127
Stalham
Guist
Cawston
128
A1065
King's Lynn
Bawdeswell
Hemsby
East Dereham
Narborough
Acle
Bure
Caister-on-Sea
A47
NORFOLK
A47
Norwich
Great Yarmouth
129
Swaffham
Stradsett
Watton
A146
Wymondham
Loddon
A134
A1117
A140
Brooke
A143
Mundford
Attleborough
Long Stratton
Lowestoft
A11
Breckland
Bungay
Beccles
Brandon
Kessingland
Brampton
Lakenheath
Thetford
A1066
Diss
Harleston
A12
A134
Scole
Halesworth
A143
Southwold
Mildenhall
Ixworth
Stanton
Eye
SUFFOLK
158
Westleton

4

Map 9

12

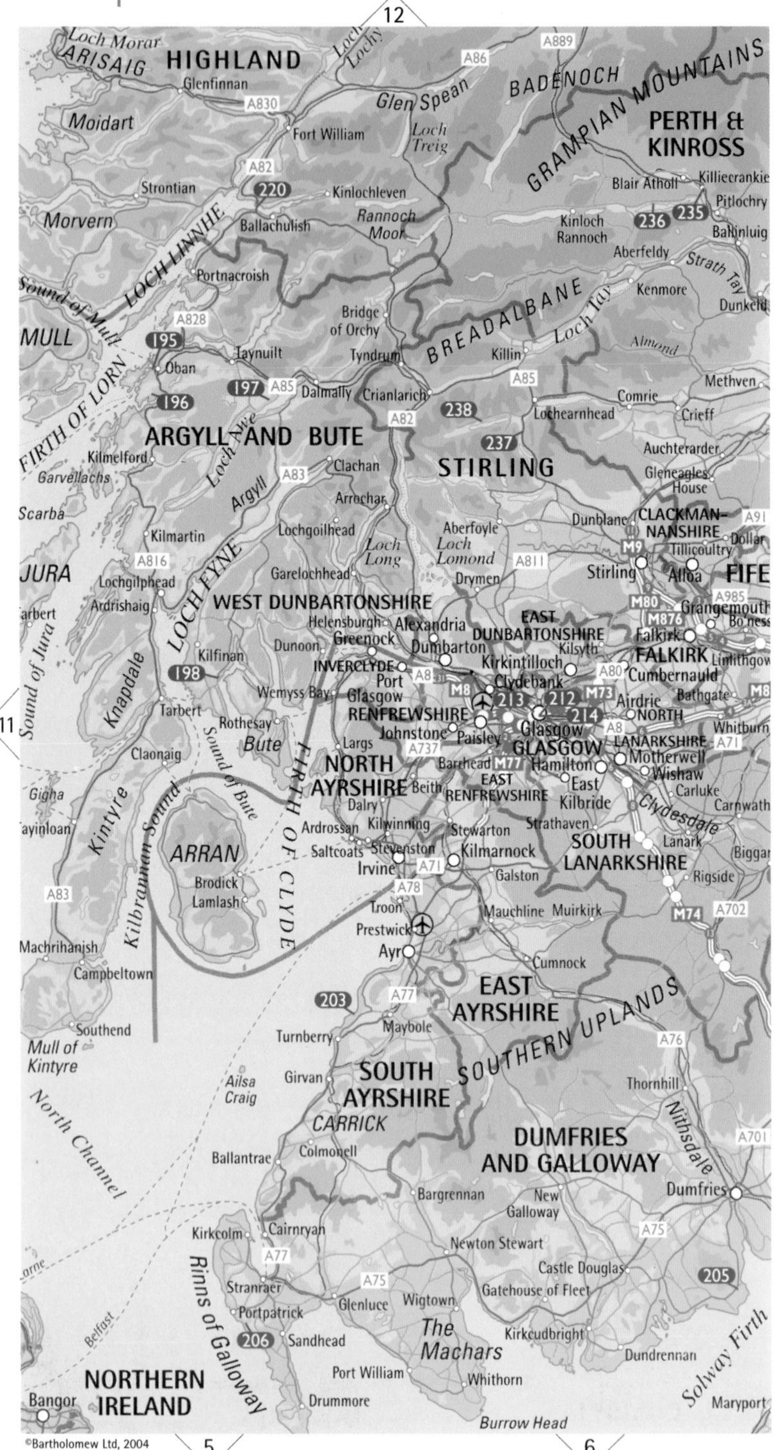
HIGHLAND
Loch Morar
ARISAIG
Glenfinnan
A830
Moidart
Fort William
Glen Spean
Loch Treig
A86
A889
BADENOCH
GRAMPIAN MOUNTAINS
PERTH & KINROSS
A82
220
Strontian
Kinlochleven
Rannoch Moor
Morvern
Ballachulish
LOCH LINNHE
Portnacroish
Blair Atholl
Killiecrankie
Pitlochry
235
236
Kinloch Rannoch
Ballinluig
Aberfeldy
Strath Tay
Kenmore
Dunkeld
BREADALBANE
Loch Tay
Almond
Sound of Mull
MULL
A828
195
Bridge of Orchy
Taynuilt
Oban
Tyndrum
Killin
196
197
A85
Dalmally
Crianlarich
Methven
Comrie
Lochearnhead
Crieff
238
237
FIRTH OF LORN
ARGYLL AND BUTE
Loch Awe
Kilmelford
Garvellachs
Argyll
A83
Clachan
STIRLING
Auchterarder
Gleneagles House
Arrochar
Scarba
Kilmartin
Lochgoilhead
Aberfoyle
Loch Long
Loch Lomond
Dunblane
CLACKMANNANSHIRE
A91
Dollar
M9
Tillicoultry
A816
JURA
Lochgilphead
LOCH FYNE
Garelochhead
Drymen
A811
Stirling
Alloa
FIFE
Tarbert
Ardrishaig
WEST DUNBARTONSHIRE
M80
A985
Grangemouth
Helensburgh
Alexandria
EAST DUNBARTONSHIRE
M876
Bo'ness
Falkirk
Sound of Jura
Knapdale
Kilfinan
Dunoon
Greenock
Dumbarton
Kilsyth
FALKIRK
Linlithgow
INVERCLYDE
Kirkintilloch
198
Port Glasgow
A8
Clydebank
A80
Cumbernauld
Wemyss Bay
M8
213
212
M73
Airdrie
Bathgate
Tarbert
Rothesay
RENFREWSHIRE
214
NORTH LANARKSHIRE
Whitburn
Sound of Bute
Bute
Johnstone
Paisley
Glasgow
Largs
GLASGOW
A71
Claonaig
FIRTH OF CLYDE
NORTH AYRSHIRE
A737
Barrhead
M77
Hamilton
Motherwell
Wishaw
EAST RENFREWSHIRE
East Kilbride
Carluke
Gigha
Beith
Dalry
Clydesdale
Carnwath
Tayinloan
Kintyre
Kilbrannan Sound
ARRAN
Ardrossan
Kilwinning
Stewarton
Strathaven
SOUTH LANARKSHIRE
Lanark
Saltcoats
Stevenston
Kilmarnock
Biggar
Irvine
A71
Galston
Brodick
Lamlash
Rigside
A83
A78
Troon
Mauchline
Muirkirk
M74
A702
Prestwick
Machrihanish
Ayr
Campbeltown
Cumnock
EAST AYRSHIRE
203
A77
Maybole
SOUTHERN UPLANDS
Southend
Mull of Kintyre
Turnberry
A76
Ailsa Craig
Girvan
SOUTH AYRSHIRE
Thornhill
North Channel
CARRICK
Nithsdale
DUMFRIES AND GALLOWAY
A701
Ballantrae
Colmonell
Dumfries
Bargrennan
New Galloway
Kirkcolm
Cairnryan
A75
A77
Newton Stewart
Rinns of Galloway
Castle Douglas
205
Stranraer
A75
Gatehouse of Fleet
Portpatrick
Glenluce
Wigtown
Belfast
206
Sandhead
The Machars
Kirkcudbright
Dundrennan
Solway Firth
NORTHERN IRELAND
Port William
Whithorn
Bangor
Drummore
Maryport
Burrow Head

11

5

6

Map 10

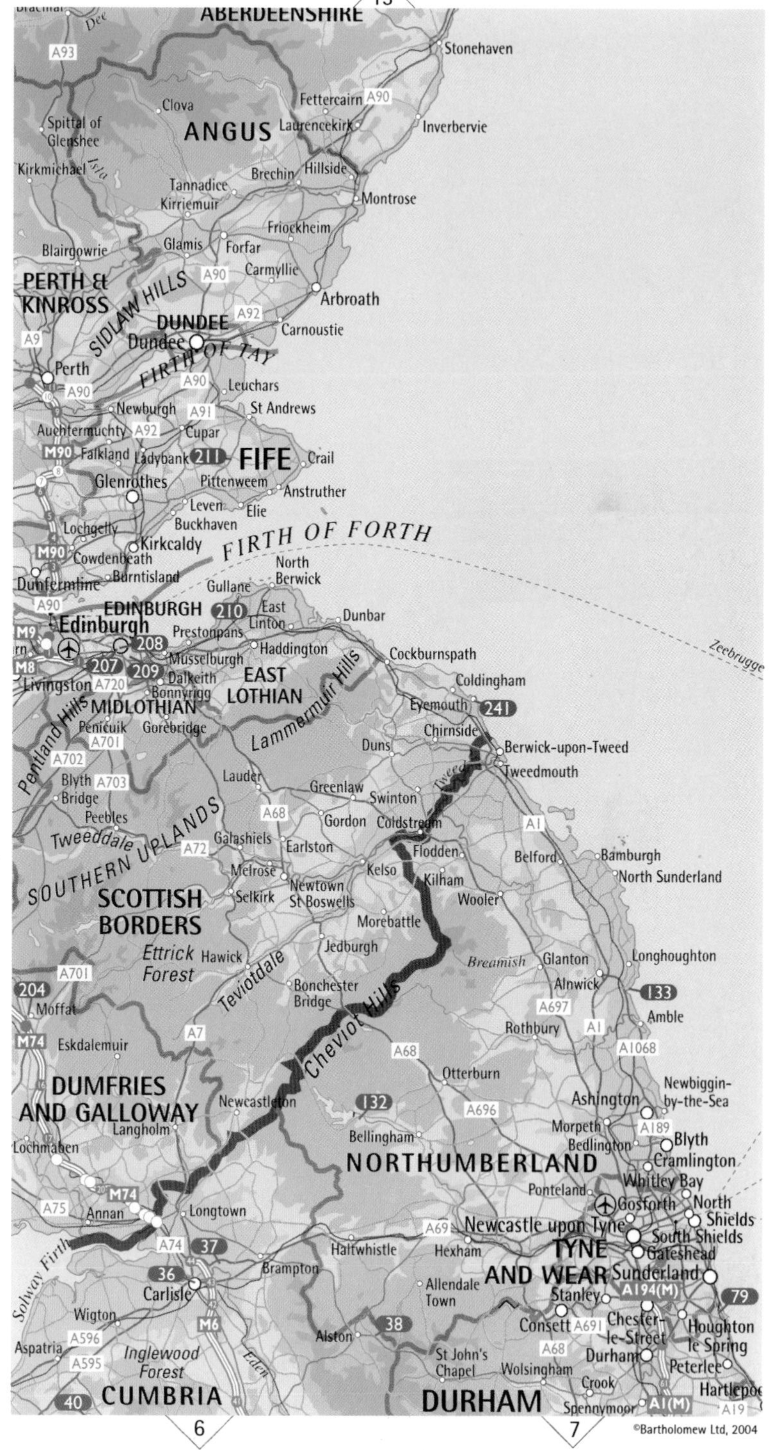
13
ABERDEENSHIRE
Stonehaven
Fettercairn
Inverbervie
Clova
Spittal of Glenshee
ANGUS
Laurencekirk
Kirkmichael
Brechin
Hillside
Tannadice
Kirriemuir
Montrose
Friockheim
Blairgowrie
Glamis
Forfar
Carmyllie
PERTH & KINROSS
SIDLAW HILLS
Arbroath
DUNDEE
Dundee
Carnoustie
FIRTH OF TAY
Perth
Leuchars
Newburgh
St Andrews
Auchtermuchty
Cupar
Falkland
Ladybank
FIFE
Crail
Glenrothes
Pittenweem
Anstruther
Leven
Elie
Buckhaven
Lochgelly
Kirkcaldy
FIRTH OF FORTH
Cowdenbeath
North Berwick
Dunfermline
Burntisland
Gullane
EDINBURGH
East Linton
Dunbar
Edinburgh
Prestonpans
Haddington
Musselburgh
Cockburnspath
Zeebrugge
Livingston
Dalkeith
EAST LOTHIAN
Coldingham
Bonnyrigg
MIDLOTHIAN
Lammermuir Hills
Eyemouth
Penicuik
Gorebridge
Chirnside
Pentland Hills
Duns
Berwick-upon-Tweed
Tweedmouth
Blyth Bridge
Lauder
Greenlaw
Swinton
Tweed
Peebles
Gordon
Coldstream
Tweeddale
Galashiels
Earlston
Flodden
Belford
Bamburgh
SOUTHERN UPLANDS
Melrose
Kelso
North Sunderland
Kilham
Newtown St Boswells
SCOTTISH BORDERS
Selkirk
Wooler
Morebattle
Jedburgh
Ettrick Forest
Hawick
Breamish
Glanton
Longhoughton
Teviotdale
Alnwick
Moffat
Bonchester Bridge
Cheviot Hills
Amble
Rothbury
Eskdalemuir
Otterburn
DUMFRIES AND GALLOWAY
Newcastleton
Newbiggin-by-the-Sea
Ashington
Langholm
Morpeth
Blyth
Bellingham
Bedlington
Lochmaben
NORTHUMBERLAND
Cramlington
Whitley Bay
Ponteland
Gosforth
North Shields
Annan
Longtown
Newcastle upon Tyne
South Shields
Haltwhistle
Hexham
TYNE AND WEAR
Gateshead
Solway Firth
Brampton
Sunderland
Carlisle
Allendale Town
Stanley
Wigton
Consett
Chester-le-Street
Houghton le Spring
Alston
Aspatria
Inglewood Forest
Eden
St John's Chapel
Wolsingham
Durham
Peterlee
Crook
Hartlepool
CUMBRIA
DURHAM
Spennymoor
A93
A90
A92
A9
A91
M90
A720
A701
A702
A703
A68
A72
A7
A74
M74
A75
M6
A596
A595
A1
A697
A1068
A696
A189
A69
A691
A194(M)
A1(M)
A19
M9
M8
211
210
208
207
209
241
204
133
132
37
36
38
79
40
6
7

Map 11

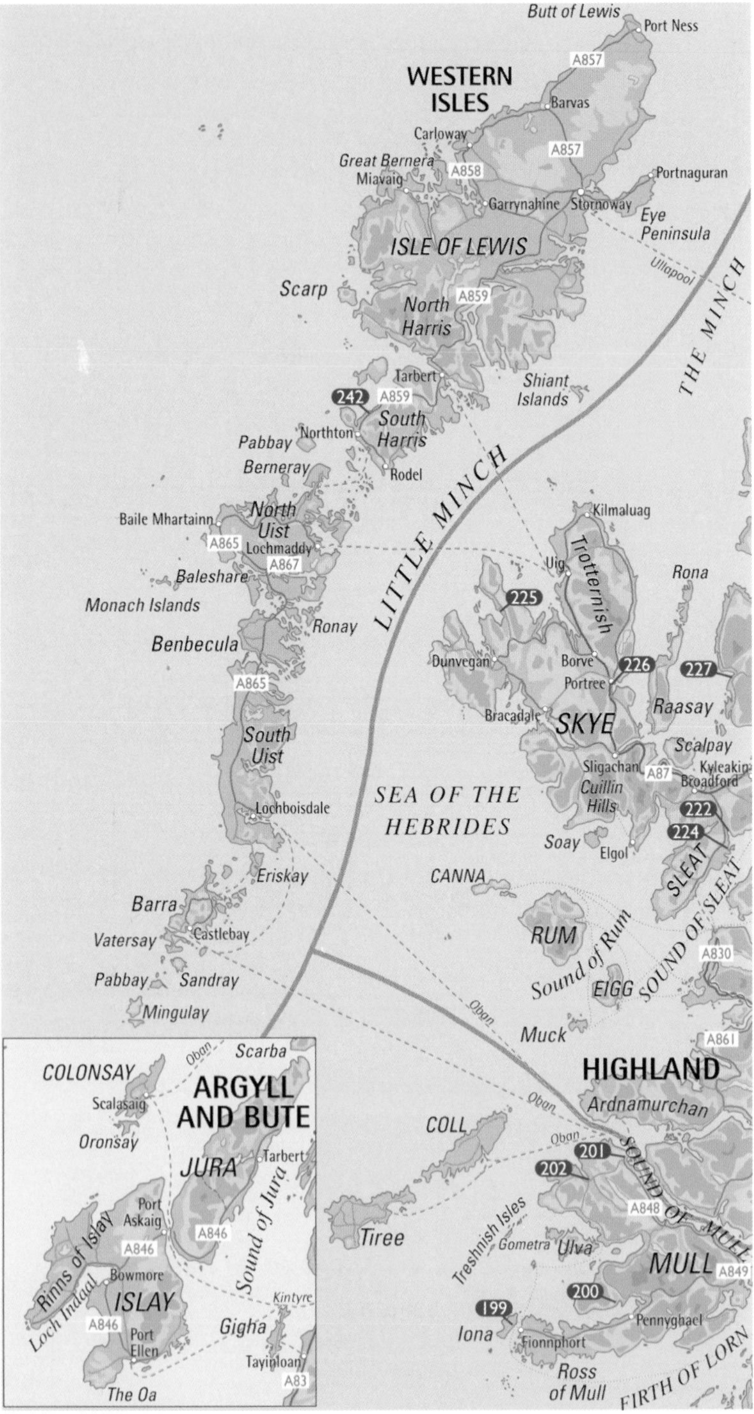

WESTERN ISLES
Butt of Lewis
Port Ness
A857
Barvas
Carloway
A857
Great Bernera
Miavaig
A858
Portnaguran
Garrynahine
Stornoway
Eye Peninsula
ISLE OF LEWIS
Ullapool
Scarp
A859
North Harris
THE MINCH
Tarbert
242
A859
Shiant Islands
South Harris
Pabbay
Northton
Berneray
Rodel
LITTLE MINCH
Baile Mhartainn
North Uist
A865
Lochmaddy
A867
Kilmaluag
Uig
Trotternish
Rona
Baleshare
Monach Islands
225
Ronay
Benbecula
Dunvegan
Borve
226
227
Portree
A865
Raasay
Bracadale
SKYE
South Uist
Scalpay
Sligachan
A87
Kyleakin
Broadford
Cuillin Hills
SEA OF THE HEBRIDES
Lochboisdale
222
224
Soay
Elgol
Eriskay
CANNA
SLEAT
Barra
RUM
Sound of Rum
SOUND OF SLEAT
Vatersay
Castlebay
A830
Pabbay
Sandray
EIGG
Oban
Mingulay
Muck
A861
Oban
HIGHLAND
Oban
Ardnamurchan
COLL
Oban
201
202
SOUND OF MULL
A848
Treshnish Isles
Tiree
Gometra
Ulva
MULL
A849
200
199
Pennyghael
Iona
Fionnphort
Ross of Mull
FIRTH OF LORN

Oban
Scarba
COLONSAY
ARGYLL AND BUTE
Scalasaig
Oronsay
JURA
Tarbert
Port Askaig
A846
Sound of Jura
A846
Rinns of Islay
Bowmore
Loch Indaal
ISLAY
Kintyre
A846
Port Ellen
Gigha
Tayinloan
A83
The Oa

Map 12

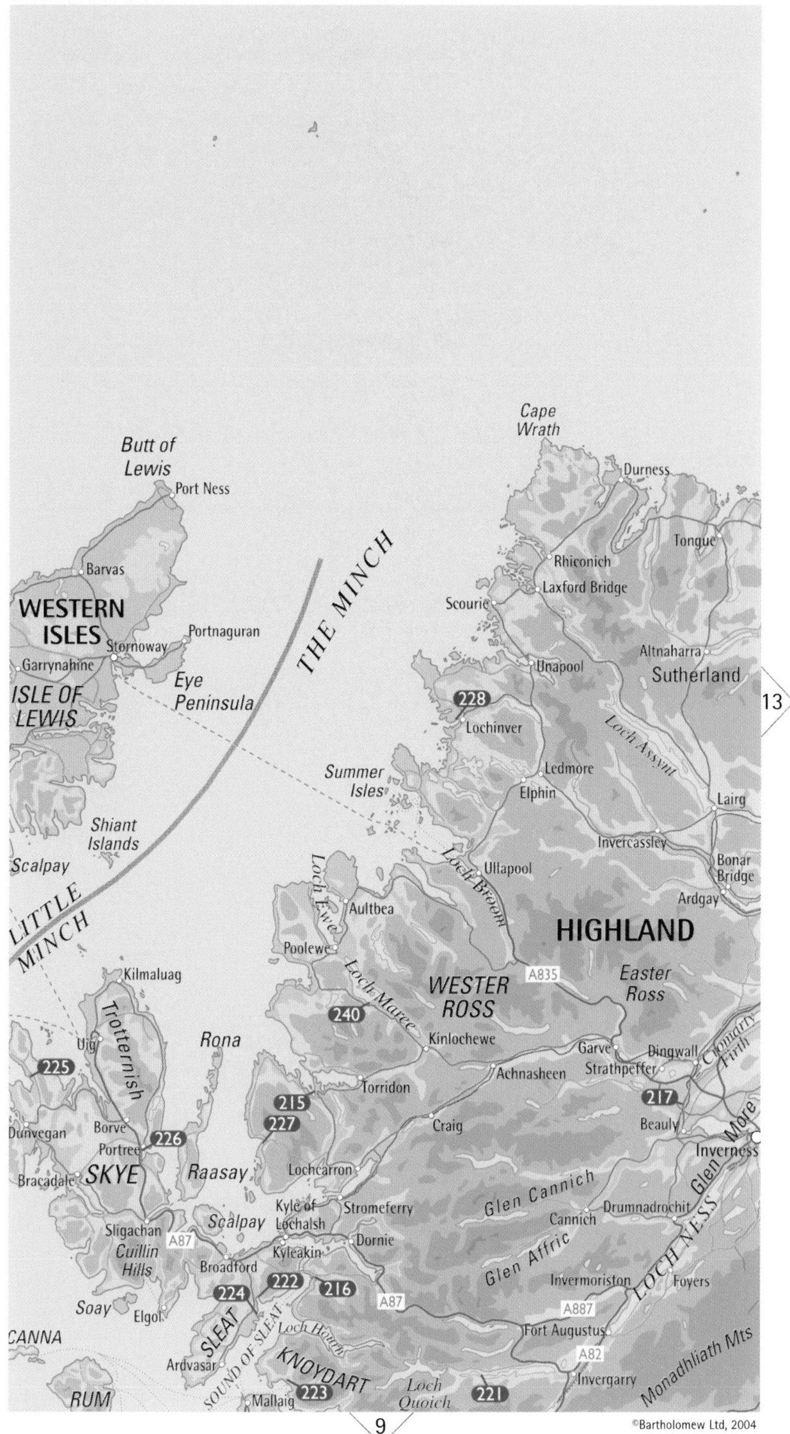

Cape Wrath
Butt of Lewis
Port Ness
Durness
Tongue
Rhiconich
Laxford Bridge
Scourie
Barvas
THE MINCH
WESTERN ISLES
Stornoway
Portnaguran
Garrynahine
ISLE OF LEWIS
Eye Peninsula
Altnaharra
Unapool
Sutherland
13
228
Lochinver
Loch Assynt
Summer Isles
Ledmore
Elphin
Lairg
Shiant Islands
Invercassley
Scalpay
Loch Broom
Ullapool
Bonar Bridge
LITTLE MINCH
Loch Ewe
Aultbea
Ardgay
HIGHLAND
Poolewe
A835
Kilmaluag
WESTER ROSS
Easter Ross
Loch Maree
240
Trotternish
Uig
Rona
Kinlochewe
Garve
Dingwall
Cromarty Firth
225
Achnasheen
Strathpeffer
Torridon
217
215
227
Craig
Beauly
Glen More
Dunvegan
Borve
226
Portree
Inverness
SKYE
Raasay
Lochcarron
Bracadale
Glen Cannich
Kyle of Lochalsh
Stromeferry
Drumnadrochit
Cannich
Sligachan
Scalpay
A87
Dornie
Kyleakin
Cuillin Hills
Broadford
Glen Affric
LOCH NESS
Invermoriston
Foyers
222
216
224
A87
Soay
Elgol
SLEAT
A887
Fort Augustus
CANNA
Loch Hourn
SOUND OF SLEAT
A82
Ardvasar
KNOYDART
Monadhliath Mts
Invergarry
Loch Quoich
RUM
Mallaig
223
221
9

Map 13

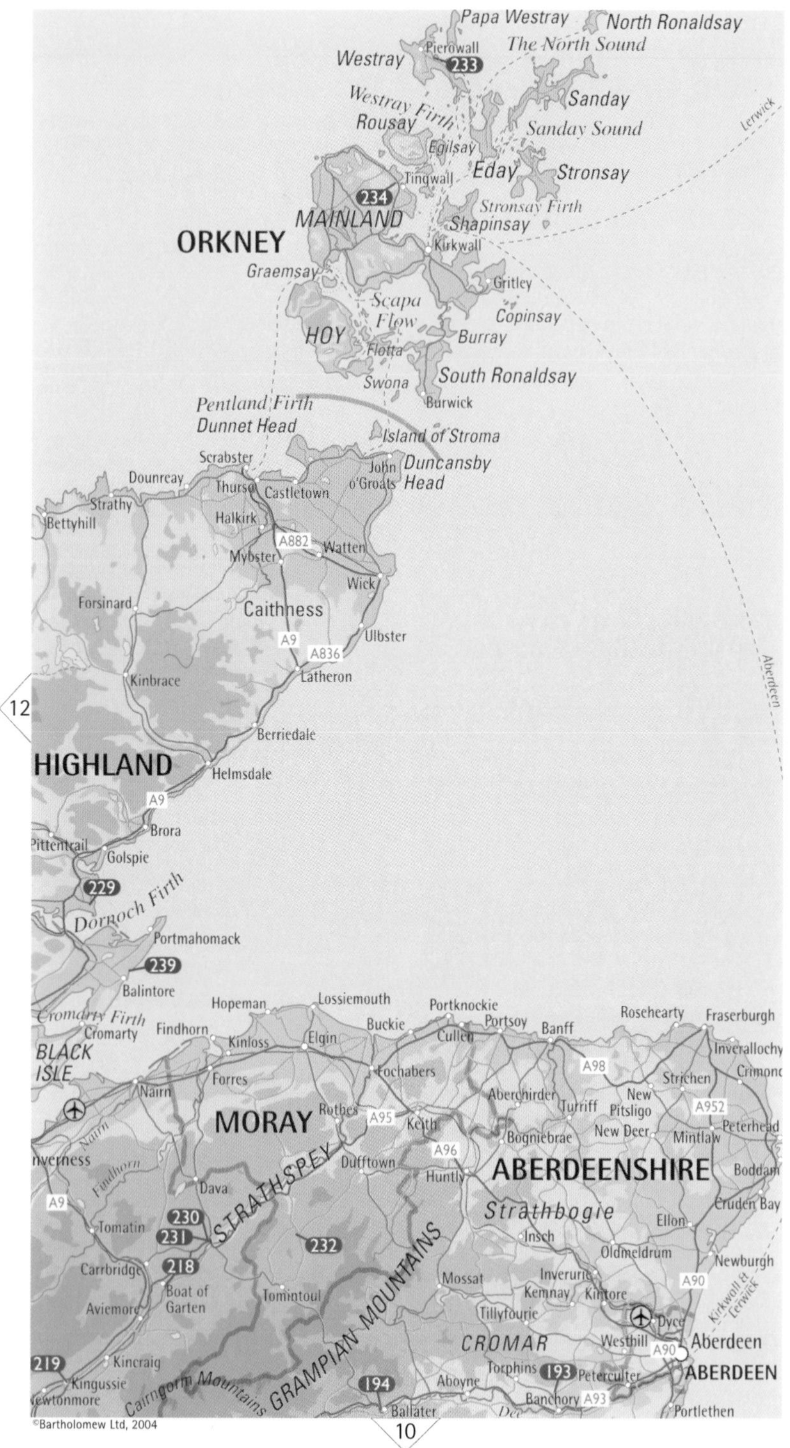

Papa Westray
North Ronaldsay
Pierowall
The North Sound
Westray
233
Westray Firth
Sanday
Rousay
Sanday Sound
Lerwick
Egilsay
Tingwall
Eday
Stronsay
234
Stronsay Firth
MAINLAND
Shapinsay
ORKNEY
Kirkwall
Graemsay
Gritley
Scapa Flow
Copinsay
HOY
Flotta
Burray
Swona
South Ronaldsay
Burwick
Pentland Firth
Dunnet Head
Island of Stroma
Scrabster
John o'Groats
Duncansby Head
Dounreay
Thurso
Castletown
Strathy
Bettyhill
Halkirk
A882
Watten
Mybster
Wick
Forsinard
Caithness
Ulbster
A9
A836
Latheron
Kinbrace
Aberdeen
12
Berriedale
HIGHLAND
Helmsdale
A9
Brora
Golspie
229
Dornoch Firth
Portmahomack
239
Balintore
Hopeman
Lossiemouth
Portknockie
Cromarty Firth
Cromarty
Findhorn
Buckie
Cullen
Portsoy
Banff
Rosehearty
Fraserburgh
BLACK ISLE
Kinloss
Elgin
Inverallochy
Forres
Fochabers
A98
Strichen
Nairn
Aberchirder
New Pitsligo
Turriff
A952
MORAY
Rothes
A95
Keith
Bogniebrae
New Deer
Mintlaw
Peterhead
A96
Dufftown
Huntly
ABERDEENSHIRE
Boddam
STRATHSPEY
Dava
Strathbogie
Cruden Bay
A9
230
231
Tomatin
Insch
Ellon
232
Oldmeldrum
Newburgh
Carrbridge
218
Boat of Garten
Mossat
Inverurie
A90
Kemnay
Kintore
Aviemore
Tomintoul
GRAMPIAN MOUNTAINS
Tillyfourie
Dyce
Kirkwall & Lerwick
CROMAR
Westhill
Aberdeen
219
Kincraig
A90
Torphins
193
Peterculter
ABERDEEN
Kingussie
Cairngorm Mountains
194
Aboyne
Banchory
A93
Dee
Portlethen
Ballater

10

How to use this book

explanations

❶ county

❷ write up
Written by us.

❸ rooms
Assume rooms are en suite; unless we state otherwise.

❹ price
The price shown is for two people sharing a room. Half-board prices are per person. A price range incorporates room/seasonal differences.

❺ meals
Prices are per person. If breakfast isn't included we give the price.

❻ closed
When given in months, this means for the whole of the named months and the time in between.

❼ directions
Use as a guide and travel with a good map.

❽ type of place
Usually either a hotel, inn or restaurant with rooms.

❾ symbols
see the last page of the book for a fuller explanation:

sample entry

❶ Yorkshire

The Star Inn
Harome, Nr Helmsley, Yorkshire YO62 5JE

❷ You know you've 'hit the jackpot' as soon as you walk into The Star – it ticks over with such modest ease and calm authority. Andrew and Jacquie arrived in 1996, baby daughters Daisy and Tilly not long after, and the Michelin star in 2002. It's been a formidable turnaround given this 14th-century inn had an iffy local reputation when they took over, yet there's no arrogance; the brochure simply says: "He cooks, and she looks after you"… and how! Andrew's food is rooted in Yorkshire tradition, refined with French flair and written in plain English on ever-changing menus: try dressed Whitby crab, beef from two miles away, Ryedale deer, or maybe Theakston ale cake. Fabulous bedrooms, all ultra-modern yet seriously rustic, are just a stroll away. Thatched and 15th-century, Black Eagle Cottage has three suites; the rest of the rooms are in Cross House Lodge, a breathtaking new barn conversion; the largest room has its own snooker table. There's also the Mousey Thompson bar, the roof mural, the deli and the Coffee Loft – just possibly the most enchanting attic in the world. Brilliant.

rooms	11: 6 doubles, 2 double/twins, 3 suites.	❸
price	£120-£195.	❹
meals	Lunch from £3.50. Dinner, à la carte, £25.	❺
closed	Mondays inc Bank Holiday Mondays. Christmas Day.	❻
directions	From Thirsk, A170 towards Scarborough. Through Helmsley, then right, signed Harome. Inn in village.	❼

Inn ❽

Andrew & Jacquie Pern
tel 01439 770397
fax 01439 771833
web www.thestaratharome.co.uk

Map 7 Entry 183

❾

- wheelchair facilities
- easily accessible bedrooms
- all children welcome
- no smoking anywhere
- cash or cheque only
- good vegetarian dinner options
- guests' pets welcome
- owners' pets live here
- pool
- bikes on the premises
- tennis on the premises
- information on local walks

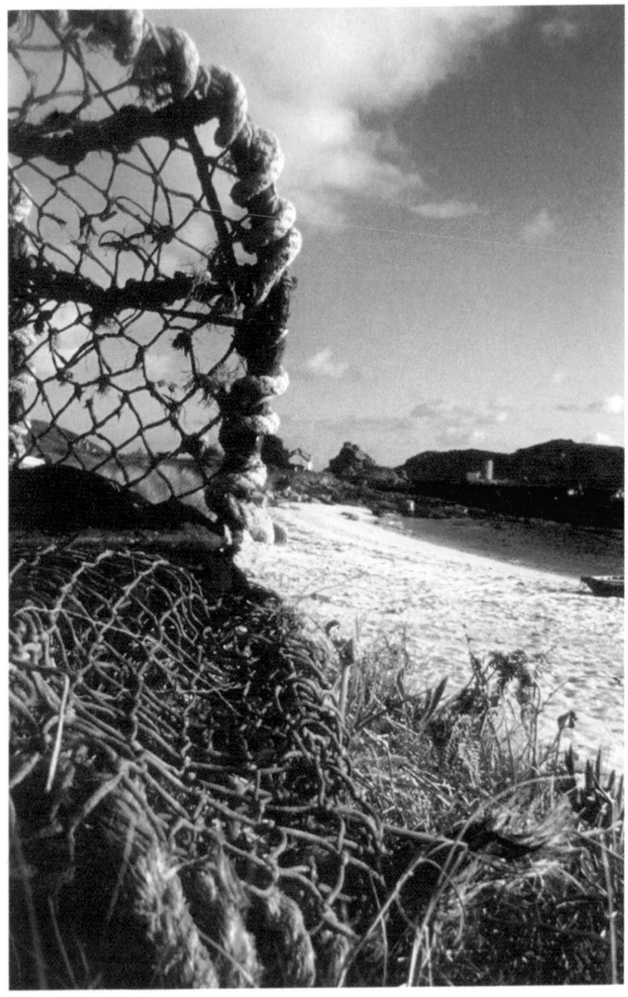

Photography courtesy of the Hell Bay Hotel, entry 26

england

The Queensberry Hotel & Olive Tree Restaurant

Russell Street, Bath, Bath & N.E. Somerset BA1 2QF

The Queensberry is an old favourite, grand but totally unpretentious and immensely enjoyable. It is rare to find a hotel of this size and elegance still in private hands: owners Laurence and Helen are enthusiastic about their new project and their staff just couldn't be nicer. Bedrooms, too, are excellent – contemporary and dramatic, with bold, inspirational colours and huge beds. If you have young children, ask for a room that's reachable by lift, and if you feel like spoiling yourself, have breakfast brought up to you: croissants, orange juice, fresh coffee, warm milk and a newspaper. Then pad around in wonderful white bathrobes feeling like a million dollars. The bath runs in seconds, the shower's a monsoon. At night, pop down to supper – the restaurant is renowned – and when you get back, your bed will have been turned down, your towels refreshed. As for the homemade fudge after supper... wonderful! All this in a John Wood house in the centre of Bath, a minute's walk from the Assembly Rooms, with the luxury of reserved on-street parking.

rooms	29: 26 twins/doubles, 1 four-poster, 2 suites.
price	£100-£195. Suites £175-£285.
meals	Breakfast £9-£14. Lunch £13.50. Dinner £26.50.
closed	Rarely.
directions	Into Bath on A4 London Road to Paragon; 1st right into Lansdown; 2nd left into Bennett Street; 1st right into Russell Street.

Hotel

Laurence & Helen Beere

tel	01225 447928
fax	01225 446065
email	reservations@thequeensberry.co.uk
web	www.thequeensberry.co.uk

Bath Paradise House Hotel

86-88 Holloway, Bath, Bath & N.E. Somerset BA2 4PX

The magical 180-degree panorama from the garden is a dazzling advertisement for Bath: the views draw you out as soon as you enter the house. The Royal Crescent and the Abbey are floodlit at night and in summer hot air balloons float by low enough for you to hear the roar of the burners... Most of the rooms make full use of the view; the best have bay windows and some have jacuzzi baths. All have a soft, luxurious country feel, with drapes, wicker chairs and good bathrooms. There are also two garden rooms in an extension that planners took years to approve – it's a remarkable achievement, in keeping with the original Bath stone house, and David is justly proud. The whole place seems to use glass in all the right places, and the sitting room has lovely stone-arched French windows that pull in the light. Two doors up on Holloway – the old Roman road into this ancient city – is the old Monastery owned by a music teacher; sit outside with afternoon tea and hear the sound of piano music drift gently across the garden. Further away, the occasional peal of bells. *Seven-minute walk down hill to centre.*

rooms	11: 4 doubles, 3 twins, 1 family, 3 four-posters.
price	£75-£155. Singles £55-£95.
meals	Restaurants in Bath.
closed	Christmas.
directions	From train station one-way system to Churchill Bridge. A367 exit from r'bout up hill. After 0.75 miles left at Andrews estate agents. Left down hill into cul-de-sac; on left.

Hotel

	David & Annie Lanz
tel	01225 317723
fax	01225 482005
email	info@paradise-house.co.uk
web	www.paradise-house.co.uk

Apsley House

141 Newbridge Hill, Bath, Bath & N. E. Somerset BA1 3PT

Apsley House takes its name from the Duke of Wellington's main London residence which had the mighty address 'No. 1, London'. The Iron Duke is thought to have built this house; the service today is as exemplary as it was then. Claire and Nicholas took two years to find Apsley but they instantly knew this was the place. The house is full of great antique furniture, a grand piano, porter chairs, gilt mirrors and rich Colefax & Fowler fabrics. Take a drink from the bar, then sink into one of the sofas in the drawing room and gaze out through a huge, arched window to the garden. The dining room shares the same, warm elegance, with fresh flowers on all the tables and thoughtful touches like jugs of iced water at breakfast (which, by the way, is superb). Most of the pretty bedrooms are large: the four-poster in gleaming carved wood is surrounded by pale blue and white drapes, there are more fresh flowers and bathrooms are a good size too. Morning papers are dropped off at your door, your clothes can be laundered, and there's a car park – precious indeed in this city. *Children welcome.*

rooms	10: 3 doubles, 5 twins/doubles, 1 four-poster, 1 family.
price	£75-£160. Singles £60-£100.
meals	Restaurants in Bath. Light supper by arrangement.
closed	Christmas.
directions	A4 west into Bath. Keep right at 1st mini-r'bout. On for 2 miles; follow 'Bristol A4' signs. Pass Total garage on right. At next lights, branch right. On left after 1 mile.

Hotel

Claire & Nicholas Potts

tel	01225 336966
fax	01225 425462
email	info@apsley-house.co.uk
web	www.apsley-house.co.uk

Dorian House

One Upper Oldfield Park, Bath, Bath & N. E. Somerset BA2 3JX

A cellist with a love of interior design is rare enough, but to find one running a hotel just above beautiful Bath is exceptional. Tim is the London Symphony Orchestra's principal cellist and was once taught by the late and great Jacqueline du Pré. Be yourself in the cosy, spoiling luxury of this converted Victorian house that feels more home than hotel. Tim and Kathryn have restored everything inside; the original tiled hallway is lovely. Sit with afternoon tea in deep sofas in the lounge, or enjoy one of six types of champagne in comfortable bedrooms all named after cellists; no surprise that the most impressive – and the most secluded – is du Pré: its huge four-poster bed is reached up a flight of stairs. Every room is decorated with beautiful fabrics and Egyptian linen; those on the first floor are traditional, those on the second and third more contemporary, with oak furniture and sloping ceilings (and four brand-new bathrooms). Tim and Kathryn's art collection is everywhere, gathered from their travels abroad. Relaxation assured, maybe some music, too.

rooms	11: 4 doubles, 3 twins/doubles, 1 family, 3 four-posters.
price	£72-£140. Singles £60-£78.
meals	Restaurants in Bath.
closed	Rarely.
directions	From Bath centre, follow signs to Shepton Mallet to sausage-shaped r'bout, then A37 up hill, 1st right. House 3rd on left, signed.

Hotel

	Kathryn & Tim Hugh
tel	01225 426336
fax	01225 444699
email	info@dorianhouse.co.uk
web	www.dorianhouse.co.uk

The County Hotel

18-19 Pulteney Road, Bath, Bath & N. E. Somerset BA2 4EZ

Maureen and her sister Sandra bought this busy roadside hotel in bustling Bath and dressed the inside in pale creams and lemons with the odd dash of chintz. It is absolutely gleaming and nothing is out of place. Furniture is reproduction but the paintings are original and part of Maureen's art collection. Bedrooms, some smaller than others, are deeply traditional with the occasional piece of French-style white furniture and views over the bowling-green from some. Bathrooms are all a good size and immaculate. There are vases of fresh flowers arranged with flair in the drawing room, reading room and dining room which has a long view over the rugby ground to the Abbey. You will eat well: Maureen arrives at the hotel at 4.45 each morning to start baking the bread and croissants for breakfast, she prefers organic ingredients and eschews the supermarkets. There's a family feel to the County that is downright old fashioned and reassuring; those who don't feel comfortable with stainless steel and smoked glass will settle down happily here. There's plenty of parking but you can walk to everything Bath has to offer.

rooms	22: 18 doubles, 2 twins, 2 singles.
price	£110-£190. Singles £75.
meals	Plenty of restaurants within walking distance.
closed	22 December-8 January.
directions	M4 junc. 18, A46 to Bath. A36 ringroad to Exeter & Wells. Right towards Holbourne Museum & straight over r'bout; 50 yds on right.

Hotel

	Mrs Maureen Kent
tel	01225 425003
email	reservations@county-hotel.co.uk
web	www.county-hotel.co.uk

SACO Serviced Apartments

2-10 Castle Crescent, Coley Hill, Reading, Berkshire RG1 6LZ

The luxury serviced apartment sector is on a roll – and not just for long-stay corporate lets. It's a brilliant, cost-conscious way for anyone to stay in a major city, whether away for work or pleasure – or, indeed, in Reading for graduation week. SACO, its apartments sprinkled from Southampton to Singapore, is one of the sector leaders – you're in professional hands. You get a fast, efficient booking service, secure entry, weekly towel and linen change, a welcome pack. The apartment is modern and open-plan: glide effortlessly from your sitting area – original Victorian features, comfortable modern furniture – to dining area to smart kitchen complete with dishwasher and white china. Bedrooms have crisp bedlinen, red cushions, framed prints; spotless shower rooms come with SACO smellies and Venetian blinds; there's a modem for your laptop, a music centre for your CDs, satellite TV and a safe. You're in a quiet residential area yet the shops and restaurants are only a step away. Windsor and its castle are a short drive, London no distance at all. *Minimum stay three nights. Long stay rates available.*

rooms	23 apartments: 17 for 2 and 6 for 4.
price	£95-£120 + VAT per night.
meals	Plenty of restaurants within walking distance.
closed	Rarely.
directions	10-minute walk from railway station.

Serviced accommodation

Jo Redman
tel 0845 122 0405
email info@sacoapartments.co.uk
web www.sacoapartments.co.uk

Red Roofs at Oldfield

Guards Club Road, Maidenhead, Berkshire SL6 8DN

A dazzling film-set of a house and garden. Built in the 1890s, later home to the Reitlinger Museum and its Egyptian, Persian and Greek artefacts, it now houses Sandy, Colin, a canny collection of Victoriana (if something takes your fancy, you can buy it) and some deeply indulged guests. Bedrooms are packed with gleaming wood, elegant watercolours, vintage fabrics, wooden floors and old knick-knacks; one of the baths has a modesty canopy, and there are fine river views from most. There isn't a reason in the world to feel tense, but just in case you do there's a serious relaxation room for massage, reiki, LaStone therapy and a whole raft of fluffy treatments. The Great Hall with its striking green woodwork and vast windows is a super place to breakfast on local organic sausages and bacon; picnic outside and listen for the swoosh of an oar. The River Thames idles past the bottom of the sweeping lawns and Colin will deliver you by boat to The Waterside at Bray or The Fat Duck for a dinner to die for. How dreamy is that?

rooms	8: 6 doubles, 2 family.
price	From £85. Singles from £70. Family £125.
meals	Available locally.
closed	Christmas.
directions	200 yds off A4 to Maidenhead at Maidenhead Bridge next to River Thames (downstream of bridge).

B&B

Colin & Sandy Brooks
tel 01628 621910
email redroofs.oldfield@virgin.net
web www.maidenhead.net/redroofsatoldfield

brightonwave

10 Madeira Place, Brighton, Brighton & Hove BN2 1TN

In a Regency parade of unremarkable guesthouses, the Victorian, funky and distinctive 'brightonwave'. Come for a fresh blast of sea air – and Shaun, who does everything: designs, cleans, cooks, greets. The feel is stylish but laid back, and friendly. Paintwork is muted, ceiling roses gleam, the guests' sitting room fireplace is sprinkled with white fairy lights, and regular art exhibitions line the walls. There are sober suede banquettes to relax on, a laptop to surf, and minimalist black tables set with white china for tarragon mushrooms on toast (or fresh blueberry pancakes); simpler breakfast may be served in your room, until 10.45 at weekends. Upstairs, fat duvets and lush linen, chocolate bars and flat-screen TVs, a pale metal four-poster (king-size) and balcony in the biggest room. Compact shower rooms have white towels from the Queen's supplier. Everyone's favourite city by the sea teems with shops, restaurants and bars; make the most of Shaun's knowledge of where to go – and have a great time sampling the results. Plans are afoot for pampering weekends and the sea is over the road.

rooms	6: 1 four-poster, 3 doubles, 2 twins/doubles.
price	£70-£180. Minimum stay 2 nights at weekends.
meals	Excellent restaurants nearby.
closed	Rarely.
directions	A23 to Brighton Pier roundabout at seafront; left towards Marina; fifth street on left.

Hotel

	Shaun Trumble & Martin Torrens
tel	01273 676794
fax	01273 608596
email	brightonwave@btconnect.com
web	www.brightonwave.com

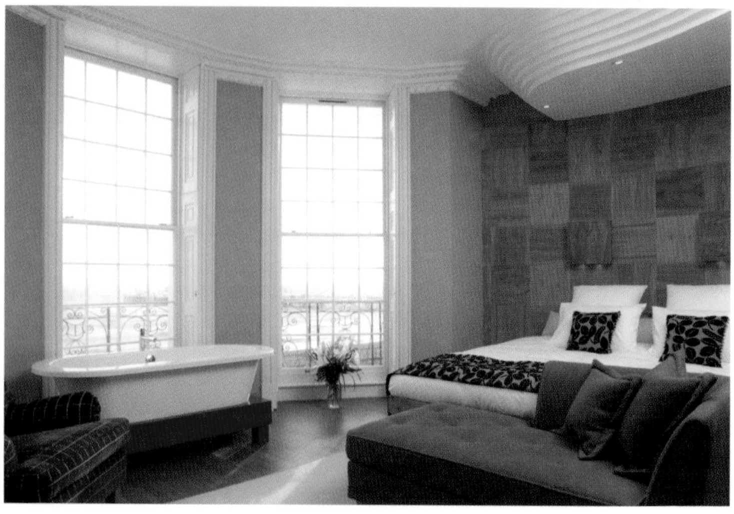

Drakes

43-44 Marine Parade, Brighton, Brighton & Hove BN2 1PE

Two Georgian townhouses facing the sea have been stripped from head to toe to create Brighton's wow-iest retreat. Mixing contemporary opulence with oriental serenity, Drakes is the first in a micro-chain of 'handmade' hotels – designer havens with a splash of individuality. Downstairs a restaurant (sister to Gingerman's) that serves such treats as local Tamworth pig with champ, pear cider and sage – and a lounge, a suave spot for pre-dinner cocktails. Then a sweeping, cantilevered staircase and a vast, dripping chandelier to link the top four floors, the 19 fabulous rooms and the gasp-worthy suite. Half have circular, sea-facing windows, others sit snugly in the attic, all combine a neutral décor with vibrant oriental colour and every little luxury: wireless connections, 'surround sound', DVDs. Staff are classy, friendly and know your needs before even you do, and the attention to detail is brilliant, from the warm pastry and morning paper outside your door to a chauffeured motor for regular guests. Stroll to the boutique-filled Lanes or the famous pier: Regency Brighton bustles at your feet.

rooms	20: 19 doubles, 1 suite.
price	£95-£320. Suite £350-£495. Minimum stay 2 nights at weekends.
meals	Dinner, 2-3 courses, £25-£30.
closed	Rarely.
directions	M23/A23 to Brighton seafront. Keep going until pier is in front of you then left; hotel 300 yds.

Hotel

	Julia Clark
tel	01273 696934
email	info@drakesofbrighton.com
web	www.drakesofbrighton.com

Paskins Town House

18/19 Charlotte Street, Brighton, Brighton & Hove BN2 1AG

Others will soon follow in the steps of Paskins – it has resolutely cast aside ordinariness in favour of its own values. It is neither grand nor chic, fancy nor smart, just easy-going and genuinely 'green' in outlook. And it is yards from the beach. Paint is used to mask some dilapidation inside, the colour schemes can be a little overwhelming and a couple of the singles are tiny, but... others are charming, with the odd four-poster, and all softly colourful, with flowery fabrics and prints, cabaret posters and the odd piece of modern art on the walls. Rambling across two handsome townhouses, the whole place is neat, clean and snug; it's fun, too. The art deco breakfast room is a joy to behold, as is breakfast: tasty tomatoes sprinkled with basil, many varieties of sausage. Vegetarians are treated royally – Paskins claims to serve the best veggie breakfasts on the south coast. All the food is organic where available, from local farms if possible. The coffee is Fair Trade, the smellies are free of the taint of animal testing and you're so close to the centre of things – let the lovely people who work here point the way.

rooms	19: 6 doubles, 2 twins/doubles, 7 singles, 1 triple, 3 four-posters.
price	£60-£125. Singles £30-£40.
meals	Sandwiches £4.20 Restaurants nearby.
closed	Rarely.
directions	M23/A23 to Brighton. Left at seafront roundabout opposite pier. Hotel 13th street on left.

Hotel

	Roger Marlowe
tel	01273 601203
fax	01273 621973
email	welcome@paskins.co.uk
web	www.paskins.co.uk

Claremont House Hotel

13 Second Avenue, Hove, Brighton & Hove BN3 2LL

A prep school during the early part of the last century, this handsome Victorian villa is being gently renovated by its new owners. They're not aiming for opulence, although original 19th-century chandeliers, fireplaces and cornices survive in many rooms and the jazzy black and white entrance steps are worthy of a film set. Russell and Michael are passionate about making guests feel welcome and cared for in their home. They're also seriously keen on food, and no special diet is too much trouble. Fresh, local, seasonal food is cooked here daily and that includes the puddings. You can eat out on the back lawn shaded by mature trees and if you need to get an early start, a breakfast tray is no problem. Flowers – outside and in – smell gorgeous. The whole place feels hugely cared for. High-ceilinged bedrooms have good beds and linen, pristine bathrooms, good showers and little extras. Hove is a classically good spot for all sorts at any time of year with nearby castles, seaside, South Downs and, of course, there's opera at Glyndebourne and the Brighton Festival.

rooms	12: 6 doubles, 5 singles, 1 four-poster.
price	£75-£130. Singles £45-£65.
meals	Dinner £17.50, book ahead.
closed	Rarely.
directions	M23/A23 to Brighton. At seafront r'bout opposite pier, right on A259 Kings Road & Kingsway for 1.5 miles, then right into Second Ave. Hotel near top of road on right.

Hotel

	Russell Brewerton & Michael Reed
tel	01273 735161
fax	01273 735161
email	info@claremonthousehotel.co.uk
web	www.claremonthousehotel.co.uk

Downlands House

33 Henleaze Gardens, Bristol BS9 4HH

A proper old-fashioned, professionally-run guesthouse in a leafy suburb near the beautiful Downs – a few bus stops or 20 minutes walk from the city centre. Mike and Jane trained as hoteliers in Chester, lived for many years in Kenya and the Caribbean then settled in this pretty Victorian villa. Downstairs is cool, neutral, light and sunny with a large drawing room that spills into a conservatory and then a courtyard garden, crammed with climbers and bulging pots. Bedrooms are not swish or luxurious but have everything you need, are freshly painted, scrupulously clean and have good beds with a mix of feather and foam duvets and pillows. Showers rather than baths, wash basins in most rooms (which are numbered) and lots of prints, pictures and family memorabilia. Breakfast is eaten at separate tables in a compact room with a good collection of china and a half door: Mike and Jane will chat to you as they rustle up a full English. Excellent local shops and restaurants and the genuine friendliness of the owners makes this a much better bet than an anonymous city hotel, and jolly good value too.

rooms	8: 4 doubles, 1 twin/double; 2 twins; 1 double with separate shower.
price	£60-£80. Singles £50-£60.
meals	Plenty of restaurants within walking distance.
closed	New Year.
directions	From M5, exit 17 onto A4018. Henleaze Gardens left after passing Badminton Girls School on right (about 3 miles from M5.)

B&B

	Mike & Jane Winterbottom
tel	0117 962 1639
fax	0117 962 1639
email	mjdownlands@blueyonder.co.uk
web	www.downlandshouse.com

The Studio

10 Hensmans Hill, Clifton, Bristol BS8 4PE

A children's clothes factory in fashionable Clifton converted into two houses, a flat, and, on the ground floor, The Studio. Step through a gate in the black iron railings to a gravelled courtyard and blue front door. Walk straight in to a large room with pretty windows, solid wooden flooring and plenty of light. Apart from the small, sparklingly bright, white-tiled bathroom, all is here: along one wall, a line of kitchen cupboards with cool blue/grey fronts, a gas hob with electric oven, microwave, fridge/freezer, washing machine and dishwasher. A stylish Conran table and chairs in checked metal sits in one corner, an easy leather chair in the other. Along the other wall, a firm double bed with pale-wood slatted headboard. That's it! Clifton village life – restaurants, cafés, shops, museums, art galleries and the Suspension Bridge are just up the road, the this is perfect for a graduation stay. For business folk there's modem access and transport to the centre; it's cosy enough for a honeymoon couple and extra special treats can be arranged. *Minimum stay two nights.*

rooms	1 double.
price	From £80; from £350 per week. Singles from £55.
meals	Continental breakfast in fridge.
closed	Rarely.
directions	2-minute walk from Clifton Village. No. 8 bus from Temple Meads station.

Self-Catering

	Anne Malindine
tel	0117 914 9508
fax	0117 914 9508
email	anne@amalindine.freeserve.co.uk
web	www.roseberyhouse.net/studio.html

Hotel Felix

Whitehouse Lane, Huntingdon Road, Cambridge, Cambridgeshire CB3 0LX

Hotel Felix is sleekly up to date, a country house with a modern twist and a mere mile (walk in, taxi back?) from the historic city. Centred around a Victorian villa in three acres, two new bedroom wings have been added at right angles to the original building (just four bedrooms in the old part), thus creating a courtyard with statue and plants in between. Bedrooms are sophisticated and luxurious: huge beds, plump pillows, soft tones, silk fabrics, feather duvets, generously proportioned bathrooms lined in slate or natural stone, hi-tech equipment that supplies CDs and films on demand, and every imaginable 'corporate' extra. Overlooking the pleasant terrace and small gardens is the light, airy, elegant Graffiti restaurant, whose chef draws on the flavoursome approach of mediterranean and Italian cooking... home-smoked salmon with black truffle and celeriac remoulade and russet apple vinaigrette is merely a starter. And there's a Conran-designed health club nearby (with spa) to work off your indulgence – ask for a day pass from reception. Contemporary style without the attitude.

rooms	52 twins/doubles.
price	£163-£270. Singles from £132.
meals	Continental breakfast included; full English £7.50. Bar meals from £4.95. Lunch about £16. Dinner from £27.
closed	Rarely.
directions	A1 north, then A1307/A14 turn-off onto Huntingdon Road into Cambridge. Hotel on left.

Hotel

Shara Ross
tel 01223 277977
fax 01223 277973
email help@hotelfelix.co.uk
web www.hotelfelix.co.uk

Frogg Manor

Fullers Moor, Broxton, Chester, Cheshire CH3 9JH

The fedora-hatted 'Chief Frog' takes full responsibility for the conversion of his sprawling 1758 manor house into eccentrically sumptuous hotel. John Sykes, dynamic, debonair and hands-on, gives you Georgian, Victorian and Edwardian all rolled into one – plus floodlit gardens, 21st-century plumbing and... frogs, living and inanimate, at every turn. If the hotel is named after a previous girlfriend, bedrooms are named after heroes. There's Wellington, dominated by an astonishingly lavish, canopied bed; Nelson, stylish with Regency cabinet and pretty chandelier; elegant Mountbatten with velvety chaise longue; and Brontë, decked in toile de Jouy and tucked under the eaves. Bathrooms flaunt shiny brass showerheads and bedrooms decanters of sherry, along with ironing boards, toiletries and vintage radios that work... extraordinary. After a glass of Scotch in the moody bar, repair to the dining room and 30 main dishes on a menu priced in guineas. Candles and lighting that dims as the evening progresses go well with food more bourgeois than modern British – all of it delicious.

rooms	6: 4 doubles, 1 suite, 1 four-poster.
price	£90-£200. Suite £200. Singles £70-£120. Half-board from £45 p.p.
meals	Breakfast £2-£17 (served 24 hours, Mon-Sat, 9-10.30am Sun). Lunch from £25. Dinner from £31.50.
closed	Rarely.
directions	South from Chester on A41; left onto A534 at r'bout. Pass Frogg Manor on right, 1st right, drive on right.

Hotel

John Sykes

tel	01829 782629
fax	01829 782459
email	info@froggmanorhotel.co.uk
web	www.froggmanorhotel.co.uk

Caradoc of Tregardock

Treligga, Delabole, Cornwall PL33 9ED

Crashing breakers, wheeling gulls, carpets of wild flowers in spring – this place is a dream for artists and a tonic for everyone. Just two fields away from the coastal path, the old farm buildings are set around a grassy courtyard with west-facing patios that catch the setting sun or gathering storm. Some bedrooms look out to sea and all are airy with huge beds, white walls and pretty linen. Caradoc's upstairs drawing room has a magnificent Atlantic view, beams and a woodburner; the farmhouse kitchen with its Rayburn has a large table that seats 12. Janet can stock the fridges with the best of Cornish for breakfast if you prefer to cook your own, and point you to good restaurants, some within walking distance along the cliffpath – or hire a chef for special occasions. Caradoc and the cottage are ideal for extended families and special interest groups – guests have use of the 60-foot studio and the Malaysian Summerhouse – for painting or yoga. There are books, music and videos too if staying in seems like a good idea. *Fully catered painting and yoga holidays available.*

rooms	6 + 1: 4 twins/doubles. Adjoining cottage with 1 double, 1 twin.
price	£70-£130. Singles £40-£65. Self-catering £375-£1,400 p.w. Studio £25 a day.
meals	Picnic £8. Cream tea £6. Dinner with wine, £35; book ahead. Private chef.
closed	Rarely.
directions	South from Delabole; 2 miles right to Treligga; 2nd farm road, signed.

Self-Catering/B&B

Janet Cant
tel 01840 213300
fax 01840 213300
email info@tregardock.com
web www.tregardock.com

The Port Gaverne Hotel

Port Gaverne, Port Isaac, Cornwall PL29 3SQ

Having successfully created the relaxed country house, Polsue Manor on the south coast of Cornwall, Graham and Annabelle have turned their attention to overhauling a seaside hotel on the north coast. It's an exciting challenge and very much work in progress but we're confident they have the flair and eye for detail to turn Port Gaverne into a stylish little enclave. The hotel is an old 17th-century inn set back from the rocky, funnel-shaped Port Gaverne near the pretty fishing village of Port Isaac – it's safe to swim. Bedrooms in the oldest part of the building have beamed character, while those in the modern wing have received the Sylvester treatment, and some have access to a small balcony. Down in the warren-like bar, snug cubby-holes are an ideal place to recuperate with a pint after a hike along the coast, or a stroll up an inland valley – both walks start outside. A wonderful stained-glass sailing rigger leads to the formal restaurant. The food has come on in leaps and bounds since they took over, cooked fresh in a modern English style. Come for the sea and quiet relaxation.

rooms	15: 8 doubles, 2 twins, 4 family, 1 triple.
price	£75-£100. Singles £45-£55.
meals	Bar meals from £4.50. Dinner £25.
closed	January-mid-February.
directions	From Wadebridge, B3314, then B3267 to Port Isaac. There, follow road right to Port Gaverne. Inn up lane from cove on left.

Hotel

	Graham & Annabelle Sylvester
tel	01872 501270
fax	01872 501177
web	www.polsuemanor.co.uk

Tregea Hotel

16-18 High Street, Padstow, Cornwall PL28 8BB

Few places have as much going for them as Padstow: pretty quayside, sandy beaches, slate-hung houses on narrow streets, fish restaurants and sailing bustle. And, at the top of the oldest, quietest part of town, the lovely Tregea Hotel. Overlooking the 13th-century church, Tregea – the 'house on the hill' – has deeds going back to 1693 when it was sold for five shillings... New owners Nick and Cazz Orchard, television actors with an eye for a dramatic setting, give you wonderful bedrooms with town or estuary views, natural colours, modern checks, white linen and a clean, metropolitan feel. There's a big sitting room with an open fire to curl up by in winter, and sofas to lounge on after a day at the beach. From sandy Harbour Cove you can watch boats bob and seagulls wheel; in the evening listen out for the gentle snuffle of the deer from the neighbouring Prideaux Manor estate. At breakfast try the daily fish special for breakfast, caught locally... a rare treat. A friendly, civilised place to stay, wonderfully near the beaches of Daymer and Polzeath.

rooms	12: 8 doubles, 4 twins/doubles.
price	£82-£98.
meals	Priority bookings at Margot's Restaurant, a 5-minute walk.
closed	Rarely.
directions	A389 west to Padstow. Pass turn to centre & docks; right after fire station, for Prideaux Place. 2nd left into Tregirls Lane; immed. right into High St. Hotel 200 yds on left.

Hotel

	Nick Orchard
tel	01841 532455
fax	01841 532542
email	tim@tregea.co.uk
web	www.tregea.co.uk

Number 6

Middle Street, Padstow, Cornwall PL28 8AP

If you dream of the Mediterranean, but don't want to leave the country, pack your bags and head to beatific Number 6. It's the sort of place you'd hope to stumble upon in the back street of an unspoilt fishing village in the south of France. Brenda and Paul came to live by the sea and fulfil the dream. Small, informal and beautifully decorated, it is not a place to come looking for spa baths and room service; it's more about style without pretension. Relax in the light, fresh, almost Bauhaus-style restaurant with its checkerboard floor and eclectic designer décor, or outside in a tiny courtyard full of bamboo, agave, cactus and lights. The restaurant caters for residents only, maybe the occasional local, so book early if you want to eat in. Upstairs, the three bedrooms vary in size but not charm: good beds, the best linen, piles of pillows, beautiful bedspreads, maybe a stainless steel propeller fan – and bathrooms that bring the beach to you, along with well-chosen soaps, oils, shower creams and luxury towels.

rooms	3 doubles.
price	£120-£130.
meals	Dinner from £26.50.
closed	Rarely.
directions	From Wadebridge, A389 west into Padstow. With inner harbour on right, right at T junction, then immediately left. Left into Middle St, 100 yards on right. Drop bags off at door; parking 5-minute walk.

Hotel

Brenda & Paul Harvey

tel	01841 532093
fax	01841 532093
web	www.number6inpadstow.co.uk

Molesworth Manor

Little Petherick, Nr Padstow, Cornwall PL27 7QT

Art, wine and rugby make a refreshing combination at this friendly, down-to-earth old rectory. Geoff and Jessica have given up the London treadmill to bring up their small child in the country, buying this family hotel from her parents; apart from the odd hankering for a curry, and Geoff's beloved London Irish, they haven't looked back, adding their own touches slowly. Both love trawling local galleries and auctions for art and interesting antiques. Geoff is also a modest wine buff with a good cellar; the local Camel Valley vintage isn't bad. The huge drawing room pulls in the morning sun; the music room with log fire blazing suits the evening. A carved staircase – no insert is the same – leads to bedrooms that vary in style and size: two at the front are grand, ones in the eaves are bright and beamed. Three in a converted barn across the courtyard are fabulous. The rectory garden is as you'd expect – mature, well-tended and peaceful. Breakfast in the gorgeous tropical-style conservatory – the freshly-made muffins are superb. You'll eat well in Padstow, too.

rooms	13: 9 doubles; 1 double, 1 twin, 1 family, 1 single all with separate shower or bath.
price	£50-£85. Whole house available.
meals	Restaurants in Padstow.
closed	November-January. Open off-season by arrangement.
directions	Off A389 between Wadebridge & Padstow. Entrance clearly signed; 300 yards from bridge in L. Petherick.

Hotel

Geoff French & Jessica Clarke
tel 01841 540292
email molesworthmanor@aol.com
web www.molesworthmanor.co.uk

Tregawne

Withiel, Bodmin, Cornwall PL30 5NR

Restored with style and multi-starred comfort, the early-18th-century farmhouse sits in a hidden valley overlooking the river Ruthern. There's a meadow for ponies, hills for sheep, a pond, a croquet lawn and a pool you can dine alongside in summer. Antiques, good paintings, tumbling cushions, fresh flowers – country-house elegance at its best. Fun, too, thanks to Peta and David who run it all with unflappable friendliness and love to entertain; delicious, accolade-winning dinners are served at the long oak table. The bedrooms in the main house are big enough to have sofas; gorgeous patterned curtains match padded headboards, walls are sunny yellow, bathrooms seduce with oodles of towels. Two cottages, set slightly apart, have been charmingly converted to provide more rooms for B&B (they're kitted out for self-catering, too). There are art courses in the next village, the Eden Project is a 20-minute drive, and golf courses at St Enodoc and Trevose are within 12 miles. David is a member of both and is delighted to take guests to play.

rooms	8: 6 twins/doubles, 2 twins (for children).
price	£80-£100. Singles £60.
meals	Dinner £27.50. Supper £22.50.
closed	Rarely.
directions	Follow A30 passed Bodmin, over r'bout, right to Withiel. Through Withiel for Wadebridge, right at T-junc. Tregawne 0.25 miles on left.

B&B

Lady Peta Linlithgow & David Jackson

tel	01208 831552
email	tregawne@aol.com
web	www.tregawne.com

Manor Cottage

Tresillian, Truro, Cornwall TR2 4BN

Don't let the slightly shabby exterior of this unpretentious restaurant with rooms put you off – locals break out in nostalgic smiles at the mere mention of the place, their memory jogged by some sublime dish that Carlton once whisked up. This is a small, relaxed operation and everything you come across is the work of either Carlton or Gillian; they painted the yellow walls, polished the wooden floors, hung the big mirror, arranged the flowers and planted the plumbago and passionflower that wander on the stone walls in the conservatory where you eat. Carlton cooks from Thursday to Saturday – the restaurant is closed for the rest of the week, presumably to let him indulge his other talents. He even put in the bathrooms; they're excellent, some with hand-painted tiles. Bedrooms are small but, for their price, superb and full of pretty things. You might have a Heal's of London bed, a hint of art deco or scented candles. Wonderful old farm quilts hang on the banister – grab one and roast away till morning. Noise from the road could disturb those who are not used to it so bring your ear plugs, it's worth it.

rooms	5: 2 doubles; 1 double with separate shower; 1 twin, 1 single sharing shower.
price	£55-£75. Singles £28-£45.
meals	Dinner £29.95; book ahead. Restaurant closed Sun-Wed.
closed	Christmas.
directions	From Truro east A390, for 3 miles. On left when entering village, signed.

Restaurant with Rooms

Carlton Moyle & Gillian Jackson
tel 01872 520212
email man.cott@boltblue.com
web www.manorcottage.com

The Summer House Restaurant with Rooms

Cornwall Terrace, Penzance, Cornwall TR18 4HL

The Summer House is a glittering find: stylish, imaginative, bustling, informal, and so, so colourful. Sunshine yellows and strong Tuscan shades bring a dreamy sense of the Mediterranean to the bustling industry of Penzance. Linda and Ciro, English and Italian respectively, run the place with energy and warmth. Food is a celebration here – dishes are fresh, simple and cooked with flair. Linda describes it as "a gentle meander through Provence and Italy", with fish bought daily from nearby Newlyn market. Clusters of shells decorate tables in the restaurant, local artists' work hangs on the walls. Outside, a walled garden of terracotta pots and swishing palm trees is a magical setting for dinner at night; alfresco breakfasts in good weather are just as good. Unwind on squashy sofas in a drawing room with gothic carvings and exotic houseplants, and chat to other guests – most do. Bedrooms combine beautiful 'collectibles' and family pieces with resourceful dabs of peppermint, or lemon stripe; some look over the garden. Fairytale luxury.

rooms	5: 4 doubles, 1 twin/double.
price	£75-£95. Singles from £70.
meals	Packed lunch from £9.50. Dinner £24.50. Restaurant closed Monday/Tuesday.
closed	December-February.
directions	With sea on left, along harbourside, past open-air pool, then immediate right after Queens Hotel. House 30yds up on left.

Restaurant with Rooms

	Linda & Ciro Zaino
tel	01736 363744
fax	01736 360959
email	reception@summerhouse-cornwall.com
web	www.summerhouse-cornwall.com

Penzance Arts Club

Chapel House, Penzance, Cornwall TR18 4AQ

Amusing, quirky and original... the Arts Club has brought a little fun to old Penzance. Belinda has created an easy-going but vital cultural centre. Fall into bed after a combination of poetry and jazz in the bar – or an intimate meal in the downstairs restaurant. The bar is a riot of paintings, ever-changing as most are for sale. There are fireplaces at either end and comfortable sofas hug an ancient wooden floor that fills with people as the laid-back party atmosphere warms up – it almost invariably does! Presiding over all in his unassuming way is Dave the barman, ready to pour a pint; the local organic beer is superb. Upstairs, charming bedrooms are as flamboyant as the bar is raffish. The house was the Portuguese embassy in the town's more prosperous days – a little garden and balcony off the bar look over the harbour. Not luxurious but good value and one of the most individual places in this book. A must for the open-minded – and for those who dream of waking up to the sound of seagulls.

rooms	7: 2 doubles; 1 double with separate bath; 1 double, 3 family, all with shower, sharing wc.
price	£60-£100. Singles £30-£45.
meals	Lunch & dinner £15-£20. Not Sun, & Mon in winter.
closed	Rarely.
directions	Along harbourside with sea on left. Opp. docks, right into Quay St. Up hill; on right opp. St Mary's Church.

Hotel

	Belinda Rushworth-Lund
tel	01736 363761
fax	01736 363761
email	reception@penzanceartsclub.co.uk
web	www.penzanceartsclub.co.uk

The Cornish Range Restaurant with Rooms

6 Chapel Street, Mousehole, Cornwall TR19 6SB

The Spanish Armada wasn't a complete failure – they sacked Mousehole. Blissfully oblivious, the Range ploughs on with its wonderful fish meals, a beacon in the darkness. The dining room is attractive but unremarkable, with straightforward furniture and a view onto the little street. But there is a bustle and purpose to it, a determination to serve excellent fish straight from the sea. Richard and Chad, old mates and ex-rugby players, are open-minded, keen and clearly enjoying themselves. They've inherited a terrific reputation and some superb bedrooms. Although above the restaurant and with the same limited views, the rooms are beautifully designed, with local handmade furniture. There are fine wooden headboards, cane chairs, wood-and-wrought-iron bedside lights and handsome wooden cupboards – all very striking. Bathrooms are almost as good with local slate, power showers and comfy bathrobes. There's even a garden with subtropical whimsy, a charming and unexpected touch. Mousehole is delightful and the harbourside is only yards away – though parking can be tricky, especially in summer!

rooms	4 doubles.
price	£50-£95.
meals	Dinner, 2 courses, from £20.
closed	Rarely.
directions	In Mousehole follow road along harbour; straight ahead passed Ship Inn. After two sharp bends Cornish Range on right.

Restaurant with Rooms

Richard O'Shea & Chad James

tel 01736 731488

fax 01736 732173

email info@cornishrange.co.uk

web www.cornishrange.com

Hell Bay

Bryher, Isles of Scilly, Cornwall TR23 0PR

Nothing stands between Bryher and America. Stand windswept on the edge of the world as the rollers crash in: the autumn gales are thrilling, and those white summer beaches are a flipflop away from your California-beachhut-style room. Hell Bay is a stylishly simple escape for anyone drawn by remote outposts and the promise of a perfect cocktail. The bedrooms are in separate buildings – elegant and fresh with nautical touches. Bleached wood, stripes, checks and pastel shades, views – from most – of the sea and masses of space, inside and out, for relaxing and for children's clutter. The high-ceilinged Lookout Lounge and bar are comfortable with Lloyd Loom furniture, and the whole place vibrant with works from the Dorrien-Smiths' modern art collection. Come for strawberries and asparagus from local suppliers, lobster and crab from the ocean – all beautifully prepared and presented, with mini dishes for children. Loll by the heated outdoor pool, be pampered by spa and sauna, spot cormorants and seals on an inter-island hop, visit neighbouring island Tresco's world-famous gardens. Special indeed.

rooms	25 suites.
price	Half-board only, £130-£240 p.p. Children in parent's room, £35 (inc. high tea). Under 2s free.
meals	3 course bar meal from £20. Lunch, 2 courses from £15. Dinner included.
closed	January-February.
directions	Ship/helicopter from Penzance, or fly to St Mary's from Bristol, Southampton, Exeter, Newquay or Land's End. Hotel can arrange.

Hotel

	Euan Rodger
tel	01720 422947
fax	01720 423004
email	contactus@hellbay.co.uk
web	www.hellbay.co.uk

Tresanton Hotel

Lower Castle Road, St Mawes, Cornwall TR2 5DR

A carved stone madonna and child guard the entrance from the little road which is all that separates Tresanton from acres of blue sea. A natural hush descends as you walk through the whitewashed opening and into a numinous world of sublime food, perfect service from graceful and intelligent staff, rooms that pretend not to be hotel rooms and modern art that will delight even the most traditional. Mostly large bedrooms come with comfortable bathrooms, simple, neutral colours and the odd stripe of lemon or blue in a blanket, and views – from all but one – of glimmering seas and bobbing boats. The whole point of being here is to unwind and recuperate from the outside world, so sprawl in the gorgeous drawing room with a book from the library, bag a deckchair on one of the terraces or simply stay in bed. Heartier folk have oodles of coastal path to ramble or yachts to sail before dinner is served with a gentle breeze overlooking the ocean or in the elegant dining room. However you decide to whimsy away your time here it will not be wasted and Tresanton will be embedded in your soul.

rooms	29 doubles and family suites.
price	From £220-£365.
meals	Lunch, 3 courses, £26; 2 courses, £20. Dinner, 3 courses, £35.
closed	Rarely.
directions	Drive past 'St Mawes' welcome sign. Right towards St Mawes Castle. Down hill & Tresanton at bottom on left hand side with four palm trees outside.

Hotel

	Olga Polizzi
tel	01326 270055
fax	01326 270053
email	info@tresanton.com
web	www.tresanton.com

Trengilly Wartha Inn

Nancenoy, Constantine, Falmouth, Cornwall TR11 5RP

It's hard to believe the Helford is navigable up to this point, simply because it's hard to navigate a car down the narrow, steep lanes to this deeply rural hideaway. Trengilly started life as a crofter's house before a small bar was added to supplement a previous owner's farming income. The pub has grown organically ever since, winning awards along the way, from 'Pub of the Year' to 'Best Dining Pub in Cornwall'. Expect honourable ales, comfy wooden settles and good meals; *all* the locals come here. Wine is important, too; Nigel knows his grapes, learning much from female wine writers – "better at telling good from bad!" Those wanting a less boisterous atmosphere can eat in a restaurant of conservative pastel colours and families can use a no-smoking conservatory. A small, cosy sitting room away from the buzz of the bar has an open fire and lots of books. Cottage-style bedrooms are well done: those above the bar have more character than quieter ones in an annexe; all bar one have valley views. The stepped garden tumbles down to the river and fills with a happy throng.

rooms	8: 5 doubles, 1 twin, 2 family.
price	£78-£96. Singles £49.
meals	Bar meals £4-£15. Dinner, 2-3 courses, £21.50-£27. Not Christmas Day or New Year's Eve.
closed	Rarely.
directions	Approaching Falmouth on A39, follow signs to Constantine. On approach to village, inn signed left, then right.

Inn

Michael & Helen Maguire
& Nigel & Isabel Logan

tel	01326 340332
fax	01326 341121
email	reception@trengilly.co.uk
web	www.trengilly.co.uk

Driftwood Hotel

Rosevine, Portscatho, Cornwall TR2 5EW

Perfectly positioned, full of curiously vibrant design, and a welcome change from the formula beach hotel. It's said the original owner of this 1930s beach villa wandered all over the Roseland Peninsula looking for the right spot and chose here. The view is wonderful: the sun rises over Nare Head, Portscatho village peeks from a small inlet, and boats criss-cross the bay. Fiona and Paul are relaxed hosts who make the place feel more like home. The refreshing Cape Cod style is clean but not clinical, full of texture, natural colours and light. The restaurant is an expanse of white and wooden floor, with simply-laid tables and driftwood 'fish' on the wall. Food is fresh and often from the sea; the chef has cooked in the best London restaurants. There's a bar with comfy window seats and a lounge with handsome driftwood lamps, luxurious sofas and a log fire. Bedrooms are simply done with neutral fabrics in sand, white and blue; views from the cabin for two are superb. Sit outside on the decked balcony for breakfast and candlelit dinner, or take a hamper to the crescent of private beach – you may see a hairy snail.

rooms	11: 7 doubles, 3 twins, 1 cabin.
price	£150-£200.
meals	Dinner £34.
closed	December & January. Open New Year.
directions	From St Austell, A390 west. Left on B3287 for St Mawes; left at Tregony on A3078 for about 7 miles. Signed left down lane.

Hotel

	Paul & Fiona Robinson
tel	01872 580644
fax	01872 580801
email	info@driftwoodhotel.co.uk
web	www.driftwoodhotel.co.uk

The Lugger Hotel

Portloe, Truro, Cornwall TR2 5RD

The Lugger, dipping its toes in the brine, is tucked tightly in to this tiny, functioning fishing village where old smuggling tales circulate still. Some of the crisply designed bedrooms and bathrooms are not huge but all have excellent beds, vim-white linen, careful lighting, deep baths and showers that aim to flatten you. The elegantly shuttered dining room with high-backed black chairs overlooks the harbour and trumpets fresh Cornish fish and locally caught lobster and crab. There's a modern seaside feel and sunny terraces to eat outdoors, but staff give good old-fashioned service with impeccable manners and Richard is always on hand to make sure everything is just so. Shelves groaning with books and a little spa room for relaxation treatments could herald a lazy break, but great walking straight from the door onto the wild coastal path may tempt you from total idleness. From every room, at every window, the sea can be heard beating out its message – relax, unwind and let the world hurtle on without you for a while. *Reductions for longer stays.*

rooms	21 doubles.
price	£150-£310.
meals	Dinner, 3 course table d'hôte, £37.50.
closed	Rarely.
directions	A390 St Austell to Truro, turn off at B3287 to Tregony. A3078 (St Mawes road); 2 miles on fork left for Portloe; left at T-junc. for Portloe.

	Sheryl & Richard Young
tel	01872 501322
fax	01872 501691
email	office@luggerhotel.com
web	www.luggerhotel.com

Trevalsa Court Hotel

School Hill Road, Mevagissey, Cornwall PL26 6TH

Oh, the stylishness of the place! A slate bar, a leather sofa, a splash of red rug on a parquet floor. Matthew is from east Germany, Klaus is from the west, and Trevalsa Court is their business and hobby rolled into one. It is immaculate, polished, spotless, but not minimalist-modern: there's a whiff of 1930s Berlin here. Bedrooms are luxurious, comfortable and varied – a shapely bed, a Deco lamp, a black and white photograph on an ochre wall. And binoculars in some rooms: the views of sea and coast demand them. Other rooms look to the garden, from which you may wend your way down to the coves and sands of Polstreath Beach. Back to food worth coming home for: two starters, two mains – tomato tartlets, pasta with scallops and sugar snap peas – fresh, caught-that-day, delicious. The dining room has dark wood on wall and floor, starched linen, discreet candles and comfy chairs, and windows through which the sun sets and the moon rises. Klaus and Matthew take an interest in every guest and fill the place with flowers. They have fulfilled their dream; relax and enjoy it.

rooms	14: 8 doubles, 2 twins, 2 singles, 2 suites.
price	£98-£150. Singles £49-£90. Suites £165.
meals	Dinner from £25.
closed	December-January.
directions	From St Austell, B3273 for Mevagissey, for 5.5 miles past beach caravan park; left at top of hill. Over mini-r'bout. On left, signed.

Hotel

Klaus Wagner & Matthew Mainka

tel	01726 842468
fax	01726 844482
email	stay@cornwall-hotel.net
web	www.cornwall-hotel.net

Marina Hotel

Esplanade, Fowey, Cornwall PL23 1HY

Follow the accolades to the Marina Hotel. Tucked into a waterfront street in Fowey, it's obvious why this was a favourite of the Bishop of Truro: some of the most gorgeous river views in Cornwall! You have three buildings in all, some grand marble pillars, and a subtly nautical décor that mixes antique with modern. Every bed is noteworthy, some are spectacular, all supremely comfortable, and most bedrooms have views – watch the boats bob by from your balcony. The new Fo'csle suite looks out over the mouth of the river past a huge sculpture of a whale's tail, the Marina's insignia. If you prefer to self-cater you can – the apartments are perfect for families – but the stripey-awned restaurant is the reason to come – for caught-that-day halibut and in-house lobster, served on Villeroy & Boch. Chef Nick Fisher, ex-Dorchester and Savoy, came to marry a Cornish girl and fulfil a long-held dream, and his dedication to the local and the organic is such that he has been known to go out and catch the fish himself. James's enthusiasm for this place is reflected in a happy supporting team.

rooms	13 + 4: 12 doubles, 1 suite. 4 self-catering apartments for 4.
price	From £134. Singles from £85. Apartments from £130.
meals	Lunch £26. Dinner £34.
closed	Rarely.
directions	Once in Fowey, hotel parking up hill.

Hotel

	James Coggan
tel	01726 833315
email	enquiries@themarinahotel.co.uk
web	www.themarinahotel.co.uk

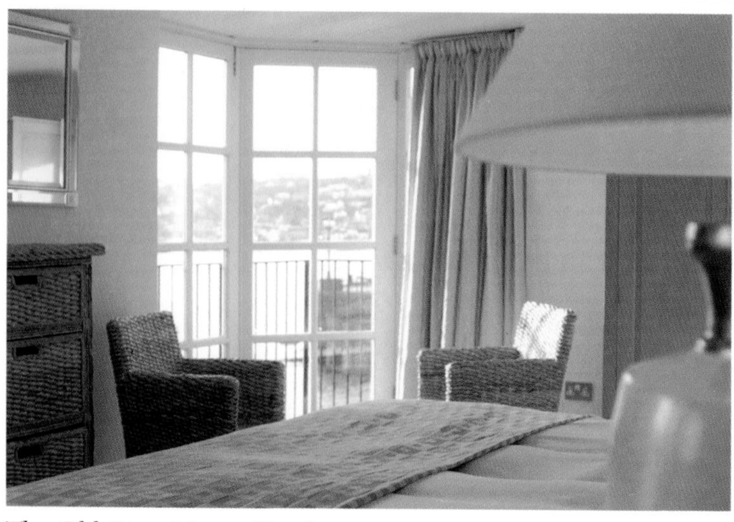

The Old Quay House Hotel

28 Fore Street, Fowey, Cornwall PL23 1AQ

The Old Quay House has everything going for it: one of the most idyllic waterfront settings in Cornwall, a colourful history dating back to 1889 and a brand new, architect-designed interior. Add to this owners passionate about good service and a loyal staff determined to deliver and you have a near-perfect small hotel. Bedrooms are blessed with the latest technology and are stylish and individual, their capacious beds and goose down duvets crisp in Egyptian white cotton. Seven have balconies with glittering estuary views, the rest look over the old rooftops of Fowey. Settle down to delicious and colourful dishes (modern British with mediterranean and north African touches), in the 'Q' restaurant, smartly decorated in neutral tones; or spill out onto the sun terrace overlooking the estuary. Fowey is enchanting and bustles with local life, passing sailors and the August regatta. Come for the best of old Cornwall – narrow cobbled streets, quaint harbour – and find, too, an excitingly contemporary and friendly place to unwind.

rooms	12 twins/doubles.
price	£120-£180. Singles £110.
meals	Lunch about £15. Dinner about £28.
closed	Rarely.
directions	Entering Fowey, follow one-way system past church. Hotel on right where road at narrowest point, opp. Old House of Foye.

Hotel

Jane & Roy Carson

tel	01726 833302
fax	01726 833668
email	info@theoldquayhouse.com
web	www.theoldquayhouse.com

Cormorant on the River

Golant, Nr Fowey, Cornwall PL23 1LL

Golant is well-hidden from Cornwall's tourist trail and the Cormorant is well-hidden from Golant. You drive along the quay, then climb a short, steep hill. The reward is a breathtaking view of the Fowey estuary, flowing through a wooded landscape. Boats tug on their moorings and birds glide lazily over the water – this is a very English paradise. The view is so good the architect made sure it leapt into every room; nine of the 11 bedrooms have picture windows, so they're fabulous to wake up in. Not bad to sleep in either, with comfy beds, pastel colours and spotless bathrooms. From the entrance, steps lead to a huge light-filled sitting room with log fire, colourful pictures and a big map of the estuary to help plan adventures – walks start from the door. There's a small bar with a good smattering of whiskies and a pretty dining room themed on the legend of Tristan, Isolde and jilted King Mark (the love story was made into an opera by Wagner: a nearby 13th-century church once belonged in the king's domain). In summer, have tea under parasols on the terraced lawn and watch the boats zip by.

rooms	11 twins/doubles.
price	£110-£180. Singles from £65 (winter only).
meals	Dinner, 4 courses, from £26.50.
closed	Rarely.
directions	A390 west for St Austell; B3269 to Fowey. After 4 miles, left to Golant. Into village, along quay, hotel signed right, up very steep hill.

B&B

Carrie & Colin King

tel 01726 833426

email relax@cormoranthotels.co.uk

web www.cormoranthotels.co.uk

Talland Bay Hotel

Talland, Porthallow, Cornwall PL13 2JB

The air is clear and fresh, the sea sparkles through the pines... there's a Mediterranean feel here, with French windows opening from the oak-panelled dining room, sitting room, library and bar onto a paved terrace and heated pool. It's a glorious spot, with two acres of subtropical gardens and a perfectly mown lawn ending in a ha-ha and a 150-foot drop to the bay. Long views stretch to the sea. Lie by the pool with a good book (from the library, perhaps), or, if you want to be alone, drift down to the end of the garden. Play croquet or badminton, or practise your putting. The bedrooms are traditional and stylish, impeccable and bathed in light, many with sea views. Some of them have a self-contained feel and their own piece of garden – this would be a super place for a small wedding or house party. The house is surprisingly ancient, mentioned in the Domesday book and once owned by the famous Trelawney family. The walking is all you'd hope for – link up with the glorious Coastal Path – as is the food; there are fresh fish and seafood from Looe, including lobster, crab and scallops.

rooms	22: 20 twins/doubles, 2 singles.
price	£90-£180. Singles £67.50-£90.
meals	Light lunch £5-£15. Packed lunch from £5. Dinner £27.50.
closed	Rarely.
directions	From Looe, A387 for Polperro. Ignore 1st sign to Talland. After 2 miles, left at crossroads; follow signs.

Hotel

	George & Mary Granville
tel	01503 272667
fax	01503 272940
email	reception@tallandbayhotel.co.uk
web	www.tallandbayhotel.co.uk

Number Thirty One

31 Howard Place, Carlisle, Cumbria CA1 1HR

It is difficult to decide which one of these two gems is the best. Is it the fine bow-fronted Victorian house in a quiet, leaf-lined street? Or Pru, who will greet you with an immaculate tray of proper tea-time treats like homemade banana bread thickly buttered? The sitting room is heaving with Victorian collectibles: brass, pot plants, a ticking grandfather clock, gilt mirrors, tasselled curtains, an ornate glass table and battalions of knick-knacks guarding every buffed surface. Bedrooms are also dressed to the nines, colour-themed and deeply comfortable. Every wall is covered in pictures and old photographs of Carlisle; make the most of Pru and her local knowledge: this is her stomping ground and she knows it inside out. Husband Mike does the cooking – a set menu of mainly British and French dishes with a mediterranean twang, served at separate tables in a dark red dining room with mahogany bookshelves and a view to a courtyard garden. The start of 81 miles of Hadrian's Wall is right outside the door and Pru will make you a solid packed lunch, probably with a starched linen napkin.

rooms 3: 2 doubles, 1 twin/double.
price £85-£100. Singles £60-£69.
meals Packed lunch £7.50. Dinner £20.
closed Rarely.
directions From M6, junc. 43, A69 Warwick Rd towards city centre. Right after 5th set of traffic lights into Howard Place. House at far end on left.

B&B

Pru & Mike Irving
tel 01228 597080
fax 01228 597080
email pruirving@aol.com
web www.number31.freeservers.com

Crosby Lodge

High Crosby, Carlisle, Cumbria CA6 4QZ

Restful, grandly comfortable, blissfully detached from the outside world, Crosby Lodge is almost like walking into a gentleman's club – only it welcomes all. Come to elope (Gretna is close) or just to escape. Patricia is everywhere, always impeccably dressed, never seeming to stop, but never seeming to hurry, either. She used to be a banker – the considerate kind, what else! – and this original 'country-house hotel' remains a laid-back family affair. Michael and Patricia came here 30-odd years ago, son James has a bistro in Low Crosby village and their daughter, Pippa, owns a wine company that supplies their wine. There could be grandchildren around as well – not that you'd mind. Inside is warm and cosy, with open fires, the odd chaise-longue, oak furniture and lots of rugs. Bedrooms are fun. They're big and bright, with good fabrics, and maybe arrow slits, or a lovely gnarled half-tester. Pat won't have "square corners" – you get arches and alcoves instead. Outside, you might find the local blacksmith, or an artist sketching a gorgeous pastoral view. Hadrian's Wall is only 10 miles away.

rooms	11: 2 doubles, 5 twins/doubles, 1 single, 3 family.
price	£130-£180. Singles £85-£95.
meals	Lunch from £5. Dinner, 4 courses, £35; à la carte, £13-£30.
closed	Christmas-mid-January.
directions	M6, junc. 44, A689 east for 3.5 miles, then right to Low Crosby. Through village. House on right.

Hotel

Michael & Patricia Sedgwick

tel	01228 573618
fax	01228 573428
email	enquiries@crosbylodge.co.uk
web	www.crosbylodge.co.uk

Lovelady Shield

Nenthead Road, Nr Alston, Cumbria CA9 3LF

From the front door of Lovelady, walk straight into an area of the High Pennines that is remote and utterly unspoilt. The River Nent runs through the garden and at the bridge, four footpaths meet. The house, hidden down a long and suitably bumpy drive, was rebuilt in 1832. The cellars date from 1690, the foundations from the 14th century when it is thought a religious order stood here. No noise, save for sheep in the fields, the birds in the trees and a burbling river that you can hear if you sleep with your window open. Peter and Marie run the place with a hint of eccentricity and masses of good-natured charm. A small rag-rolled bar and pretty sitting rooms full of clocks and log fires give a low-key, country-house feel. Long windows in all rooms bring the views inside and French windows open up for Pimms on the lawn. The food is superb, Barrie is a Master Chef and you dine surrounded by gilt mirrors, sash windows and fresh flowers. Upstairs, dark hallways lead through old pine doors to bright bedrooms with window seats, maybe a sofa, good furniture and Scrabble; most have gorgeous views.

rooms	12: 9 doubles, 2 twins, 1 four-poster.
price	Half-board only, £60-£130 p.p.
meals	Dinner, 4 courses, inc; non-residents £34.50. Lunch by arrangement.
closed	Rarely.
directions	From Alston, A689 east for 2 miles. House on left at junction of B6294, signed.

Hotel

	Peter & Marie Haynes
tel	01434 381203
fax	01434 381515
email	enquiries@lovelady.co.uk
web	www.lovelady.co.uk

Augill Castle

Brough, Kirkby Stephen, Cumbria CA17 4DE

In our fair quest to find places for you to stay, fate led us to a castle in the garden of Eden... well, almost. Augill Castle is an early Victorian folly in Cumbria's beautiful Eden Valley. It was completed in 1841 for John Bagot Pearson, the eldest of two brothers; he was determined to build a bigger and better house overlooking the family pile at Park House after a sibling row. The result is wonderfully over the top, with turrets, arched fairytale windows, a castellated tower and monstrously large rooms – how green with envy his brother must have been! Simon and Wendy rescued the building after years of neglect in 1997 and decorated the whole caboodle; there's no stinting on anything here, be it fabric, colour, food or welcome. Big bedrooms ooze gothic style: four-posters, roll-top baths, swagged curtains, maybe a turret wardrobe or a piano. Downstairs, relax in the elegant library bar, and banquet around a huge table in the grand dining room beneath a panelled ceiling of stunning blues. Perfect for weddings or house parties with seating for up to 40 or roaming feasts for 60 – the food will be perfect.

rooms	12: 4 twins/doubles, 6 doubles, 2 four-posters.
price	£140-£250. Singles £100.
meals	Dinner, £35; most Fridays & Saturdays, or by arrangement.
closed	Christmas & New Year.
directions	M6 junc. 38; A685 through Kirkby Stephen. Just before Brough, right for South Stainmore; signed on left after 1 mile.

B&B

Simon & Wendy Bennett

tel	01768 341937
email	augill@aol.com
web	www.stayinacastle.com

The Pheasant

Bassenthwaite Lake, Nr Cockermouth, Cumbria CA13 9YE

The snug at The Pheasant is wonderful, a treasured relic of times past as a busy coaching inn. A barman guards 40 malts at a low-slung wooden bar and walls shine from a combination of 300 years of tobacco smoke and polish. The inn has since turned into a hotel, and drinks are now usually served in sitting rooms of understated elegance: gilt mirrors, sprays of garden flowers, trim carpets, fresh, yellow walls and fine furniture – all immaculate, yet immediately relaxing. The bedrooms have been beautifully remodelled, too, revealing the odd hidden beam; mellow lighting has been added, warm colours put on the walls and a rug or two thrown in for good measure. Most are in the main part of the inn; three are in a nearby garden lodge... and though pristine throughout, you'll still come across Housekeeping armed with feather dusters! There's a kennel for visiting dogs, Skiddaw to be scaled and Bassenthwaite Lake to be paddled. A perfect place to take your time. *Children over eight welcome.*

rooms	15: 11 twins/doubles, 1 single, 3 suites.
price	£140-£170. Half-board (minimum 2 nights) from £95 p.p. Singles £80-£95. Suites from £160.
meals	Light lunch from £5. Dinner, à la carte, about £30.
closed	Christmas Day.
directions	From Keswick, A66 north-west for 7 miles. Hotel on left, signed.

Inn

	Matthew Wylie
tel	01768 776234
fax	01768 776002
email	info@the-pheasant.co.uk
web	www.the-pheasant.co.uk

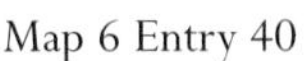

The Mill Hotel

Mungrisdale, Nr Penrith, Cumbria CA11 0XR

A small, eclectic bolt hole, this 1651 mill house on the northern border of the lakes has a stream racing past that is fed by fells that rise behind. Richard and Eleanor belong to that band of innkeepers who do their own thing instinctively and naturally – this is the antithesis of a big, impersonal hotel. Richard comes out to greet you at the car, to help with the bags, to show you up to your room, and finally, invites you down for drinks "whenever you're ready". Downstairs you'll find a tiny library and a homely lounge with rocking chair, ancient stone fireplace, wood carvings and piles of reference books on every subject under the sun. Meanwhile Eleanor has been cooking five courses of heaven for your supper, all homemade and organic where possible, from the olive bread to the watercress soup; breakfasts are first class. Bedrooms, on three floors, vary in size and style; some come with beams, all with bowls of fruit, African art, fresh flowers and good linen. The two in the old mill, wrapped in Clematis montana, share a sitting room where you can fall asleep to the sound of the river.

rooms	9: 4 doubles, 3 twins; 1 double, 1 twin, sharing bath and sitting room (let only to same party).
price	Half-board only, £59-£79 p.p.
meals	Dinner, 5 courses, included.
closed	November-February.
directions	M6, junc. 40 (Penrith), A66 west for Keswick for 7 miles, then right, for Mungrisdale. Hotel next door to Mill Inn.

Hotel

	Richard & Eleanor Quinlan
tel	01768 779659
fax	01768 779155
email	quinlan@evemail.net
web	www.themillhotel.com

Old Dungeon Ghyll

Great Langdale, Ambleside, Cumbria LA22 9JY

This is an old favourite of hardy mountaineers and it comes as no surprise to learn that Tenzing and Hilary stayed here. The hotel is at the head of the valley, surrounded by spectacular peaks, heaven for hikers and climbers, a place to escape to. The scenery is breathtaking, and this is a solid and genuine base from which to plan your ascent. Eclectic bedrooms are decorated with the odd brass bed, patchwork quilts, floral wallpaper and patterned carpets. All are blissfully free of phones and TVs – you wouldn't want them here, not when there's so much going on downstairs. In winter, a fire crackles in the sitting room, all the food is home-cooked – fresh bread, teacakes and flapjacks every day – and there's a small snug resident's bar. Best of all is the famous hiker's bar – hotel wedding parties always seem to end up here. Guitars and fiddles appear – do they carry them over the mountain? – *ceilidhs* break out and laughter fills the rafters, all overseen by Neil, Jane and great staff. Come to walk and to leave the city far behind.

rooms	14: 4 doubles, 4 twins/doubles, 1 twin, 2 family, 3 singles, all sharing 4 baths & 1 shower.
price	£82-£88. Singles from £41.
meals	Packed lunch £3.95. Bar meals from £8. Dinner £20.
closed	Christmas.
directions	From Ambleside, A593 for Coniston, right on B5343. Hotel on right after 5 miles, signed, passed Great Langdale campsite.

Inn

Neil Walmsley
tel 01539 437272
fax 01539 437272
email neil.odg@lineone.net
web www.odg.co.uk

White Moss House

Rydal Water, Grasmere, Cumbria LA22 9SE

At the epicentre of Wordsworth country; walk north a mile to his home at Dove Cottage or south to his somewhat more salubrious house at Rydal Mount. The paths are old and you can follow his footsteps up fell and through wood. He knew White Moss, too – he bought it for his son and came here to escape. The Dixons have lived here for a quarter century and they have kept the feel of a home: flowers everywhere, a woodburning stove, pretty floral fabrics and lots of comfy sofas and chairs. There's a small bar in an old linen cupboard, and after-dinner coffee in the sitting room brings out the house-party feel. Bedrooms range in size, but not comfort. All are different and have good views; a glazed pine-panelled bay window maybe, an old wooden bed, a sprinkling of books and magazines, and a bathroom, with Radox to soothe fell-worn feet. The cottage is in a quiet, beautiful spot further up the hill, with the best view of all right out across Rydal Water. Then there's the small matter of food, all cooked by Peter – five courses of famed indulgence await, and superb wines. *Children over five welcome.*

rooms	5 + 1: 2 doubles, 3 twins/doubles. 1 cottage for 4.
price	Half-board only, £65-£99 p.p.
meals	Dinner, 5 courses, included; non-residents £30. Restaurant closed Sunday night.
closed	December-mid-February.
directions	From Ambleside, north on A591. House signed on right at far end of Rydal Water.

Hotel

Susan & Peter Dixon

tel	01539 435295
fax	01539 435516
email	sue@whitemoss.com
web	www.whitemoss.com

The Samling

Ambleside Road, Windermere, Cumbria LA23 1LR

Possibly the best hotel in Britain? It's hard not to reach this conclusion after you've been to The Samling. The brochure for once is telling the truth: "it's like no other place you've stayed" – especially in the Lakes, which has been gasping for an alternative to chintz and rhododendron for years. There's not a swirly carpet in sight, just lots of good taste in 67 acres overlooking Lake Windermere – Wordsworth came here to pay his rent. The Maxfields are great patrons of the arts so you'll find beautiful paintings inside and sculptures to contemplate on garden wanderings. Nothing's showy or grand, it's about relaxing in style – hotel policy encourages breakfast in bed! Designer Amanda Rosa did the interiors – in the autumnal sitting room there are checked sofas, fresh lilies, a bowl of apricots and a big, open fire. Fabulous bedrooms named after the Cumbrian counting system are full of texture, colour and surprises: stucco walls of orange ochre, slate floors, candles in every bathroom and most have lake views; suites in the "bothy" are superb... so are the food and the service. Worth every penny.

rooms	10: 7 doubles, 1 twin/double, 2 suites.
price	£175-£375. Half-board from £245 p.p. Singles from £175. Suite £375.
meals	Dinner, à la carte, £40; menu gourmand, 8 courses, £60.
closed	Rarely.
directions	From Windermere, A59 for Ambleside for 3 miles. On right up steep drive, signed.

Hotel

	Tom Maxfield
tel	015394 31922
fax	015394 30400
email	info@thesamling.com
web	www.thesamling.com

Aynsome Manor Hotel

Cartmel, Nr Grange-over-Sands, Cumbria LA11 6HH

Stand at the front door of Aynsome and look across ancient meadows to Cartmel Priory, still magnificent after 800 years, and still the heart of a small, thriving community. Strike out across the fields to the village – a three-quarter-mile walk – and discover its gentle secrets. The house, too, echoes with history: it was home to the descendants of the Earl of Pembroke; in 1930, it gave up a long-held secret when a suit of chain armour dating back to 1335 was found behind a wall. Dine on the best of local produce in the gorgeous, panelled, candlelit dining room with its ornate tongue-and-ball ceiling. In the hall, a melodious grandfather clock, a wood and coal fire and carved oak panels, the gift of an 1839 storm. A cantilevered spiral staircase with a cupola-domed window leads up to the old-fashioned lounge where fires burn in a marble Adams-style fireplace. Bedrooms are simple, comfortable, and some are small; beamy no. 13, in the attic, was the 'wig room'. Race-goers will love the National Hunt racecourse, and the Varley family is delightful. *No under fives in restaurant.*

rooms	12: 5 doubles, 4 twins, 2 family, 1 four-poster.
price	£75-£90. Singles from £45. Half-board £52-£76 p.p.
meals	Dinner, 4 courses, £23.
closed	January.
directions	From M6 junc. 36 take A590 for Barrow. At top of Lindale Hill, follow signs left to Cartmel. Hotel on right 3 miles from A590.

Hotel

	Christopher & Andrea Varley
tel	01539 536653
fax	01539 536016
email	info@aynsomemanorhotel.co.uk
web	www.aynsomemanorhotel.co.uk

Riber Hall

Matlock, Derbyshire DE4 5JU

Alex is wonderfully 'old school', and has run this 14th-century Elizabethan manor house for 30 years with one foot firmly in the past. Fires gently smoulder all year in the sitting room and dining room, giving the grandeur of Riber a warm intimacy. Bedrooms are great fun; most have antique four-posters, timber-framed walls, beams, mullioned windows, thick fabrics, good furniture. And you're pampered rotten: beds turned down discreetly, super bathrooms with Gilchrist & Soames toiletries, umbrellas, fresh fruit and homemade shortbread. There's a secret conservatory full of colour and scent, and a walled orchard garden with long views – pure tranquillity – look out for the grafted 180-year-old weeping copper beech that lets you walk under its stunning canopy. The food has won many awards and the cellar is stocked with some of the best wine in Britain. Alex is a gentle, engaging host, who speaks with passion about Spain, wine and the 37 species of bird that live in the garden. Darley Dale, for one of the best views in Derbyshire, is five minutes on foot. *Children over 10 welcome.*

rooms	14: 3 doubles, 2 twins, 9 four-posters.
price	£136-£182. Singles £101-£116.
meals	Continental breakfast included; full English £8. Lunch from £13. Dinner, 2-3 courses, £32-£37.
closed	Rarely.
directions	From Matlock, A615 to Tansley, turn at Royal Oak into Alders Lane. Wind up hill for 1 mile to hotel.

Hotel

	Alex Biggin
tel	01629 582795
fax	01629 580475
email	info@riber-hall.co.uk
web	www.riber-hall.co.uk

The Peacock at Rowsley

Bakewell Road, Rowsley, Matlock, Derbyshire DE4 2EB

Deep in its river valley, the old dower house to Haddon Hall had strayed, of late, from atmospheric fishing lodge to dullish hotel. Until the MacKenzies, Jenni and Ian, blew in from the Brecons and set about re-energising the place. A triumph! The timeworn sofas have gone, the mullioned windows and the dreamy timelessness remain: fisherman have been striding in here to buy their Fishing Tickets for the past 200 years. Now the hall is sisal-clad as young city types join more antiquated guests before the open fire. The feel is intimate, even hushed, the standards are high, the bedrooms chic and jaunty (big beds with crisp linen, zany armchairs in wild colours, the odd lovely antique), the waiters attentive, the menu fabulous. This modern British food is imaginative, fresh, seasonal. Hot waffles at breakfast, for dinner venison and elegant wines, and scrumptuous packed lunches for those who may be spotted wading silently in the dark waters under the bridge. Views are to a terraced garden rich in hidden corners and subtle planting. An unusual marriage of old and new, a heart-lifting place to unwind.

rooms	16: 6 doubles, 7 twins, 2 singles, 1 four-poster.
price	£110-165. Singles £65-£85. Minimum stay 2 nights at weekends.
meals	Breakfast buffet inc. (cooked dishes extra). Lunch £16-£20.50. Dinner à la carte from £25.
closed	Rarely.
directions	A6 north through Matlock, then to Rowsley. On right in village.

Hotel

	Jenni MacKenzie
tel	01629 733518
fax	01629 732671
email	office@thepeacockatrowsley.com
web	www.thepeacockatrowsley.com

Tor Cottage

Chillaton, Tavistock, Devon PL16 0JE

Maureen gives you space yet pampers you in her lovely old Devon longhouse with its wild woodland walks and themed rooms. One room is simple and rustic, one filled with art deco, one straight out of *House and Garden*; there's a cottage wing in the main house – and a freshly furnished woodland cabin in its own valley with hammocks in the trees, a gypsy caravan to play in and steps down to the stream. Wander through the gardens to the heated outdoor pool, breakfast with others in the pretty conservatory – or hole up in your own space with the trug of goodies that waits on your bed. Breakfast is the best: homemade muesli, local sausages and bacon, and flavoursome orange-yolked eggs. Everything you might need is in your room – log-burning stove, fridge, trays of smoked salmon sandwiches that appear as if by magic when you get peckish – and each room has its own little garden or terrace. Resist the temptation to stay put: the beaches are a short drive, there are miles of superb walking and the market town of Tavistock is a good find for book-lovers and antique-seekers. *Minimum stay two nights. Special deals available.*

rooms	5: 3 doubles, 1 twin/double, 1 suite, all with private garden or conservatory.
price	£130. Singles £89. Suite £140.
meals	3 miles to nearest pubs/restaurants.
closed	Christmas & New Year.
directions	In Chillaton keep pub & PO on left, up hill towards Tavistock. After 300 yds, right (bridlepath sign). Cottage at end of lane.

B&B

Maureen Rowlatt

tel	01822 860248
fax	01822 860126
email	info@torcottage.co.uk
web	www.torcottage.co.uk

The Arundell Arms

Lifton, Devon PL16 0AA

A tiny interest in fishing would not go amiss – though the people here are so kind, they welcome anyone. Anne has been at the helm for 40 years – an MBE for services to tourism is richly deserved – while chef Philip Burgess has been here for half that time. This is a *very* settled hotel, with Mrs VB, as staff call her fondly, quietly presiding over all: during a superb lunch – St Enodoc asparagus, scallops and homemade chocs – she asked after an 80th birthday party, ensuring their day was memorable. Over the years, the hotel has resuscitated buildings at the heart of the village: the old police station and magistrates court is a pub, the old school a conference centre. Pride of place is the funnel-roofed cock-fighting pit, one of only two left in England and now the rod room where novice and hardy fisherfolk alike begin salmon and trout fishing courses; spy otter and kingfisher on 20 miles of their own water on the Tamar and five tributaries. No surprise it's probably the best fishing hotel in England – Anne's late husband wrote about fly-fishing for *The Times*; Ambrosia rice started life just down the road.

rooms	27: 8 doubles, 11 twins, 7 singles, 1 suite.
price	£104-£136. Singles from £52.
meals	Bar meals £7-£15. Dinner from £34; à la carte from £39.
closed	Christmas.
directions	A30 south-west from Exeter, passed Okehampton. Lifton 0.5 miles off A30, 3 miles east of Launceston & signed. Hotel in centre of village.

Hotel

	Anne Voss-Bark
tel	01566 784666
fax	01566 784494
email	reservations@arundellarms.com
web	www.arundellarms.com

Lewtrenchard Manor

Lewdown, Okehampton, Devon EX20 4PN

A thrilling, historical pastiche set in a Tudor mansion; only Edwardian radiators and soft-towelled bathrobes belie the fact you're not in 16th-century England. Entering the hall, your senses explode with the magnificence of it all... you almost expect to be set upon by hounds. Nothing so ill is in store, however. Most of what you see was put together in the late 1800s by the Reverend Sabine Baring-Gould, author of *Onward Christian Soldiers*. He was an avid collector of ornamental wooden friezes – the ones in the dining room are extraordinary – but he left no record of where they came from. One fabulous room follows another until you reach the 1602 gallery, with the salvaged, honeycombed, plaster-moulded ceiling, grand piano and 1725 Bible – one of the most beautiful rooms you will see in this book. Bedrooms are large, ornately plastered, oak-panelled or both, filled with bowls of fruit and flowers from the garden. One has Queen Henrietta Maria's four-poster. Follow breakfast with a stroll round the gardens; they are outstanding – as is sixth-century St Petroc's church next door.

rooms 15: 9 doubles, 7 suites.
price From £140. Singles from £100.
meals Lunch from £12-£18, Tues to Sun. Dinner from £35.
closed Rarely.
directions From Exeter, exit A30 for A386. At T-junc., right, then 1st left, for Lewdown. After 6 miles, left for Lewtrenchard. House signed left after 0.75 miles.

Hotel

Sarah Harvey
tel 01566 783222
fax 01566 783332
email info@lewtrenchard.co.uk
web www.lewtrenchard.co.uk

The Hoops Country Inn & Hotel

Horns Cross, Bideford, Devon EX39 5DL

Blissfully out of kilter with the outside world – entering Hoops Inn is like stepping into a timewarp. It's changed little in 800 years – there are just fewer smugglers rubbing shoulders with the local gentry at the bar these days. The lack of road signs to say you've arrived in this tiny hamlet – Hoops comes from 'hoopspink', the Devon word for bullfinch – adds to the splendid sense of disorientation. The signs were taken down to confuse an enemy invasion during the Second World War and never put back. The bar has a mellow tick-tock atmosphere, with lots of irregular beams, uneven floors, snug corners, low-hung doorways and blazing fires in winter; newspapers are there to browse over a pint. Above the bar, baroque-style bedrooms are magnificent; the four-poster beds were made from one massive oak – one originally slept up to 20 (sic). Pass a pretty courtyard – lovely for afternoon tea – to bedrooms in an old coach house. They're smaller, but have the same luxurious period feel. Fresh fish, an ample vegetarian menu and the friendliest welcome add to the specialness.

rooms	12: 7 doubles, 2 twins/doubles, 1 twin, 1 family, 1 suite.
price	£90-£140. Singles £50-£85. Suite £170.
meals	Bar lunch from £8.50. Dinner £12-£24.
closed	Christmas Day.
directions	From Bideford, A39 towards Bude for 6 miles. Just past Horns Cross, road dips. Inn on right.

Hotel

Gay Marriott
tel 01237 451222
fax 01237 451247
email sales@hoopsinn.co.uk
web www.hoopsinn.co.uk

The Red Lion Hotel

The Quay, Clovelly, Bideford, Devon EX39 5TF

Clovelly has been spared time's march, partly because of its position – and partly because it is a tenanted estate. It is completely car-free. The houses perch like seagulls' nests on ledges cut into the cliff and many still have original cob walls of red earth and straw. A steep cobbled path snakes down to a small harbour, and there's the Red Lion, right on the quayside, looking out across the Atlantic – you'll hear the sound of the sea from every room. It's an eccentric place, but pleasantly so, with laid-back staff and friendly management. Smart bedrooms with nautical touches are up-to-date, thanks to a recent makeover, and every single one has sea or harbour views. Wonderful seafood is delivered straight from the fishing boat to the kitchen. Travel out to Lundy Island, a wildlife sanctuary, or walk along Hobby Drive, a beautiful coastal walk laid out in the early 1800s. The late Christine Hamlyn, anointed 'Queen of Clovelly', restored many of the cottages and is still loved by villagers. There's nowhere quite like it.

rooms	11: 7 doubles, 2 twins, 2 family.
price	£87.50-£108. Half-board (minimum 2 nights) £113.50-£149 p.p. Singles from £43.75.
meals	Bar lunch from £3.25. Dinner £25.
closed	Rarely.
directions	From Bideford, A39 for Bude for 12 miles, right at r'bout, for Clovelly. Left fork before Visitor Centre, left at white rails down steep hill.

Hotel

	John Rous
tel	01237 431237
fax	01237 431044
email	redlion@clovelly.co.uk
web	www.redlion-clovelly.co.uk

Northcote Manor

Burrington, Umberleigh, Devon EX37 9LZ

As it was for the monks who came here in the 15th century, Northcote remains a haven from the bedlam of life. The setting is magical, reached by a long driveway that climbs lazily through woodland. The hotel is surrounded by 20 acres of lawn and garden and dreamy views that stretch across the soft, yielding countryside of the Taw River Valley. All is deliriously peaceful: beautiful specimen trees, sweet birdsong and the faint smell of wood smoke on the breeze. The older half of the building was completed in 1716, the rest was added in the Victorian era; enter a studded oak door to an open hallway with lilies, newspapers and an open fire which welcomes all year. Stairs lead to bedrooms in matching fabrics; no surprises but all is smart. Cheryl manages with genuine care, while Richie stars in the kitchen. The formal dining room is in the oldest part, down carpeted steps; hand-painted murals on the wall bathe one corner in a warm, pinky glow. We can but look forward to the advent of flying monks shown in one; in the meantime, let your spirits soar.

rooms	11: 4 doubles, 1 twin/double, 1 twin, 1 four-poster, 4 suites.
price	£140-£240. Half-board (minimum 2 nights) from £95 p.p. Singles from £80.
meals	Dinner £35.
closed	Rarely.
directions	M5, junc. 27, A361 to S. Molton. Fork left onto B3227; right on A377 for Barnstaple. 6 miles on left, signed.

Hotel

	Cheryl Hinksman
tel	01769 560501
fax	01769 560770
email	rest@northcotemanor.co.uk
web	www.northcotemanor.co.uk

Eastacott Barton

Umberleigh, Devon EX37 9AJ

A small, intimate country-house hotel – without the meals but with stacks of special touches. Sue and James used to oversee the unconscionably grand Lewtrenchard Manor, so could probably run most places standing on their heads. Log fires in two sitting rooms, three lakes, views down the Taw Valley, a new larch wood… and loo rolls as perfectly folded as the sheets on the beds. The Victorian house, once an estate cottage, had been renovated with no expense spared; now the Murrays have added a terracotta-floored garden room for morning feasts concocted by Sue: sausage, bacon, fried bread, tomato, mushrooms, hog's pudding – the works. Bedrooms are immaculate (carpets brand new, windows south-facing, big beds) and are divided between those in the house (toile de Jouy quilts, elegantly dressed windows, sumptuous baths) and those in the barn, less glam but with characterful beams and as-lovely views. These 27 acres lie at the end of a lane in deepest Devon – and the beach is 10 minutes away. James and Sue can also steer you in cultural and gastronomic directions: their welcome is first-class.

rooms	4 doubles.
price	£60-£115. Singles £50-£95.
meals	Pubs/restaurants a short drive away.
closed	Rarely.
directions	From South Molton B3227 for Torrington. After 6 miles, left to Eastacott. Continue for 1-2 miles. Do not turn left at stone cross (to Eastacott!); go straight; entrance 700 yds on left.

Hotel

	Sue Murray
tel	01769 540545
email	stay@eastacott.com
web	www.eastacott.com

Halmpstone Manor

Bishop's Tawton, Barnstaple, Devon EX32 0EA

Charles and Jane are preserving a long tradition of farmhouse hospitality at Halmpstone that's gently at odds with the 21st century – in 1630, John Westcote described his stay here as "delightful". The handsome Queen Anne manor you see today was completed in 1701, after fire destroyed much of the original house of 22 rooms in 1633; its proportions remain charming. Fresh flowers adorn every room, pink walls cheer, family photos beam from silver frames, china figures stand on parade… all is traditional. Bedrooms in pink and peach are immaculate, with floral coronets, draped four-posters, a decanter of sherry, fresh fruit and more flowers. Afternoon tea is included, as are the newspapers. Dine by candlelight in the lovely panelled dining room. Jane's cooking has won heaps of awards: try Clovelly scallops, local lamb, and a selection of north Devon cheeses. Charles was born here and has run the farm for much of his life. Both are 'hands-on' and welcoming. Halmpstone means 'Holy Boundary Stone' and the building faces south to Dartmoor. Walk in the pretty garden, or stray further.

rooms	5: 3 twins/doubles, 2 four-posters.
price	£100-£140. Singles £70.
meals	Dinner, 5 courses, £27.50.
closed	Christmas & New Year.
directions	From Barnstaple, south on A377. Left opp. petrol station, after Bishop's Tawton, signed Cobbaton & Chittlehampton. After 2 miles, right. House on left after 200 yds.

B&B

	Jane & Charles Stanbury
tel	01271 830321
fax	01271 830826
email	charles@halmpstonemanor.co.uk
web	www.halmpstonemanor.co.uk

Broomhill Art Hotel & Sculpture Gardens

Muddiford, Devon EX31 4EX

An important and inspiring gallery gently dominates the ground floor of this rambling Victorian house; eight international exhibitions a year haul in thousands of art lovers, and it doesn't stop there. The informal, terraced, 10-acre garden has a cool, tree-lined lake around which geese puttle and 150 contemporary sculptures lurk. Some are huge and scary, some amusing, but all are for gasping at (and taking home if you're feeling flush). Rinus and Aniet run house, gallery, garden and energetic young children with kind, relaxed, enthusiasm and very few rules. Wander at will, ask questions if you want – you won't be bothered in any way. The bedrooms have one or two ugly hangovers from the 1970s but the beds are new, the lighting modern and the art original. Rinus cooks good, award-winning mediterranean food and can be generous with wine and hospitality! It's clear that he and Aniet are passionate about their subject: live jazz, a ceramics shop, be-bop, lectures and poetry... if it comes along they put it on. A unique experience.

rooms	6: 4 doubles, 2 twins.
price	£60-£70. Singles £35-£45.
meals	Lunch from £5. Dinner, 2 courses, £16. Restaurant closed Sundays & Monday evenings.
closed	20 December-mid-January.
directions	From Barnstable, A39 north towards Lynton, then left onto B3230, following brown signs to Sculpture Gardens & hotel.

Hotel

Rinus & Aniet Van de Sande
tel 01271 850262
fax 01271 850575
email info@broomhillart.co.uk
web www.broomhillart.co.uk

The Old Rectory

Martinhoe, Devon EX31 4QT

As you quietly succumb to the wonderful sense of spiritual calm, it's hard to conceive that one field away the land skids to a halt and spectacular cliffs drop 800 feet. The Exmoor plateau meets the sea abruptly at the village of Martinhoe – 'hoe' is Saxon for high ground – creating a breathtaking view as you approach. This lovely understated hotel stands next to an 11th-century church in three acres of mature garden. Nurtured by clergy past, the garden now occupies the affection of Christopher and Enid: birdsong, waterfalls, scented azaleas and the bizarre gunnera only hint at its allure. This is a gentle retreat, dedicated to food and marvellous hospitality. Enid has been cooking since she was a child and makes her own marmalade, bread and cakes, biscuits and ice cream. Meat is fresh, local and organic; even the water, filtered and purified, is from a local borehole. Traditional bedrooms have Laura Ashley wallpaper and the odd Waring & Gillow antique, and one has a balcony; bathrooms sparkle. Grapes from the 200-year-old vine above your head fill fruit bowls in season.

rooms	9: 5 doubles, 1 twin, 2 twins/doubles, 1 suite.
price	£90-£124. Singles £60-£82. Half-board £65-£92 p.p.
meals	Dinner, 5 courses, £30.
closed	November-February.
directions	A39 for Lynton, bypass Parracombe, left after 2 miles, for Martinhoe. Across common, left into village, entrance 1st on right by church.

Hotel

Christopher & Enid Richmond

tel 01598 763368
fax 01598 763567
email info@oldrectoryhotel.co.uk
web www.oldrectoryhotel.co.uk

St Vincent House Hotel & Restaurant

Castle Hill, Lynton, Devon EX35 6JA

After working in the Andalucian village of Gaucin, Jean-Paul and Lin have been happily embraced by the villagers of Lynton. It could be something to do with the excellent range of classic Belgian beers, the Fête du Poisson (and lobsters from Lynmouth) every weekend, or the role that chocolate plays on the pudding menu – whatever, they have brought an invigorating breath of fresh air to this charming house built by Captain Green with monies from the battle of Cape St Vincent. Tucked between the Exmoor Museum and a pretty front garden, the place has been cleared of clutter, the floorboards stripped and the bedrooms and bathrooms given a modern lift with good lighting, white linen and neutral colours. Fresh flowers in jugs, old and modern art on the walls, a charming dining room with original art deco lighting, a drawing room with working fire and books – there's a relaxed feel. Get out and about and discover Exmoor National park, the 'Little Switzerland', so loved by Coleridge, Wordsworth and Shelley. And do take the water-powered Victorian cliff railway down to Lynmouth.

rooms	6: 4 doubles, 1 twin, 1 family.
price	£50-£60. Singles £38.
meals	Dinner £18.95-£20.95.
closed	January.
directions	In Lynton, ignore first sign to left; follow signs for carparks. Up hill, see car park on left, thatched house on right; on left after car park, next to Exmoor Museum.

Hotel

Jean-Paul Salpetier & Lin Cameron
tel 01598 752244
fax 01598 752244
email welcome@st-vincent-hotel.co.uk
web www.st-vincent-hotel.co.uk

Bark House Hotel

Oakfordbridge, Nr Bampton, Devon EX16 9HZ

Alastair describes this small hotel as "a little haven where you can unwind and enjoy good cooking for a few days." He nips smartly across the main, but not busy, road to help you with your luggage; Justine is waiting inside to offer tea and homemade cake. The low-ceilinged sitting and dining rooms are comfortable and warm with patterned carpets and curtains. Bedrooms are cottagey with good beds upon which lie teddies and one has a fine bay window; all have rural, pretty views. Apart from being incredibly spoilt you will be bowled over by the food. Alastair makes almost everything himself and is a true enthusiast – ask him! Meat, fish and vegetables are local and seasonal; canapes, ice creams, sorbets and little sweets are homemade. Wine is taken seriously and the list evolves regularly, so if you are sybaritic by nature and adore a bit of attention you will love it here. A garden to explore or sit in, the gorgeous wooded valley surrounding the River Exe to wander through and birds, lots of birds, will keep nature-lovers happy.

rooms	5: 2 doubles, 2 twins/doubles; 1 double with separate bath.
price	£85-£115. Half-board from £70 p.p. Singles £47.50-£57.50.
meals	Dinner £27.50.
closed	Occasionally.
directions	From Tiverton, A396 north towards Minehead. Hotel on right, 1 mile north of junction with B3227.

Hotel

Alastair Kameen & Justine Hill
tel 01398 351236
web www.barkhouse.co.uk

Kings Arms

Stockland, Nr. Honiton, Devon EX14 9BS

Stay for a week and you'll almost be a fully-fledged local – this is a cross between a pub and a community centre with a vast overflowing notice board to fill you in on the gossip you didn't catch at the bar. You'll also be a stone or two heavier with seemingly endless menus, masses of fish, locally-reared game and even ostrich. Ramble at will past crackling fires, beams, gilt-framed mirrors, stone walls, cosy low ceilings and, eventually, the stone-flagged Farmer's Bar where you meet the "fair-minded, fun-loving locals". One comes from as far as Birmingham to take his place at the bar; they'll have you playing darts in no time. As for Paul, "he's a tyrant to work for," said one of his staff with an enormous smile on his face. Bedrooms are not grand but perfectly traditional, with maybe a walnut bed or a cushioned window seat. It is a working pub and won't be quiet until about 11pm so don't try to sleep earlier, just join in. Lose yourself in the Blackdown Hills or simply laze around inside with Princess Ida, the cat. If you like inns, stay here.

rooms	3: 2 doubles, 1 twin.
price	£60. Singles £40.
meals	Lunch from £4. Dinner, 3 courses, from £15.50.
closed	Christmas Day.
directions	From centre of Honiton, head north-east out of town. Stockland signed right just before junction with A30. Straight ahead for 6 miles to village.

Inn

	Paul Diviani, John O'Leary & Heinz Kiefer
tel	01404 881361
fax	01404 881732
email	reserve@kingsarms.net
web	www.kingsarms.net

Combe House Hotel & Restaurant

Gittisham, Honiton, Nr Exeter, Devon EX14 3AD

If the spirit of Combe House could be bottled and sprinkled over the world, good would surely come of it. As it is, Ruth and Ken have distilled their own worldly experience to create a sublime place to stay. Globe-trotting careers have seen them put Australia's Hunter Valley on the map and Ken cook in the Antarctic for three years. But what makes here so special is the modest way they apply themselves to each task, big or small. Their latest project has been the faithful restoration of a Georgian kitchen – a deliciously romantic spot for a private party. By the light of the Tilly lamp you are treated to the finest Devon produce, fresh as can be, with the chef finishing your main course on the huge wood-burning range. The rest of the house is just as fabulous – meet history at every turn as Elizabethan and Restoration eras meld into one: cavernous fireplace, mullioned windows, oak panelling, ancestral portraits – not theirs! – antique-furnished bedrooms, trompe l'œil murals. All this on 3,500 acres with a 'lost' arboretum. The long, wooded drive that brings you here will unravel all.

rooms	15: 11 twins/doubles, 1 four-poster, 3 suites.
price	£140-£198. Half-board from £99 p.p. Singles from £125. Suites £275.
meals	Lunch £18-£22.50. Dinner £36. Parties in Georgian kitchen £38 p.p. plus room hire.
closed	Rarely.
directions	A30 south from Honiton for 2 miles; A375 for Sidmouth & Branscombe. Signed through woods.

Hotel

	Ruth & Ken Hunt
tel	01404 540400
fax	01404 46004
email	stay@thishotel.com
web	www.thishotel.com

Bickleigh Castle

Bickleigh, Tiverton, Devon EX16 8RP

The bride gets to stay in the castle, you stay in the cottages – they're thatched, just-renovated and gorgeous. With its 15th-century film set looks, Bickleigh is one of the south-west's most beautiful castles – and its 1096 chapel the oldest place in Devon in which to exchange vows. The Hays have swept in full of energy and ideas – for speciality dinners, charity balls, wine weekends, country fairs, vintage car rallies, and the occasional talk about Matters Ghostly. You get 30 acres of grounds, five of which are landscaped (great banks of rhododendrons with fine views to the Exe, a knot garden just planted) and terrific food; organic Devon pork in west country cider with honey apples and cream caught our eye. The Great Hall (perfect for big functions) has a fireplace of carved stone, the bridal suite a four-poster clothed in rich yellow. Cottage bedrooms couldn't be prettier: walls freshly painted, curtains and cushions strewn with flowers, soft lamps, embroidered quilts, the odd fireplace or beam. There's history here in bucket-loads – and peace, romance and fabulous food. New and special.

rooms	16: 2 doubles, 2 twins, 2 singles; 1 four-poster with separate bath; .
price	£100-£175. Singles £50-£100.
meals	Dinner from £30.
closed	Rarely.
directions	M5 junc. 27 to Tiverton. Clearly signposted 'Bickleigh Castle' on road.

B&B

	Sarah & Robert Hay
tel	01884 855363
fax	01884 855771
email	info@bickleighcastle.com
web	www.bickleighcastle.com

Alias Hotel Barcelona

Magdalen Street, Exeter, Devon EX2 4HY

This extraordinary place reinvents the British hotel experience. Hotel Barcelona belongs to an exciting new breed that uses fresh design and classic memorabilia to put folk up in affordable style – without losing its sense of humour in the process. Barcelona is the brainchild of hotel visionary Nigel Chapman. Here, he has taken a former Victorian eye infirmary and turned it into a psychedelic ark of shape and colour that heals all the senses, even the most jaded. Nothing says 'Barcelona' directly, except the odd Jujol-inspired handrail and bedroom doors taken from Gaudi's Casa Mila. More, it's the vibrant buzz of the Catalan capital that's arrived in this terribly English city. A stunning collection of 50s and 60s furniture in the lobby, Café Paradiso with its rainbow-coloured mural, the Kino cabaret club performing every weekend, and elegant bedrooms that curve, angle and slope. Amazing cocktails, smiling staff and fabulous food, right through from the wood-oven pizzas to the chocolate fondant pudding. A word of advice: pay extra for a bigger room. *¡Arriva! ¡Arriva!*

rooms	46: 20 twins/doubles, 19 doubles, 7 singles.
price	£85-£105. Singles £75.
meals	Continental breakfast inc.; full English £10.50. Lunch £12. Dinner £22.25.
closed	Rarely.
directions	A379 for Exeter, 3rd exit at Countess Wear r'bout, for Centre; 2 miles to main traffic junc. Right lane into Magdalen St; on right.

Hotel

	Fiona Dolan
tel	01392 281000
fax	01392 281001
email	info@hotelbarcelona-uk.com
web	www.hotelbarcelona-uk.com

Bel Alp House

Haytor, Devon TQ13 9XX

Mark and his partner, an interior designer, moved from the comfort of Yeoman's House in Salcombe to a gorgeous Edwardian house on the slopes of the National Park – with absolutely everything to do. Self-confessed house and garden addicts they plan to leave no corner unchanged. The bones are impressive: Dame Violet Wills' old country house – 1,000 feet above sea level – with distant views to the coast has unusual arched doorways, a stained-glass window of saints at the foot of the oak staircase and large bay windows. Huge bedrooms have comfortable chairs, good beds and linens, and thoughtful extras like binoculars and Molton Brown goodies in the gleaming bathrooms. Mark is a good cook and breakfasts, which can be taken late, will be free-range, organic and seasonal; bread, preserves and muesli are homemade. It won't feel like staying in a hotel, more like a weekend house party with friends. Clotted cream teas in the gazebo in the summer and beside the roaring log fire in the winter. Stroll through the secret garden to the pub or walk in the Park. Great fun.

rooms	3 doubles.
price	£130-£200.
meals	Dinner £40 p.p. (min. 6 people). Good local pub/restaurant short walk away.
closed	Christmas.
directions	Just off the B3387 Haytor road, 2.5 miles from Bovey Tracey.

Hotel

	Mark Andrews
tel	01364 661217
fax	01364 661292
email	belalphouse@aol.com
web	www.belalp.co.uk

Kingston House

Staverton, Totnes, Devon TQ9 6AR

It's hard to know where to begin describing this stupendous house – the history in one bathroom alone would fill a small book. "It's like visiting a National Trust home where you can get into bed," offers Elizabeth, your gentle and erudite host. Set in a flawless Devon valley, Kingston is one of the finest surviving examples of early 18th-century architecture in England. Arrive down a long country lane that rises and falls, increasing your expectations; at the brow of the last hill, the house comes into view... utterly majestic, demanding your attention – as do the Great Danes that come to greet you. Completed in 1735 for a wealthy wool merchant, many original features remain, including the 24 chimneys. The craftsman who carved the marble hallway later worked on the White House in Washington DC, the marquetry staircase is the best example in Europe, and the magnificent bed in the Green Room has stood there since 1830. There's a thunder-box loo, an Angel tester bed, a painted china closet, ancient wall paintings... The cooking is historic, too – devilled kidneys, syllabub and proper trifle. Genuine and welcoming.

rooms	3 doubles.
price	£140-£160. Singles £90-£100.
meals	Dinner, 4 courses, £34.50.
closed	Christmas & New Year.
directions	From A38, A384 to Staverton. At Sea Trout Inn, left fork for Kingston; halfway up hill right fork; at top of hill, straight ahead at x-roads. Road goes up, then down to house; right to front of house.

B&B

	Michael & Elizabeth Corfield
tel	01803 762235
fax	01803 762444
email	info@kingston-estate.co.uk
web	www.kingston-estate.co.uk

Fingals

Dittisham, Dartmouth, Devon TQ6 0JA

Richard miraculously combines a laissez-faire management style with a passionate commitment to doing things well. He is ever-present without intruding, fun without being challenging, spontaneous without being demanding. This is his place, his style, his gesture of defiance to the rest of the hotel world. He does things his way, and most people love it. And he is backed by Sheila, whose kindness and perennial good nature are a constant source of wonder. The food is good, with a Gallic appeal, and the meals around the big table memorable. This is a place to mingle with kindred spirits into the early hours; though the accent is on conviviality, you can eat at separate tables if you prefer. You find children wandering freely, happy adults, certainly, mooching dogs, and Sheila's ducks being marshalled home in the evening. Ask for rooms in the main house – they're bigger. The indoor pool beckons, and sauna and jacuzzi, ping-pong and croquet for all, perhaps tennis on the lawn and cosy conversation in the bar. But don't be misled, you can do peace and quiet here, too. Perfect for the open-hearted.

rooms	10 + 1: 8 doubles, 1 twin, 1 family. Self-catering barn for 4.
price	£70-£140. Barn £500-£800 p.w.
meals	Dinner £27.50.
closed	2 January-26 March.
directions	From Totnes, A381 south; left for Cornworthy. Right at x-roads for Cornworthy; right at ruined gatehouse for Dittisham. Down hill, over bridge. Signed on right.

Hotel

	Richard Johnston
tel	01803 722398
fax	01803 722401
email	richard@fingals.co.uk
web	www.fingals.co.uk

The Little Admiral

27-29 Victoria Road, Dartmouth, Devon TQ6 9RT

Bang in the centre of bustling Dartmouth, this painted Georgian townhouse with pretty windows appears unremarkable. But inside is a large, airy space with vibrant James Stewart paintings on otherwise unadorned cream and lilac walls, cast-iron fireplaces, squashy sofas, books and magazines and no reception desk – it's relaxed and unstuffy. The dining room is charming, with good sized tables, modern lighting and more bright paintings. Bedrooms have pocket-sprung mattresses, plain colours with the odd funky headboard or zebra-striped screen, super snazzy bathrooms and modern art. James and Clare have a young family, and are obviously delighted with their latest 'baby', for which they have left behind a corporate lifestyle. Mission statement? "To be happy and make a living". James does the cooking, Spanish-style but taking his pick of Devon's finest fish, meat and veg. Sailing can be organised, there are arduous walks, great beaches and all the shops and restaurants of pretty Dartmouth. Check their web site before you come: it's packed with good advice about what you can do.

rooms	10: 8 doubles, 1 twin, 1 four-poster.
price	£79.50-£135. Single occ. £60-£75.
meals	Tapas dinners Thurs, Fri & Sat night: 3 courses £18.
closed	January.
directions	From M5 A38 for Plymouth; A385 for Totnes then to Dartmouth. There, 3rd right (Townstal Road) & down into town. On right hand side.

Restaurant with Rooms

	James & Clare Brown
tel	01803 832572
fax	01803 835815
email	info@little-admiral.co.uk
web	www.little-admiral.co.uk

Barrington House

Mount Boone, Dartmouth, Devon TQ6 9HZ

Rumour has it that General Eisenhower stayed here before the Normandy landings; one can only assume he left this blissful spot feeling restored and ready for battle. The south-facing garden overlooks the Dart estuary and has magnificent views across to Kingswear and out to sea past the castle. Chrissie and John are charming, easy-going and relaxed. You'll be left to your own devices with your own key; a short walk down narrow lanes and steps will bring you out in the centre of Dartmouth with all its chi chi shops and restaurants. The Dart Valley Trail passes the house, there's a boat for sailing (with a picnic if you want) and beaches galore. Breakfast is a flexible feast and includes old favourites like boiled eggs with marmite soldiers or a thoroughly modern smorgasbord. Bedrooms are plain and well-proportioned, filled with light and unashamedly lacking in frills and fuss; bathrooms are simple and clean. The views are the thing, and the laid-back feeling of being on holiday – which settles as you clamber up the drive after a coastal hike to the big white house on the hill.

rooms	4: 3 doubles, 1 twin.
price	£90-£110. Singles from £60.
meals	Dinner, 3 courses, £25. Book ahead.
closed	Rarely.
directions	Arrive in Dartmouth on A3122, past B.P. garage on right, 4th right into Townstal Rd, 1st left into Mount Boone. 3rd house on left behind high stone wall.

B&B

	John Smither
tel	01803 835545
fax	01803 835545
email	enq@barrington-house.com
web	www.barrington-house.com

Hazelwood House

Loddiswell, Nr Kingsbridge, Devon TQ7 4EB

In 67 acres of woodland, meadows and orchards in an untamed river valley, Hazelwood House is no ordinary hotel. It is a place of exceptional peace and natural beauty, created more as a relaxed, unpretentious country house. It might not be for everyone, but those who like it, love it. Through the front door, past rows of books and paintings, and enter a world to revive the spirit. Chances are Daisy the dog will be there to roll over and greet you. Lectures and courses and evenings of music from classical to jazz play a big part – they have a knack of attracting the best – and all is carried off with a friendly approach. Anabel and Gillian, who are involved with 'Through the Heart to Peace', a peace initiative started in 1993, came here some years ago and the place has evolved ever since. The atmosphere outweighs any decorative shortfalls, the food is delicious and fully organic and they produce their own spring water. Cream tea on the veranda is wonderful, or roam past ancient rhododendrons and huge camellias to fields of wild flowers and grazing sheep.

rooms	15: 1 family, 1 twin, both with separate baths. 3 family, 5 double, 4 twin, 1 single, sharing 4 baths.
price	£59-£135. Singles £41.
meals	Lunch from £10. Packed lunch £5-£8. Dinner £18-£29.
closed	Rarely.
directions	From Exeter, A38 south; A3121 south. Left onto B3196 south. At California Cross, 1st left after petrol station. After 0.75 miles, left.

B&B

Janie Bowman, Gillian Kean & Anabel Watson

tel	01548 821232
fax	01548 821318
email	info@hazelwoodhouse.com
web	www.hazelwoodhouse.com

The Henley

Folly Hill, Bigbury-on-Sea, Devon TQ7 4AR

The view from this Edwardian summer house is truly uplifting, a glorious vision of sand, sea and a lush patchwork of fields. The garden falls away gently, disappearing over a shallow cliff to an inviting expanse of golden sand and white surf – nothing jars the eye and a private footpath leads the way down. The hotel entrance creates the second good impression: bold red walls lead to two sitting areas and a conservatory, all decorated with a homely elegance. A dining room of Lloyd Loom chairs, pot plants, seagrass and candles pulls in the view to maximum effect; every table has its own special portion. Martyn conjures up flavoursome, fresh, beautiful-looking food: one reviewer said the view and dinner combined were enough to make her feel at peace with the world. Bedrooms are small and adequate; bathrooms shine. The beaches are popular with surfers and sun-seekers, and you can reach Burgh Island by a sandy causeway at low tide, by sea tractor at high tide – great fun. A special setting, lovely people... and visiting pets are fussed over. *Children over 12 welcome.*

rooms	6 doubles.
price	£78-£88. Singles £49-£54.
meals	Dinner £20.
closed	November-March.
directions	From A38, A3121 to Modbury, then B3392 to Bigbury-on-Sea. Hotel on left as road slopes down to sea.

Hotel

	Martyn Scarterfield & Petra Lampe
tel	01548 810240
fax	01548 810240
email	enquiries@thehenleyhotel.co.uk
web	www.thehenleyhotel.co.uk

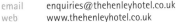

Burgh Island

Bigbury-on-Sea, Devon TQ7 4BG

The walk over the sand with a golden beach to either side is dramatic and at high tide you must arrive by sea tractor. On the island, the little Pilchard Inn seems cowed by the rocks, and, towering over it all, the splendid white building that was Archie Nettlefold's eccentric playpen for naughty theatrical folk in the 1930s. Inside is no less impressive: the Peacock Bar with its intricate ceiling, the cool, dazzling, Palm Court, the glamorous Ballroom and the charming Captain's Cabin – all have been rescued and there's more to do. Everything is in the art deco style, meticulously restored or painstakingly tracked down by Tony, who understands and adores the era, and Deborah who fizzes with fun and organises great balls and evenings of dance. Bedrooms, some of which are not huge, are totally authentic and delightful with plenty of room for bathing and putting on make-up. Stacks to do, from tottering down to the freshwater Mermaid Pool to a game of tennis or a brisk walk. At night, plenty of frothy dash and glamour, with a touch of decadence and a jolly good dinner. Very Agatha Christie.

rooms	23 suites & doubles.
price	Half board only, £275-£420.
meals	Lunch £30. Dinner £45 (non-residents).
closed	Rarely.
directions	Drive to Bigbury-on-sea. At high tide you are transported by sea tractor, at low tide by Landrover. Walking takes three minutes.

Hotel

Deborah Clark & Tony Orchard

tel	01548 810514
fax	01548 810243
email	reception@burghisland.com
web	www.burghisland.com

Bridge House Hotel

3 Prout Bridge, Beaminster, Dorset DT8 3AY

There is much here to make one happy – good food, award-winning hospitality and the inestimable beauty of Hardy country. At the heart of Bridge House is the food – traditional and as local as possible, and probably not for slimmers. You eat in the panelled, Georgian dining room, with a fine Adam fireplace and the palest of pink linen. Bedrooms hold no surprises but have stacks of space and are solidly traditional, with padded headboards and floral duvet covers and curtains. Peter is very much the convivial host; his good-natured professionalism has won him accolades and rightly so. The Pinksters have a gift for inspiring loyalty: their staff enjoy their work and they stay. The history of this ancient building gives it a sense of dignity and solidity; an ancient monument first, probably a 13th-century priest's house next, a dwelling house in the Tudor period which explains the variety of mullioned windows… later eras saw the creation of a priest's hole. Beaminster is a pretty town not far from the south coast and there's llama trekking nearby if you crave a little adventure.

rooms	14: 3 doubles, 9 twins/doubles, 1 single, 1 family.
price	£102-£134. Half-board (minimum 2 nights) from £75 p.p. Singles £54-£96.
meals	Lunch £11. Dinner, 5 courses, £28.50.
closed	Rarely.
directions	From Yeovil, A30 west; A3066 for Bridport to Beaminster. Hotel at far end of town, as road bends to right.

Hotel

	Peter Pinkster
tel	01308 862200
fax	01308 863700
email	enquiries@bridge-house.co.uk
web	www.bridge-house.co.uk

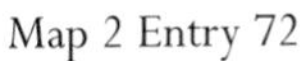

Innsacre Farmhouse

Shipton Gorge, Bridport, Dorset DT6 4LJ

This is a perfect little place, alone in its 21 acres of orchard, valley and wooded hills, elegant without pretension and wrapped in peace and quiet. Inside, 17th-century open-stone walls, low-beamed ceilings, a warm country feel. Behind it all are Sydney and Jayne, two easy-going francophiles who share a gift for unwinding city-stressed souls. Come to relax – bedrooms (not huge) with antique French beds, bold colours and soft lights will help unravel the tightest knot. You get your own tables at breakfast and dinner, and there's a small bar in the sitting room – Sydney is keen on his wines, knowledgeable too – along with colourful pictures, open fire and chairs to sink into. In summer, spill out onto the terrace with your pre-dinner drink and watch the setting sun. The orchard is heavy, in season, with fruit that Jayne turns into delicious compotes – have them at breakfast along with cured ham sausages and American-style pancakes. Walk the fields and you may bump into the Jacob sheep – you can buy their undyed wool – or keep going for superb beaches and the Dorset Coastal Path. *Arrival after 4pm.*

rooms	4: 3 doubles, 1 twin.
price	£75-£85. Singles from £50.
meals	Dinner £19.50. Late arrival supper £16.50.
closed	October, Christmas & New Year.
directions	From Dorchester A35 for Bridport. After 13 miles 2nd road signed left to Shipton Gorge & Burton Bradstock. 1st left up long drive to farmhouse.

B&B

	Sydney & Jayne Davies
tel	01308 456137
email	innsacre.farmhouse@btinternet.com
web	www.innsacre.com

The Fox Inn

Corscombe, Nr Dorchester, Dorset DT2 0NS

Clive, an ex-accountant, is now a licensee and his 17th-century thatched inn is in the hands of a man who feels privileged to be running one of the most sought-after places to stay and eat in the south of England. Everything about the Fox makes you feel good: the food, the people, the setting – Hardy's Wessex at its most peaceful and beautiful. The beers are not bad either, and there are farm ciders and excellent wines. In the old days, drovers on the way to market would wash their sheep in the stream opposite and stop for a pint of cider; the inn only received a full licence 40 years ago. In spite of modern changes the old feel has been kept, with clever additions like a slate-topped bar, a flower-filled and benched conservatory and a long table made from a single oak felled by the storms of 1987. Be charmed by stuffed owls in glass cases, gingham tablecloths, paintings, flowers, flagstones, fires and six fish dishes a day. Bedrooms have simple country charm with floral and mahogany touches; one in a converted loft is reached by stone steps. Special, indeed, and you can almost smell the sea.

rooms	4: 3 doubles, 1 twin.
price	£80-£100. Singles £55-£75.
meals	Dinner, à la carte, about £20.
closed	Christmas Day.
directions	From Yeovil, A37 for Dorchester for 1 mile, then right, for Corscombe, for 5.5 miles. Inn on left on outskirts of village. Use kitchen door to left of main entrance if arriving before 7pm.

Inn

Clive Webb

tel 01935 891330

fax 01935 891330

email dine@fox-inn.co.uk

web www.fox-inn.co.uk

Plumber Manor

Sturminster Newton, Dorset DT10 2AF

Best of all at Plumber is the family triumvirate of Brian in the kitchen, Richard behind the bar cracking jokes and Alison, who is simply everywhere. They know exactly how to make you feel at home. This has been *their* family home for 300 years, though ancestors have lived "in the area" since they arrived with William the Conquerer. Outside, a large, sloping lawn, a white bridge over the river and deckchairs scattered about the well-groomed garden. Inside, the house remains more home than hotel with huge family portraits crammed on the walls; everything in this house seems to be *big*. The atmosphere is relaxed without a trace of pomposity. Stay in the main house if you can; bedrooms have had a recent makeover with fresh colours and fabrics, similar to those in the converted stables which are bigger but have less character. The stone path between the two came from a local river bed, and kept one guest amused for hours looking for dinosaur fossils... The enormous old sofa on the landing may be the most uncomfortable ever made – but this is the *only* discomfort you'll find. *Pets by arrangement.*

rooms	16: 2 doubles, 13 twins/doubles; 1 twin/double with separate bath.
price	£110-£170. Singles from £95.
meals	Dinner, 3 courses, £26.
closed	February.
directions	From Sturminster Newton, follow signs to hotel & Hazlebury Bryan for 2 miles. Entrance on left, signed.

Hotel

Richard, Alison & Brian Prideaux-Brune

tel	01258 472507
fax	01258 473370
email	book@plumbermanor.com
web	www.plumbermanor.com

The Museum Inn

Farnham, Blandford Forum, Dorset DT11 8DE

This delightful, part-thatched 17th-century inn owes its name to General Augustus Lane Fox Pitt Rivers, the 'father of archaeology'; it fed and bed folk who came to see his museum in the 1800s. He opened three museums to house his fabulous collection; only the Pitt Rivers in Oxford survives. No sign either of the yaks and zebu that the General once released into a nearby pleasure park. What you will discover is one of the best inns in the south of England. Vicky and Mark work well together to create a wonderfully warm and friendly place to stay: she does bubbly, he does laid-back. The smart refit has a lovely period feel, with flagstones, inglenook, fresh flowers and a mismatch of wooden tables and chairs. Leading from the restaurant is a gorgeous drawing room filled with books. Bright, comfortable bedrooms are impeccably done, those upstairs (there are four more in the stables) have antique beds and masses of character. Chef Mark Treasure is as brilliant as his name suggests; breakfasts, too, are amazing. Farnham is a thatched idyll in the middle of Cranborne Chase, ideal for walks and horses.

rooms	8 doubles.
price	£75-£120. Singles £65.
meals	Light lunch from £3.95. Dinner, à la carte, about £24.
closed	Christmas Day & New Year's Eve.
directions	From Blandford, A354 for Salisbury for 6.5 miles, then left, signed Farnham. Inn on left in village.

Inn

	Vicky Elliot & Mark Stephenson
tel	01725 516261
fax	01725 516988
email	enquiries@museuminn.co.uk
web	www.museuminn.co.uk

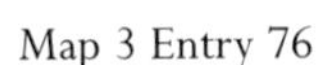

Mortons House Hotel

Corfe Castle, Wareham, Dorset BH20 5EE

One day the old railway will reach Wareham and collect you from your London train. Meanwhile, just enjoy the passing steam from the terrace of this wonderful 1590 manor house – the station is below. Mortons was built from Purbeck stone in the shape of an 'E' to honour Queen Elizabeth I and overlooks the ruins of Corfe Castle. Bit by bit, these hugely enthusiastic owners have undertaken a complete overhaul of the old house, and recently added two rooms for the less able-bodied in a lovely quiet corner of the grounds. Traditional bedrooms make good use of four-posters and original stone fireplaces, one suite has its own private staircase and the finest views. The food is another draw, as are the friendly staff. Spend a wintry evening before a log fire among the oak panelling after a delicious meal, or strike out along the Jurassic coast, recently granted World Heritage status. Keen golfers get preferential rates with the local club. The village is protected and perfect, the old 'capital' of the Isle of Purbeck... you've even a sunny micro-climate here.

rooms	19: 13 doubles, 3 twins, 3 suites.
price	£126-£200. Half-board £146-£195 for 2 people per night (min. 2 night stay). Singles £75-£120.
meals	Lunch, 3 courses, £20. Dinner, 5 courses from £25. Bar meals from £5.
closed	Rarely.
directions	From Wareham, A351 to Corfe Castle. Hotel on left 50 yds from market square.

Hotel

Andy & Ally Hageman,
Ted & Beverly Clayton

tel	01929 480988
fax	01929 480820
email	stay@mortonshouse.co.uk
web	www.mortonshouse.co.uk

Lord Bute Hotel

Lymington Road, Christchurch, Highcliffe, Dorset BH23 4JS

Tucked away behind the original entrance lodges to Highcliffe Castle, Lord Bute Hotel and Restaurant is causing a big stir. You need to book well in advance now to eat their fresh, locally sourced food- a daily changing menu of modern English with a continental twist. The restaurant is glamorous with black carpets and crisp white and gold linen – Raffles with a dramatic spin. Light spills in from the gorgeous wooden-floored orangery and the conservatory which overlook the garden. Here, Thai-style pots sprout bamboo and colourful acers sit on terracotta-block paving terraced down to a pretty grassed area. Air-conditioned, double-glazed bedrooms are smart with mahogany furniture, spotless tiled bathrooms and all mod cons. Gary and Simon are fun and work hard to give you a good time – all this and monthly cabaret evenings with famous names, or live music on most weekends. If you have any energy left over then take the path down to the beach behind the castle, or drive into the New Forest. Bournemouth is nearby for shopping or clubbing.

rooms	11: 10 twins/doubles; 1 suite. 1 family room in the Coach House.
price	From £85. Singles from £65. Suite from £140. Family room from £120.
meals	Lunch £11.95. Dinner £26.95; à la carte also available.
closed	Rarely.
directions	From Christchurch, A337 towards Lymington to Highcliffe. 200 yds past castle.

Hotel

Gary Payne & Simon Box

tel	01425 278884
email	mail@lordbute.co.uk
web	www.lordbute.co.uk

Seaham Hall Hotel

Lord Byron's Walk, Seaham, Durham SR7 7AG

Seaham Hall is designed to make you feel *you* own the place – and we bet you never feel so spoiled. One of the remarkable things about this ever so modern hotel is that there are so few rooms for such a large building. Texture, shape and electronic gadgets knit together to create a stunning series of set-piece designs; every bedroom is behind two thick oak doors, and every bath fits two. The building was once a hospital; it was also where Lord Byron was married. You feel enormously good here. Get lost and cosy with a newspaper in the huge drawing room – the ceiling feels several double decker buses high. Tall French windows open onto a wide and formal garden terrace with stone steps leading to the bleak and beautiful coast. The owner is a great patron of the arts: sculptures and paintings are added all the time. Pride of place goes to Charybdis, a water sculpture by William Pye, outside the front entrance. The cone-shaped spa is arguably the best in the country, the food is exceptional – and why bother to get up when breakfast in bed is all part of the service? Sit back and enjoy it all.

rooms	19: 13 doubles, 5 suites, 1 penthouse.
price	£195-£325. Suites £365-£435. Penthouse £525.
meals	Full English breakfast £9. Dinner £40; à la carte from £40.
closed	Rarely.
directions	A1(M), junc. 62, A690 through Houghton le Spring, A19 south on to Seaham. At seafront, left on B1287 for 2 miles. On left.

Hotel

	Tom & Jocelyn Maxfield
tel	01915 161400
fax	01915 161410
email	reservations@seaham-hall.com
web	www.seaham-hall.com

The Bell Inn & Hill House

High Road, Horndon-on-the-Hill, Essex SS17 8LD

Christine's parents ran the Bell for years and she was born here. John is also a key figure, much admired in the trade, as is Joanne, their loyal manager of 17 years – an industry award for hospitality has proved what folk have known for a long time. Christine's beautifully decorated suites upstairs are by far the best places to stay – they're named after famous mistresses: Lady Hamilton, Madame du Barry and Anne Boleyn, who's said to be buried in the local church. The other bedrooms are next door in Hill House; all are comfortable. Dining areas suit the mood of the day. The breakfast room is light and airy, with elegant white table and chair coverings; the flagstoned bar, with oak panelled walls and French wood carvings – part of a huge collection built up by Christine's father – bustles with working folk at lunchtime; and the smart restaurant is busy in the evening. Waiters serve in white aprons and black ties under the close eye of the Master Sommelier, Joanne. The food rightly picks up awards, too, as should Christine's flower arangements. Great value and so close to London.

rooms	15: 7 doubles, 3 twins, 5 suites.
price	£50-£60. Suites £75-£85.
meals	Breakfast £4.50-£9.50. Bar meals from £6.50. Dinner, à la carte, about £23. No food on Bank Holidays.
closed	Christmas.
directions	M25, junc. 30/31. A13 to Southend for 3 miles; B1007 to Horndon. On left in village.

Inn

	Christine & John Vereker
tel	01375 642463
fax	01375 361611
email	info@bell-inn.co.uk
web	www.bell-inn.co.uk

The Pier at Harwich

The Quay, Harwich, Essex CO12 3HH

The Pier stands smartly on the quayside in the historic port of Harwich. Owners the Milsoms took over the next-door pub in 2000 to carve out a handsome lounge: loads of space, seagrass matting, simple bold colours and deep sofas around an open fire. The Harbourside Restaurant upstairs takes the pick of the views over the harbour and the Stour and Orwell estuaries and fresh fish is, of course, what you should eat. Chris and Vreni Oakley – he's the seafood expert, she, his charming Swiss-born wife, does front of house – have been here nearly 25 years; they clearly love the place and go out of their way to see that guests do too. Informal eating takes place in the H'apenny Bistro (very fresh fish and chips) and on the buzzing quayside. Bedrooms are beautifully done: more seagrass, painted tongue and groove panelling, great colour, good quality fabrics – splash out on the Mayflower suite for the best views. The hall and bar have a modern feel and a maritime sprinkling of ships' wheels and brass portholes. Book a mooring.

rooms	14 doubles.
price	£95-£170. Half-board (minimum 2 nights) from £100 p.p. Singles £70-£90.
meals	Lunch £16. Dinner, à la carte, £25-£28.
closed	Rarely.
directions	M25, junc. 28, A12 to Colchester bypass, then A120 to Harwich. Head for quay. Hotel opposite pier.

Hotel

	Chris & Vreni Oakley
tel	01255 241212
fax	01255 551922
email	pier@milsomhotels.com
web	www.milsomhotels.com

Three Choirs Vineyards

Newent, Gloucestershire GL18 1LS

A fondness for cooking and wine-making will equip you for the full-bodied and very English experience of Three Choirs. Thomas has run the pesticide-free vineyard with thoughtful and gentle reserve for almost a decade. There are 100 acres of grounds, of which 75 grow 16 varieties of grape; the rest have been left to encourage wildlife, including birds of prey. The wine from here went to the wedding of Charles and Diana and still lubricates British embassies; the hotel and restaurant evolved more recently as an addition to the winery. The bedrooms are in a modern building and are crisply clean and comfortable, each with French windows opening to a small patio and cast-iron furniture: relax with a glass of wine and enjoy the peaceful views that produced it. At breakfast, don't be embarrassed to ask for more wine with your smoked salmon and scrambled eggs – it's a house special. Chef Darren cooks like a dream, has won many accolades and runs monthly cookery courses. Dick Whittington was born up the road – you may wonder why he ever left.

rooms	8 twins/doubles.
price	From £85. Half-board £135 p.p. (minimum 2 nights). Singles £75.
meals	Lunch about £16. Dinner, à la carte, about £28.
closed	Christmas & New Year.
directions	From Newent, north on B4215 for about 1.5 miles, follow brown signs to vineyard.

Hotel

	Thomas Shaw
tel	01531 890223
fax	01531 890877
email	info@threechoirs.com
web	www.threechoirs.com

Corse Lawn House Hotel

Corse Lawn, Gloucestershire GL19 4LZ

It would be fun to arrive here by carriage – preferably a mud-streaked one. The last circular 'wash' for cleaning your wheels and horses sits serenely outside this Queen Anne house. Ducks, pheasants, doves and squirrels potter about it now in this quietest part of Gloucestershire. The Hine family (of Cognac fame) run the hotel – also their home – like clockwork. Baba is in the kitchen making everything from scratch: bread, sausages, jams, marmalades, ice creams, sorbets, and even smoking her own salmon and chicken. A vegetable and herb garden provides greens and the fields and hedgerows around are trawled for mushrooms, elderflowers and other goodies. The lovely flowers, arranged with flair, are all grown in the cutting bed here. Denis and Giles operate front of house and a superb wine cellar. Comfortable rooms downstairs are stuffed with good antiques and pictures, old-fashioned and elegant, the colours mainly greens and pinks. Bedrooms are large, immaculate and traditional – "we don't follow trends particularly," says Giles. A lot of people will be thrilled about that.

rooms	19: 14 twins/doubles, 2 four-posters, 2 suites, 1 single.
price	£130-£165. Singles from £85. Suites £170.
meals	Dinner £29.50; à la carte from £32.50.
closed	Christmas.
directions	From Tewkesbury A438 to Ledbury. After 3 miles left onto B4211. Hotel on right after nearly 2 miles.

Hotel

	Giles Hine
tel	01452 780771
fax	01452 780840
email	enquiries@corselawn.com
web	www.corselawn.com

Hotel on the Park

Evesham Road, Cheltenham, Gloucestershire GL52 2AH

Symmetry and style to please the eye in the centre of the spa town of Cheltenham. The attention to detail is staggering – everything has a place and is just where it should be. The style is crisp and dramatic, a homage to the Regency period in which the house was built, but there's plenty of good humour floating around, not least in Darryl, who's brilliant at encouraging people to dive in and enjoy it all. There are lovely touches too: piles of fresh hand towels in the gents' cloakroom, where there's a sink with no plug hole – you'll work it out; newspapers hang on poles, so grab one and head into the drawing room where drapes swirl across big windows. Lose yourself in a book from the library, dine on poached salmon with lemon noodles, chocolate marquise with mint ice cream... the restaurant is sumptuous, with Doric columns and Greek and Roman busts, fun too. Upstairs, bedrooms are fabulous, crisp and artistic, all furnished to fit the period, one blessed with a jacuzzi and an adjustable massaging bed. The whole house is classically dramatic – a huge treat.

rooms	12: 5 doubles, 4 twins, 3 suites.
price	£114-£139. Singles £88.50. Suites £144-£164.
meals	Breakfast £7.25-£9.50. Dinner, à la carte, from £27.50.
closed	Rarely.
directions	From town centre, join one-way system, & exit signed Evesham. On down Evesham Road. Hotel on left opposite park, signed.

Hotel

	Darryl Gregory
tel	01242 518898
fax	01242 511526
email	stay@hotelonthepark.co.uk
web	www.hotelonthepark.com

Alias Hotel Kandinsky

Bayshill Road, Montpellier, Cheltenham, Gloucestershire GL50 3AS

Kandinsky, Russian painter, theorist and pioneer of the abstract – a fitting name for a hotel pushing back the boundaries of British hospitality. The first hotel to come from the Alias stable has hotel innovator Nigel Chapman's signature written all over it. Like its sister hotel in Exeter, Kandinsky gives free rein to Nigel's design-obsession with sitting down in the right chair in the right surroundings; marionettes from Bali in the quirky-chic reception prepare you for a vibrant port of call. Bedrooms are compact, coir-floored, delightful, with all mod cons; ask for one of the quieter ones at the weekend. The bar and lounge are in the Raffles colonial style: rugs on painted wooden floors, antique sofas, palms, gilt mirrors, chandeliers... and bamboo in the conservatory. Gates from a French monastery lead to the restaurant with its trademark Neapolitan pizza oven. The private club downstairs feels like a New York lounge, with soft lighting, black leather couches, brilliant cocktails, and 50s party dresses in the ladies loo that are there to be worn by all, and are! Welcome to the party.

rooms	48: 14 doubles, 26 twins/doubles, 8 singles.
price	£89-£115. Singles £79. B&B 2 nights + 1 dinner from £105 p.p.
meals	Breakfast £7.75-£10.95. Lunch £14-£25. Dinner, à la carte, £20-£30.
closed	Rarely.
directions	M5, junc. 11, A40 to centre; left at r'bout end of Lansdown Rd for Montpellier. Road veers to left, hotel ahead.

Hotel

	Lorraine Jarvie
tel	01242 527788
fax	01242 226412
email	info@hotelkandinsky.com
web	www.hotelkandinsky.com

Heaven's Above at The Mad Hatters

3 Cossack Square, Nailsworth, Gloucestershire GL6 0DB

In Carolyn's words, you "never know what's coming next" at this exceptional, fully organic restaurant with rooms. Arrive to a bowl of cherries one day, some fragrant sweet peas picked from the garden the next. She and Mike were smallholders once. They lived at the top of the hill, worked the land, kept livestock, made bellows and earned next to nothing. In the early Nineties, they came down the hill to open a restaurant. Locals flocked in, and still do. The food is delicious, consistently so, some still grown back up the hill: try fabulous fish soup, lamb with garlic and rosemary, and a mouth-puckering lemon tart. *Cotswold Life* has given it 'chef of the year' award but it's a place with heart, not designed to impress, which is probably why it does, and full of rustic charm: cookery books squashed into a pretty pine dresser, mellow stone walls, big bay windows, stripped wooden floors, simple ash and elm tables and exceptional art. Bedrooms are delightful – huge, like an artist's studio, with wooden floors, whitewashed walls and rag-rolled beams.

rooms	3: 1 double; 1 double, 1 twin sharing bath.
price	£60. Singles £35.
meals	Lunch £15. Dinner, à la carte, £25. Restaurant closed Sunday evenings, Mondays & Tuesdays.
closed	Rarely.
directions	M5, junc. 13, A419 to Stroud; A46 south to Nailsworth. Right at r'bout & immed. left; opp. Britannia Pub.

Restaurant with Rooms

Carolyn & Mike Findlay

tel 01453 832615

email mafindlay@waitrose.com

The Priory

Priory Fields, Horsley, Stroud, Gloucestershire GL6 0PT

Suzie does good company and long, lazy meals with the odd glass or two so well that one guest even recommends the Priory hangover! A Cotswold stone house which defies an obvious label, Suzie is someone you immediately warm to: she's such an exuberant hostess that you want to feel a part of the fun and energy here. There's a well-stocked bar and deep feather-filled sofas to sink into for chats by the log fire. Take your time over traditional English meals around a walnut table in the splendid terracotta dining room with sparkling chandelier, big mirrors, gold sconces and cut glass. Fresh flowers and plants are everywhere. Suzie has laboured heroically to transform a dilapidated home into a sophisticated country house. Her eclectic style and quirky sense of humour have brought together an elegant hotchpotch of treasures collected over the years. The comfortable, smallish bedrooms come with impeccable bathrooms; some have tree-top views, all have the dawn chorus. The garden is being restored and the local pub is a pleasant stroll away. A great place for that special house party, too.

rooms	10: 4 doubles, 3 twins, 3 singles.
price	£75. Singles £45. House party rates on application.
meals	Dinner by arrangement. Restaurants nearby.
closed	24-26 December.
directions	M4, junc. 18, towards A46 north for Stroud. Enter Nailsworth on B4058, signed Horsley. Left at Bell & Castle pub. Entrance 200 yds on right.

B&B

Suzie Lamplough

tel 01453 834282

fax 01453 833750

email horsleypriory@onetel.com

web www.theprioryhorsley.com

No. 12

Park Street, Cirencester, Gloucestershire GL7 2BW

No. 12 is another of those pleasing British phenomena, not a hotel but a small place run with enormous thought and care. (The offer of tea and homemade cake on arrival is a typical touch.) Sarah has lavishly converted this splendid, listed Georgian townhouse, with its beams dating back to the early 1600s, right down to the last detail. Bedrooms mix antique and contemporary furniture, while feather pillows, merino wool blankets and fine bed linen spoil further… extra-long beds include a *bateau lit* and a leather sleigh bed. Ultra-modern bathrooms, almost minimalist in style, come with dressing gowns and Molton Brown goodies. Cranberry-red walls and white china make a striking contrast in the dining room at breakfast, while checked sofas, fresh flowers and *Condé Nast Traveller* and *Vogue* in the sitting room encourage you to linger. It is quietly immaculate. As is old Cirencester, 'capital of the Cotswolds', a favourite destination for travellers since Roman times and civilised in every way. *Children over 12 welcome.*

rooms	3 doubles.
price	£80. Singles £60.
meals	Restaurants in Cirencester.
closed	Rarely.
directions	M4 junc. 15, A419 to Cirencester. M5 junc. 11a, for Cirencester.

B&B

Sarah Beckerlegge
tel 01285 640232
email no12cirencester@ukgateway.net
web www.no12cirencester.co.uk

Barnsley House

Barnsley, Cirencester, Gloucestershire GL7 5EE

'BB' is carved in stone above the door: Brereton Bouchier built Barnsley in 1697. A succession of rich rectors followed... until 1952, when Prince Charles's favourite gardener, Rosemary Verey, blew in. Her desire: that the garden should "curtsey to the house"; now eight gardeners dance in attendance. Inside, Tim and Rupert are creating a new form of perfection: expect a stone urn topped with a slab of glass at 'reception', scarlet bucket chairs, Bose sound systems, his and her freestanding baths; this is a Cotswold haven of a chic and unfussy persuasion. Not a whisper of chintz, just a cool symphony of new art on plain walls in restful colours, old, old beams and mullioned windows. Sip cocktails in the satin-and-chrome boudoir-bar, or Chablis on the patio in summer; then retire to your generous, minimalist bed and indulge in ice cream and champagne (little extras on the house). Bedrooms are big, with sofas; the sitting room, with logs, is small. In the cool, green dining room, the menu is sensuous, seasonal and short, with herbs, veg and berries straight from the garden. Prepare to be hopelessly spoiled.

rooms	9 doubles.
price	£260-£450.
meals	Lunch, 2 courses, £19.50. Dinner, 3 courses, £39.50.
closed	Rarely.
directions	M4, junc. 15; A419 for Gloucester. Exit at Cirencester junc., B4425 to Bibury. Barnsley 2 miles on.

Hotel

	Tim Haigh & Rupert Pendered
tel	01285 740000
fax	01285 740900
email	info@barnsleyhouse.com
web	www.barnsleyhouse.com

The New Inn at Coln

Coln St Aldwyns, Nr Cirencester, Gloucestershire GL7 5AN

Built by decree of Elizabeth I, this lovely coaching inn of roaring fires, low beams and oil paintings by Angela Kimmett provides old-fashioned hospitality at its most appealing. The New Inn at Coln is a real way of life for the Kimmett family. They and their friendly staff take the time to talk you through a local walk, the ales on tap, the imaginative menu – the food is traditional with a continental twist. The bedrooms, bisected by ancient beams, have everything – Jacobean-style four-posters or half-testers with a romantic floral theme; those in the converted dovecote have views across meadows to where the River Coln splashes along. In summer, sip drinks outside under the generous shade of parasols. Brown-trout-fishing on the river at the bottom of the meadow can be arranged and golf, biking and horse riding are all nearby. Walk from the front door through this sleepy Cotswold village, past grazing cows and gliding swans, into some of England's most tucked-away countryside; nothing too dramatic, just a classic of its type, inspiration to the artist, the poet… and maybe you.

rooms	14: 10 doubles, 3 twins/doubles, 1 single.
price	£120-£155. Singles £90-£104.
meals	Bar lunch from £8.50. Dinner, 2-3 courses, £29-£35.
closed	Rarely.
directions	From Oxford, A40 passed Burford, B4425 for Bibury. Left after Aldsworth to Coln St Aldwyns.

Inn

	Roger & Angela Kimmett
tel	01285 750651
fax	01285 750657
email	stay@new-inn.co.uk
web	www.new-inn.co.uk

The Dial House

The Chestnuts, Bourton-on-the-Water, Gloucestershire GL54 2AN

The 'Venice of the Cotswolds' and such a peaceful setting, with sandstone Georgian houses and the slow, meandering River Windrush drifting by. Cotswolds' travellers are drawn to the genteel buzz of Bourton village life. There's lots going on, and right in its midst stands The Dial House, built in 1698 by architect Andrew Paxford – his and his wife's initials are carved on the front. Originally The Vinehouse, it was renamed after the large sundial above the front door. Inside, Jane and Adrian have created an oasis of old world charm, with Jacobean-style furniture, wonderful four-posters, old portrait paintings and impressive stone fireplaces. Elegant yet friendly, it epitomises the traditional country-house hotel. The best bedrooms are in the main house, with lovely antiques, a refreshing lack of chintz, Penhaligon smellies and organic chocolates, and views of the village and river through leaded window panes. Rooms in an extension look out onto the walled garden, a lovely spot to keep the world at arm's length for a while, and the classic English menu takes a lot of beating.

rooms	13: 9 doubles, 1 four-poster suite with private sitting room, 3 four-posters.
price	£110-£120. Suite £175. Half-board (minimum 2 nights) £75 p.p.
meals	Packed lunch available. Dinner, à la carte, from £35 for 3 courses.
closed	Rarely.
directions	From Oxford, A40 to Northleach, right on A429 to Bourton. Hotel set back from High St opp. main bridge.

Hotel

	Jane & Adrian Campbell-Howard
tel	01451 822244
fax	01451 810126
email	info@dialhousehotel.com
web	www.dialhousehotel.com

Wesley House

High Street, Winchcombe, Gloucestershire GL54 5LJ

Wesley House, a 15th-century half-timbered townhouse, entices you off the street and seduces you once inside. Old timber-framed white walls, a terracotta-tiled floor, a big open fire and a cosy bar were made for lazy afternoons flicking through the papers. Downstairs is open-plan; the split-level dining area stretches back in search of the gentle countryside – and finds it. French windows lead out to an atrium-ed terrace where breakfast and lunch, or evening drinks, are enjoyed; it's also perfect for private parties. Winchcombe was once the sixth-century capital of Mercia. Bedrooms, each with its own shower room, have more of those ancient whitewashed, timber-framed walls that need little decoration. They are warm, smart, well-lit and compact, with good wooden beds, crisp cotton sheets, new carpets and the occasional head-cracking bathroom door; one room has a lovely balcony. Find fresh milk and coffee in every room, and indulge in breakfast in bed, with home-baked bread, croissants, pains au chocolat… even kumquat, orange and whisky marmalade. *Children over seven and babies welcome.*

rooms	5 doubles.
price	Half-board only, £150-£180. Singles £90-£120.
meals	Lunch from £12.50. Dinner £29.50-£35.
closed	Christmas.
directions	From Cheltenham, B4632 to Winchcombe. Restaurant on right. Drop off luggage, parking nearby.

Restaurant with Rooms

	Matthew Brown
tel	01242 602366
fax	01242 609046
email	enquiries@wesleyhouse.co.uk
web	www.wesleyhouse.co.uk

The White Hart Inn & Restaurant

High Street, Winchcombe, Gloucestershire GL54 5LJ

The Swedes have arrived in Gloucestershire but they come in peace, bearing a smorgasbord of vibrant chic and warm hospitality. It's a far cry from the sixth century when this Cotswold village was the Saxon capital of Mercia; any mention of Scandinavians on the loose would have resulted in a call to arms! Not anymore. Locals have welcomed their arrival at this 16th-century coaching inn. Thanks to the discerning interior design of Nicole's mother Ursula, it feels more like a stylish rural hotel in Sweden: scrubbed wooden floors, sisal matting, big windows and Gustavian style blue-grey furniture in the restaurant. Bedrooms smell inviting; the best have views of the high street. One named after Swedish painter Carl Larsson has a stunning four-poster in the middle of the room, just as the artist did, with green checked fabric and fresh flowers. Nicole employs solely Swedish staff on six-month stints to improve their English; all take it in turns to serve, clean, or cook authentic food: *sil*, marinated herring, is superb. They've even introduced Santa Lucia, a winter festival of song and candles.

rooms	8: 2 doubles, 4 twins/doubles, 2 four-posters.
price	£65-£125. Half-board (minimum 2 nights) £75 p.p. Singles £55-£115.
meals	Lunch about £10. Dinner, à la carte, about £25.
closed	Christmas Day.
directions	From Cheltenham, B4632 to Winchcombe. Inn on right.

Inn

	Nicole Burr
tel	01242 602359
fax	01242 602703
email	enquiries@the-white-hart-inn.com
web	www.the-white-hart-inn.com

The Malt House

Broad Campden, Chipping Campden , Gloucestershire GL55 6UU

You could imagine that one of the Famous Five lived in this substantial English house in the middle of an untouched Cotswold village, with climbing roses, magnolia trees and deckchairs on the lawn. A place that so echoes to the past, you almost expect the vicar to call for tea, or a post boy to bring a telegram to say the London train is running late. Still much in evidence is that very English ritual of sipping gin in a lovely setting: the manicured garden has its own 'gin and tonic' bench! A thatched summer house for afternoon tea, a walled kitchen garden that grows figs and a small brook complete the idyllic scene. The house itself has a mellow grandeur: polished wooden floors, ancient oak panelling, walls of shimmering gold and a 17th-century fireplace beneath a mantelpiece that rises to within a foot of the ceiling. Bedrooms vary, with mullioned windows, sloping floors, gilt mirrors, and muralled bathrooms; some have painted floorboards. Judi is very English, too. Friendly staff and excellent food, locally sourced, will keep you smiling for days.

rooms	7: 1 double, 4 twins/doubles, 1 four-poster, 1 suite.
price	£118.50-£139.50. Singles from £91. Suite from £139.
meals	Available locally.
closed	Christmas.
directions	A44 through Moreton-in-Marsh; left on B408 to Chipping Campden. Entering village, 1st right for Broad Campden. Hotel 1 mile on left.

Hotel

Judi Wilkes

tel 01386 840295

fax 01386 841334

email info@the-malt-house.freeserve.co.uk

web www.malt-house.co.uk

The Churchill Arms

Paxford, Chipping Campden, Gloucestershire GL55 6XH

Above all, The Churchill is fun, an engaging mixture of the old and new that creates a relaxed, informal atmosphere. Walk into the bar, with stone floors and wooden tables, and find a hub of happy chatter. Leo and Sonya are proud of their creation – one guest described it as "Fulham in the country", and the locals sipping their well-kept Hook Norton like it that way. Many were reluctantly starting to leave when our inspector arrived just after lunch. Bedrooms right above the bar are equally fun and stylish; two are small but good use of space won't leave you feeling hemmed in. "Frills and drapes are not us," says Sonya. Beams, old radiators and uneven floors obviously are. Add good fabrics, pastel colours and country views from the heart of this picture-perfect village and this is a place worth getting away for. The food is quite superb, too. One usually cantankerous Sunday critic conceded that the sticky toffee pudding was perfect, the salmon organic, the chips crispy and golden. Such perfection might explain the prayer stool in one corner.

rooms	4 doubles.
price	£70. Singles £40.
meals	Lunch from £10.50. Dinner from £14.50.
closed	Rarely.
directions	From Moreton-in-Marsh, A44 for Worcester & Evesham. Through Bourton-on-the-Hill, right at end to Paxford. Through Blockley, over railway & tiny bridge into Paxford.

Inn

	Leo & Sonya Brooke-Little
tel	01386 594000
fax	01386 594005
email	info@thechurchillarms.com
web	www.thechurchillarms.com

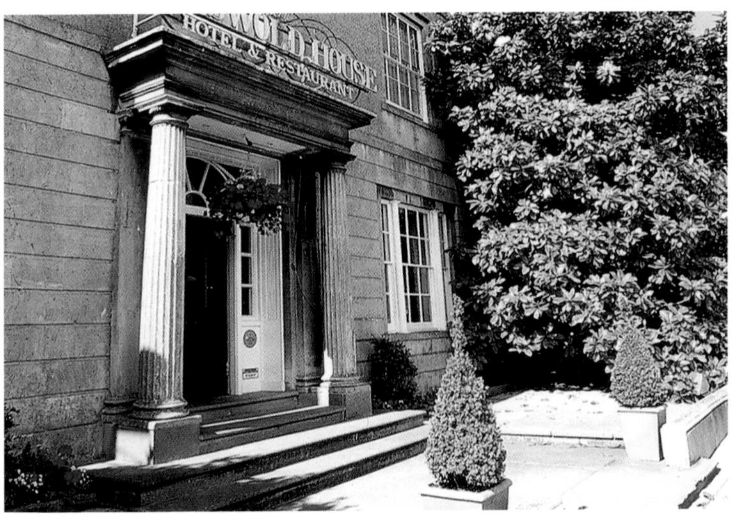

The Cotswold House Hotel

The Square, Chipping Campden, Gloucestershire GL55 6AN

Few brochures quite capture the spirit of a place, Cotswold House's is one exception. It pulls out like a concertina, revealing a tantalising glimpse of what to expect behind the impressive colonnaded entrance of this 19th-century wool merchant's house. Ian and Christa's philosophy was to create a hotel where the bedrooms felt better than your own room at home – they've succeeded. National Trust colours, cashmere underblankets and Frette linen sheets on luxurious beds, French colognes and lotions in stylish bathrooms, fresh coffee percolators, Bang & Olufsen film and stereo systems, remote controls to fine-tune your viewing and listening pleasure... even a Pillow Menu. Downstairs, relax in red and terracotta drawing rooms, with antiques, fresh flowers and paintings, or stroll in two acres of walled garden, with meandering paths and secluded spots; the vegetable garden supports a well-regarded menu in season. Wine, music and celebrity events are held through the year; the village has chi chi shops to browse – and you can park free. Go on, spoil yourself.

rooms	22: 2 doubles, 16 twins/doubles, 2 four-posters, 2 suites.
price	£190-£595.
meals	Brasserie meals from £9. Dinner £45.
closed	Rarely.
directions	From Oxford, A44 north for Evesham. 5 miles after Moreton-in-Marsh, right on B4081 to Chipping Campden. Hotel in square by town hall.

Hotel

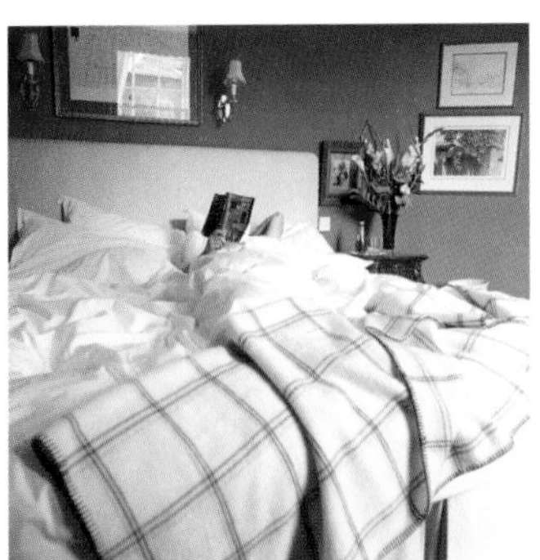

	Ian & Christa Taylor
tel	01386 840330
fax	01386 840310
email	reception@cotswoldhouse.com
web	www.cotswoldhouse.com

Master Builder's House Hotel

Bucklers Hard, Beaulieu, Hampshire SO42 7XB

By the River Beaulieu in a timeless end-of-the-road idyll, Master Builder's has the feel of a well-heeled yacht club. The hotel shares this blissful spot with two rows of cottages still lived in by workers of the nearby Montague Estate. Yachts and sailing boats glide past on their way to the Solent following the same route taken by Nelson's fleet two centuries before. It was here that the great shipwright Henry Adams built many of the warships which would go on to fight in the Battle of Trafalgar; ancient slipways that launched the ships still survive at the river's edge. Bedrooms in a wing named after Adams are uniformly done to a high standard, each with a king-size bed. More expensive bedrooms in the characterful main part of the hotel have darker colour schemes and lovely river views. There's a traditional pub, full of sailors in summer, a hall that seems to tumble down to the water, a restaurant with a view, and a terrace for meals outside. Beaulieu is a one-hour walk upstream past marshland teeming with birdlife and the New Forest stretches to the west. Also charter a boat to their other hotel on the Isle of Wight.

rooms	25 twins/doubles.
price	£175-£235. Singles £130.
meals	Bar lunch from £4.95. Lunch from £16.95. Dinner from £29.50.
closed	Rarely.
directions	From Lyndhurst, B3056 south passed Beaulieu turn-off, then 1st left, signed Bucklers Hard. Hotel signed left after 1 mile.

Hotel

	Samanatha Brinkman
tel	01590 616253
fax	01590 616297
email	res@themasterbuilders.co.uk
web	www.themasterbuilders.co.uk

Westover Hall

Park Lane, Lymington, Hampshire SO41 0PT

A hotel, but family-run and without the slightest hint of stuffiness. It was built for the German industrialist Siemens in 1897 to be the most luxurious house on the south coast; a fortune was lavished on wood alone. It is still vibrant with gleaming oak and exquisite stained glass and it's hard to stifle a gasp when you enter the hall – it's a controlled explosion of wood. The Mechems are generous and open-minded, keen that people should come to unwind and treat the place as home. Private parties can take over completely and throw the rule book towards the window. Bedrooms are exemplary: some have sea views, all are furnished with a mix of the old and the contemporary; bathrooms are spotless. The whole place indulges you. Romantics can take to the bar or restaurant and gaze out to sea. The more active can dive outside and walk up the beach to Hurst Castle. Alternatively, sink into a sofa on the sunny balcony for great views of the Needles, or visit their nearby mediterranean beach hut.

rooms	12: 8 doubles, 2 twins, 1 family, 1 single.
price	£165-£230. Half-board £112.50-£145 p.p.
meals	Light lunch £10-£15. Dinner £35.50.
closed	Rarely.
directions	From Lymington, B3058 to Milford-on-Sea. On through village. House on left up hill.

Hotel

	Nicola & Stewart Mechem
tel	01590 643044
fax	01590 644490
email	info@westoverhallhotel.com
web	www.westoverhallhotel.com

The Ancient Camp Inn

Ruckhall, Eaton Bishop, Hereford, Herefordshire HR2 9QX

Buried down a maze of cowparsleyed lanes is this old inn. Named after a neighbouring Iron Age hill fort, the Ancient Camp is now a thoroughly modernised restaurant with rooms, surrounded by an astonishing verdancy. In the distance, the Herefordshire hills appear to dip and rise for ever. Kathryn and Charles gave up France for this, though Charles still works there and comes back at weekends, laden with bottles of olive oil. You'd be mad not to eat in; the delightful Mackintoshes have brought with them a Gallic-trained chef and a love of simple, delicious food. Low-ceilinged dining room, sitting room and snug bar flow into each other warmly – cream sofas, white walls, lilies in an enamel jug – while beds upstairs sport goose or duckdown pillows and duvets dressed in snowy white. Cottage windows freshly painted have stunning views to the Wye that meanders below – 300 yards of riverside fishing, all yours). Bedrooms at the back are smaller, but full of Kathryn's modern touches. A lawned garden with a very pretty terrace and more views – what a spot for summer breakfasts!

rooms	5: 4 doubles, 1 twin.
price	£70-£90. Singles £60.
meals	Lunch £15. Dinner £25.
closed	Two weeks in February.
directions	From Hereford A465 to Abergavenny. After 0.5 miles right to Ruckhall & Belmont Golf course. Pass Belmont Abbey & golf course. Cross small bridge, right for Ruckhall; inn signed.

Inn

Charles & Kathryn Mackintosh

tel	01981 250449
email	reservations@theancientcampinn.co.uk
web	www.theancientcampinn.co.uk

Glewstone Court Country House Hotel & Restaurant

Glewstone, Ross-on-Wye, Herefordshire HR9 6AW

Grand, yet relaxed enough to have no rule book. Bill does front of house, Christine cooks – brilliantly; they are charming and fun. There's faded glamour and an easy conviviality in the drawing room bar, full of squashy sofas, interesting things and an open log fire in front of which resident dogs lounge. The centre of the house is early Georgian, with a stunning stair that spirals up to a galleried landing. Big bedrooms have patchwork quilts, period pieces, Christine's pretty stencil work, comfy chairs and good reading lights. The Rose Room is wonderful and the Victoria Room enormous. All look over fruit orchards to the Wye Valley and the Forest of Dean beyond. Dominating the croquet lawn at the front is the largest cedar of Lebanon in the west; there's a modest helipad, too. Dine in the lovely restaurant with open fires in winter, or outside in good weather. The easy dress code welcomes all styles, except baseball caps and mobile phones. Most food is locally sourced – the Hereford beef is exceptional – some organic, some from the potager. Heaven for those in search of the small and friendly.

rooms	8: 5 doubles, 1 single, 2 suites.
price	£99-£115. Singles £49-£65.
meals	Lunch about £20. Dinner, 3 courses, about £27. Sunday lunch £17.
closed	Christmas.
directions	From Ross-on-Wye, A40 towards Monmouth, right 1 mile south of Wilton r'bout, for Glewstone. Hotel on left after 0.5 miles.

Hotel

Christine & Bill Reeve-Tucker

tel 01989 770367
fax 01989 770282
email glewstone@aol.com
web www.glewstonecourt.com

Kilverts Hotel

The Bullring, Hay-on-Wye, Herefordshire HR3 5AG

Those wanting to stay in the thick of this literary outpost bang on the Welsh border could do no better than check into Kilverts. The hotel sits in narrow streets teeming with bookshops, art galleries and antique shops... they wind round the town's crumbling castle which peers over all. Hay is the second-hand bookshop capital of Britain, and holds an internationally famous literary festival every May. The front terrace of the hotel is the place to people-watch with a drink or a meal; the bar is a cosy retreat if the weather drives you inside – stone floor, wooden tables, local ales and homemade pizzas. The more formal restaurant has a mural on the wall of a ballroom in chaos! The menu is the same wherever you eat and has daily specials. There's also the quieter garden out back – the biggest undeveloped plot in the town. Upstairs, go for one of two lovely beamed attic rooms at the top; one has an 18th-century oak tester. The rest have few surprises but all are comfortable. Colin is a likeable chap, as is Tired Ted the hotel cat. And the countryside seduces.

rooms	11: 6 doubles, 3 twins/doubles, 2 twins.
price	£70-£90. Singles £50.
meals	Bar meals from £3.25. Lunch & dinner, à la carte, about £19.
closed	Christmas Day.
directions	On entering Hay pass Nat West Bank, next right & downhill for 40 yds. Kilverts on right. Car park at rear.

Hotel

	Colin Thomson
tel	01497 821042
fax	01497 821580
email	info@kilverts.co.uk
web	www.kilverts.co.uk

Penrhos Hotel

Kington, Herefordshire HR5 3LH

The architecture is magnificent. The medieval cruck hall (1280) was the first of the buildings to make up Penrhos Court; since then, each generation has added or adapted to suit the needs of the times. The result of 700 years of farm-building evolution is a black-timbered house facing ancient barns around a large grassy courtyard with a puddleduck pond in the middle. The ancient farmstead has remained true to its roots, and suppers, served on long oak tables in the great hall, are fittingly local and organic. Owner Daphne Lambert is one of the most creative chefs in the country and her food resonates with natural flavours and nutritional value. The home-baked bread is superb, the ingredients entirely seasonal: line-caught fish comes overnight from Cornwall, organic chicken is from Graig Farm, vegetables are from the surrounding area and herbs and fruit from the garden, picked and dug that day. Bedrooms have field views, lovely in summer, there is a snug sitting room from the 14th century and authenticity at every turn. *Green Cuisine food and health courses held here.*

rooms	15: 9 doubles, 4 twins, 2 four-posters.
price	£95-£120. Singles from £65.
meals	Dinner, 4 courses, £31.50.
closed	January.
directions	From Leominster, A44 for Kington. Hotel 1 mile before Kington on left, 200 yds up drive, signed.

Hotel

Martin Griffiths & Daphne Lambert

tel	01544 230720
fax	01544 230754
email	martin@penrhos.co.uk
web	www.penrhos.co.uk

The George Hotel

Quay Street, Yarmouth, Isle of Wight PO41 0PE

The position is fabulous, with the old castle on one side, the sea at the end of a sunny garden, and the centre of Yarmouth, the island's oldest town, just beyond the front door – handy if you're a corrupt governor intent on sacking passing ships. Admiral Sir Robert Holmes moved here for that very reason in 1668, demolishing a bit of the castle to improve his view. The house has been rebuilt since Sir Robert's day but a grand feel still lingers: the entrance is large, light and stone-flagged; a drawing room next door is panelled, with kilim-covered sofas. Six newly refurbished bedrooms were done in Colefax and Jane Churchill, while the bigger, more expensive bedrooms are also beautifully panelled; one has a huge four-poster, and two have timber balconies with views out to sea. Meals can be taken outside in the garden bar; or else eat in the buzzy, cheerful, yellow-and-wood brasserie, or the sumptuous, burgundy dining room. Dig even deeper into your pocket and charter a private boat to take you to lunch at their other hotel on the mainland.

rooms	17: 15 twins/doubles, 2 singles.
price	£175-£235. Singles from £125.
meals	Lunch & dinner in brasserie from £25. Dinner in restaurant, 4 courses, £45. Restaurant closed Sundays & Mondays.
closed	Rarely.
directions	Lymington ferry to Yarmouth, then follow signs to town centre.

Hotel

	Jacki Everest
tel	01983 760331
fax	01983 760425
email	res@thegeorge.co.uk
web	www.thegeorge.co.uk

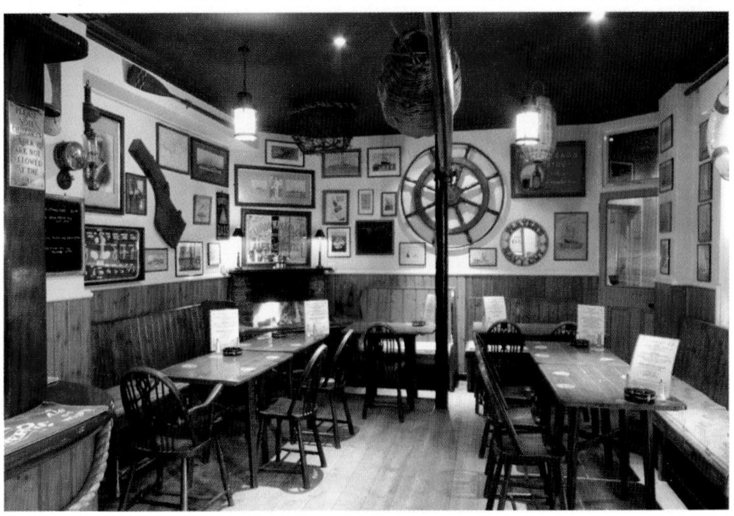

Seaview Hotel and Restaurant

High Street, Seaview, Isle of Wight PO34 5EX

The Seaview's reputation has spread beyond the isle and its yachtsmen; they organise gourmet cycling breaks, and you can put up here and 'walk the Wight' in May. The terrace, with its railings, mast and flag, is like the prow of a boat, and the nautical theme continues inside. Wander past portholes, ships' wheels, lanterns and sails into the restaurant – for seabass with spinach mash and lemon oil, organic salmon and their very special tomato summer pudding; in the bar, order island-brewed Goddard's Special and the famous hot crab ramekin. Food is taken seriously here, eight chefs dancing attendance in the kitchen. The sitting room is lovely and antique-cosy with binoculars and papers; bedrooms are smartly colour coordinated and have all you need, the bigger ones at the front with sea views, the smaller ones at the back nice and quiet. But it's the service that sets the place apart. Beds are turned down, a full cooked breakfast can be brought to your room and staff couldn't be nicer. And you get day membership of a fabulous health club, with pool, nearby. Great for families.

rooms	16: 3 doubles, 11 twins/doubles, 2 family suites.
price	£74-£179. Singles from £58. Suites £194-£252.
meals	Lunch & dinner £5-£30.
closed	Christmas.
directions	From Ryde, B3330 south for 1.5 miles. Hotel signed left.

Hotel

Nicholas & Nicola Hayward

tel 01983 612711
fax 01983 613729
email reception@seaviewhotel.co.uk
web www.seaviewhotel.co.uk

Priory Bay Hotel

Priory Drive, Nettlestone, Isle of Wight PO34 5BU

Medieval monks thought Priory Bay special, so did Tudor farmers and Georgian gentry; all helped to mould this tranquil landscape. Parkland rolls down from the main house and tithe barns to a ridge of trees. The land then drops down to a long, clean sandy beach and a shallow sea; it's as mediterranean as Britain gets. Fishermen land their catch here for the freshest grilled seafood. Huge rooms in the house mix classical French and contemporary English styles. The sun-filled drawing room has tall windows – exquisite rococo-style chairs obligingly face out to sea, and afternoon cream teas by the winter log fire are a treat. The dining room has a mural of the bay on the wall, and elaborate flower decorations at each table. Bedrooms in the main house are luxurious; some have a fresh and modern feel, others oak panelling, maybe a crow's nest balcony and telescope. Bedrooms in nearby outbuildings are less enticing but much cheaper. Andrew is a humorous host, and a supporter of the organic movement – they grow as much as they can. The grounds also support falcon and red squirrel, and the odd golfer.

rooms	26: 16 twins/doubles, 10 family.
price	£90-£270. Half-board £65-£125 p.p. Singles from £65.
meals	Lunch & dinner £25. Picnic hampers available.
closed	Rarely.
directions	From Ryde, B3330 south through Nettlestone, then left up road, signed to Nodes Holiday Camp. Entrance on left, signed.

Hotel

	Andrew Palmer
tel	01983 613146
fax	01983 616539
email	reception@priorybay.co.uk
web	www.priorybay.co.uk

The Walpole Bay Hotel

Fifth Avenue, Cliftonville, Kent CT9 2JJ

Edwardian through and through... and as much a museum as a hotel, The Walpole is splendidly faded and run with true devotion. It's been Jane and Peter's long ambition to preserve that period between the wars when genteel English folk flocked to the seaside in their best attire. Step back in time as you walk up marble steps to a beautiful wrought-iron veranda with wicker chairs and old sedans. Inside, swirly carpets, flowery wallpaper, huge palms, working gas lights, Lincrusta panelling and old photos of guests posing outside with their charabancs; many of the museum's artefacts were donated. The ballroom with its sprung maple floor is retro heaven – the 20s and 40s nights are recommended! The 1927 gated Otis lift travels three floors to bedrooms with sea views; the balconies are next to be restored. Jane and Peter live in the butler's quarters and are as fun as the hotel is authentic – everything fits so well, you can't help falling for its nostalgic charm. There's lots to do as well. Visit the extraordinary shell grotto, or stroll along the Thanet coastline and find an 80-million-year-old fossil.

rooms	42: 34 doubles, 3 four-posters, 5 suites.
price	£60-£105. Singles £40-£75. Suites £65-£75.
meals	Lunch from £3.50. Dinner, à la carte, from £15. Afternoon tea from £3.50.
closed	Rarely.
directions	From Margate, to Cliftonville along road with beach on left, pass Winter Gardens & Lido. Fifth Ave. on left after Butlins Hotel.

Hotel

Jane & Peter Bishop

tel	01843 221703
fax	01843 297399
email	info@walpolebayhotel.co.uk
web	www.walpolebayhotel.co.uk

The Ringlestone Inn

Ringlestone Hamlet, Nr Harrietsham, Kent ME17 1NX

Two old sisters once ran The Ringlestone; if they liked the look of you, they'd lock you in; if they didn't, they'd shoot at you. Michael and his daughter Michelle have let that tradition slip, preferring to run their 1635 ale house with a breezy conviviality. Glass tankards dangle above the bar, a woodburner throws out heat from the inglenook and old *Punch* cartoons hang on the original brick and flint walls between oak beams and stripped wooden floors. They stock 30 fruit wines and liqueurs as well as excellent local ales to sup in settles or on quirky, tiny, yet very comfy chairs. Across the lane in the farmhouse, bedrooms are perfect: oak furniture, sublime beds, crisp linen and big, luxurious bathrooms. The food is good – panini or penne for lunch, maybe, game pie (they specialise in pies) with redcurrant wine for dinner. There are waterfalls and *pétanque* in the garden, space for big parties, a children's licence and the occasional vintage car rally. Good walking, fabulous Leeds castle close, and breakfasts that will keep your strength up for a week.

rooms	3: 2 twins/doubles, 1 four-poster.
price	£99-£120. Singles £89.
meals	Breakfast £12-£15. Lunch from £5.50. Dinner £8-£25.
closed	Christmas Day.
directions	M20, junc. 8. Left after 0.25 miles at 2nd r'bout to Hollingbourne. Through Hollingbourne, up hill, then right at brown 'Knife and Fork' sign. Pub on right after 1.5 miles.

Inn

Michelle Stanley
tel 01622 859900
fax 01622 859966
email bookings@ringlestone.com
web www.ringlestone.com

Wallett's Court Country House Hotel

Westcliffe, St Margaret's at Cliffe, Dover, Kent CT15 6EW

Wallett's Court is *old*. Odo, half-brother of William the Conqueror, lived on the land in Norman times, then Jacobeans left their mark in 1627. When Chris and Lea renovated in 1975, the house gave up long-held secrets: tobacco pipes fell from a ceiling and 17th-century paintings were found in a blocked-off passageway, still hanging on the wall. Gavin, their son, now runs the business with the same passion and commitment – all feels warm and genuine... even the ghost is well-behaved. Old features catch the eye: ancient red-brick walls in the drawing room, an oak staircase with worn, shallow steps in the hall. Bedrooms in the main house are big, with heaps of character, those in the barn and cottages are smaller and quiet. Above the spa complex – indoor pool, sauna, steam room and massage, aromatherapy and treatment suite – four excellent, contemporary rooms have been recently added. There's tennis, a terrace with views towards a distant sea and white cliffs within a mile for breezy walks, rolling mists and wheeling gulls. Great food, too, and puddings to diet for. Popular with golfers.

rooms	16: 13 doubles, 2 twins, 1 family.
price	£99-£159. Singles £79-£119.
meals	Lunch £17.50. Dinner £27.50.
closed	Christmas.
directions	From Dover, A2/A20, then A258 towards Deal, then right, signed St Margaret's at Cliffe. House 1 mile on right, signed.

Hotel

Chris, Lea & Gavin Oakley

tel	01304 852424
fax	01304 853430
email	stay@wallettscourt.com
web	www.wallettscourt.com

Romney Bay House

Coast Road, New Romney, Kent TN28 8QY

The library look-out upstairs has a telescope so you can spy on France on a clear day. Designed by Clough Williams-Ellis – creator of Portmeirion – for American film star Hedda Hopper, this ethereal dreamscape is as stunning as the photograph suggests. Inside, the whole place has a lingering 1920s house-party feel. There's an honesty bar full of colour, a drawing room with sofas to sink into, a conservatory for cream teas, a dining room where Clinton serves up great things. Two years ago he and Lisa swapped jobs in London hotels for the Good Life in Kent; they have impeccable pedigrees both, and know what works... whether you're here for a conference, a wedding or a great escape, you'll love their relaxed perfectionism. Curl up by the fire with a book or a game – there are plenty to borrow; go for a bracing shingleside walk; whack a few balls on the tennis court, drive the fairways on the neighbouring green. Bedrooms are elegant and full of everything you'd hope for: pretty furniture, half-testers, sleigh beds and views – some to the links, some to the sea. An unpretentiously intimate place.

rooms	10: 8 doubles, 2 twins.
price	£85-£150. Singles £60-£95.
meals	Dinner, 4 courses, £35. Cream teas from £5.75.
closed	One week at Christmas.
directions	M20, junc. 10, A2070 south, then A259 east through New Romney. Right to Littlestone; left at sea & on for 1 mile.

Hotel

Clinton & Lisa Lovell
tel 01797 364747

Cloth Hall Oast

Cranbrook, Kent TN17 3NR

Sweep up the rhododendron-lined drive to this immaculate Kentish oast house and barn. For 40 years Mrs Morgan lived in the 15th-century manor next door, where she tended both guests and garden; now she has turned her perfectionist's eye upon these five acres. There are well-groomed lawns, a carp-filled pond, pergola, summer house, pool and flowers – two beds of orange and yellow, four all-white. Light shimmers through swathes of glass in the dining room; off-white walls and pale beams that soar from floor to rafter. Mrs Morgan is a courteous hostess and an excellent cook; discuss in the morning what you'd like for dinner – duck with cherries, sole Veronique... later you dine at an antique table gleaming with crystal and candelabra. There are two bedrooms for guests: a four-poster on the ground floor, a triple on the first. Colours are soft, fabrics are frilled but nothing is busy or overdone; you are spoiled with good bathrooms and fine mattresses, crisp linen and flowered chintz. And there's a sitting room for guests, made snug by a log fire on winter nights.

rooms	2: 1 four-poster, 1 triple.
price	£110-£120.
meals	Dinner £20-£22.
closed	Rarely.
directions	1 mile SE of Cranbrook off Golford Road to Tenterden. Private road to right alongside the cemetery.

B&B

Mrs Katherine Morgan

tel 01580 712220

email clothhalloast@aol.com

The Inn at Whitewell

Whitewell, Clitheroe, Lancashire BB7 3AT

Richard was advised not to touch this inn with a bargepole, which must qualify as among the worst advice ever given, because you'll be hard-pressed to find anywhere better than this. The inn sits just above the River Hodder with views across parkland to rising fells in the distance. Merchants used to stop at this old deerkeeper's lodge and fill up with wine, food and song before heading north through notorious bandit country; superb hospitality is still assured but the most that will hold you up today is a stubborn sheep. Back at the inn, Richard, officially the Bowman of Bowland, wears an MCC tie and peers over half-moon glasses with a soft, slightly mischievous smile on his face, master of all this informal pleasure. The bedrooms are warm and cosy, some with fabulous Victorian showers, others with deep cast-iron baths and Benesson fabrics; all have art and Bose music systems; the biggest look onto the river. The food is a treat and the restaurant drinks in the view. There are also seven miles of private fishing, even their own well-priced Vintner's. Mildly eccentric, great fun.

rooms	17: 11 twins/doubles, 5 four-posters, 1 suite.
price	£94-£120. Singles £69-£110. Suite £110-£140.
meals	Bar meals from £5.50. Dinner, à la carte, from £23.50.
closed	Rarely.
directions	M6, junc. 31a, then B6243 east through Longridge, then follow signs to Whitewell for 9 miles.

Inn

Richard Bowman
tel 01200 448222
fax 01200 448298

The Victoria

10 West Temple Sheen, Richmond, London SW14 7RT

This is a cool, contemporary gastropub, that manages to be both down-to-earth and quietly vibrant. Big airy rooms are full of pretty things: expect Designers Guild leather armchairs, comfy sofas, Bonzini table football, painted floorboards and splashy modern oils. The locals love it and have turned it into a *de facto* community centre. Mothers gather for coffee after they've dropped the kids off at school – but they come for the food, too, and for good reason. Mark and Clare have transformed the place in the years they've been here; the hallmarks now are fine rooms, good food and helpful staff. Treat yourself to *caldo verde*, bouillabaisse, and poached pear with chocolate for about £25, then retire to stylish bedrooms. You'll find white walls, Egyptian cotton, beechwood beds, suede bedheads, goose down pillows, cashmere blankets and high-pressure showers. Every room has a PC and broadband internet connection... all free. Great value for money, and with the Sheen Gate entrance to Richmond Park close by, you can walk off your indulgence lost to the world. A great little place.

rooms	7: 5 doubles, 2 twins/doubles.
price	£98.50. Singles £82.50.
meals	Lunch & dinner £10-£35.
closed	Christmas.
directions	Train: Waterloo to Mortlake. Buses: 33, 337, 485.

Restaurant with Rooms

	Mark Chester & Clare Lumley
tel	020 8876 4238
fax	020 8878 3464
email	mark@thevictoria.net
web	www.thevictoria.net

Twenty Nevern Square

Earl's Court, London SW5 9PD

This is a great place, a fusion of classical and minimalist styles, with a clean, cool contemporary interior and beautiful things all around: Victorian birdcages, gilt mirrors, porcelain vases, a bowl full of dried rose petals. There's a real flow to the downstairs, all the way though to the conservatory-bar, with its stained glass, ceiling fans, cane chairs and glass tables. Bedrooms are equally stylish, with natural colours on the walls, cedar-wood blinds and rich fabrics throughout: silks, cottons and linens – nothing here is synthetic. CD players and TVs have been cleverly hidden away in pretty wooden cabinets; there is no clutter. Rooms come in different shapes and sizes, each with something to elate: an Indonesian hand-carved wooden headboard, an Egyptian sleigh bed, a colonial four-poster, some sweeping blue and gold silk curtains. A couple of the rooms have balconies, there are marble bathrooms, too. An open fire warms the sitting room in winter. Good value for money, very friendly staff, and close to the tube.

rooms	20: 13 doubles, 3 twins, 1 suite, 3 four-posters.
price	£99-£140. Four-posters from £120. Suite £160-£190. Singles £80-£110.
meals	Continental breakfast included, full English £5-£9. Room service.
closed	Rarely.
directions	Two-minute walk from Earl's Court tube station. Parking £20 a day, off-street (2pm-11am)

Hotel

	Sadik Saloojee
tel	020 7565 9555
fax	020 7565 9444
email	hotel@twentynevernsquare.co.uk
web	www.twentynevernsquare.co.uk

The Mayflower Hotel

26-28 Trebovir Road, Earl's Court, London SW5 9NJ

Simply amazing, a steal of a hotel that gives great style at knockdown prices with no catches. Harry's Bar in New York was the inspiration for the interior of the juice bar, while in reception an enormous wood carving from Jaipur frames a sculpted waterfall. Wander at will and come across creamy stone floors, leather sofas, American walnut and original art. Bedrooms are not huge but wonderfully designed, with shiny red marble bathrooms and exceptional walk-in showers. Most are filled with unusual antiques from India and the Far East, with lots of carved wood, gorgeous Andrew Martin fabrics and light wood floors. You get swish curtains, Merino wool blankets, Egyptian cotton and ceiling fans. The technology is state-of-the-art, the use of space is clever. Rooms at the front flood with light and a couple have balconies. Family rooms are super-funky with bunk beds and good lighting. The tube is a two-minute walk and Earl's Court is on your doorstep. Don't miss the Troubadour for live music and great food; Bob Dylan, Jimi Hendrix and Joni Mitchell all played here in the 60s.

rooms	47: 28 doubles, 11 twins, 3 singles, 5 family.
price	£89. Singles £59-£79. Family £120.
meals	Continental breakfast included; English breakfast £5-£10.
closed	Rarely.
directions	Tube: Earl's Court. Bus: 74, 328, C1, C3. Parking: Tesco car park (5-minute walk), £25 for 24 hours.

Hotel

	Faisal Saloojee
tel	020 7370 0991
fax	020 7370 0994
email	info@mayflower-group.co.uk
web	www.mayflowerhotel.co.uk

The Cranley Hotel

10 Bina Gardens, South Kensington, London SW5 OLA

In a charming quiet London street of brightly painted Georgian houses, the Cranley has a neat front garden with wooden tables and chairs, clipped bay trees and wide steps up to the front door. The hall leads straight into a calm drawing room with deep Wedgewood-blue walls, original fireplaces, good antiques, coir carpets and the odd lively rug. Bedrooms are extremely comfortable: pale carpets, lilac walls, embroidered headboards over huge beds, plain cream curtains with bedspreads to match, pretty windows and cream-tiled snazzy bathrooms. Robes and slippers, state-of-the-art technology, air conditioning, prettily-laid tables for continental breakfast if you don't want it in bed and lovely Penhaligon smellies as a link back to the family who once owned the house. A cream tea with warm scones and clotted cream in the afternoon comes with the package, along with champagne and canapés at 7pm before you go off to an excellent local restaurant booked by the friendly staff. A treasure. *Weekend rates from £145, breakfast included.*

rooms	39: 4 singles, 15 doubles, 10 twins, 9 four-posters, 1 suite.
price	£165-£285. Suite £285-£345. Singles £141-£180.
meals	Continental breakfast £9.95. 24-hour room service. Restaurants close by.
closed	Rarely.
directions	4-minute walk from Gloucester Road tube. Parking 2 minutes away.

Hotel

	Robert Wauters
tel	020 7373 0123
fax	020 7373 9497
email	info@thecranley.com
web	www.thecranley.com

L'Hotel

28 Basil Street, Knightsbridge, London SW3 1AS

L'Hotel is well-named – it has the feel of a small Parisian hotel, but chief among its many bounties is Isabel, who has proved it is not only what you do, but how you do it that matters. Her way is infectious; she is kind and open and nothing is too much trouble. The hotel's not bad either. No lounge, but a great little restaurant/bar – the social hub of the place – where the odd note of jazz rings out and where wines come direct from the hotel's French vineyard. You can have breakfast down there (excellent coffee in big bowls, pains au chocolat and hot croissants from the hotel bakery), or up in your room, while you laze about on vast beds that are covered in Egyptian cotton, with Nina Campbell fabric on the walls, little box trees on the mantlepiece and original art on the walls. Turn left on your way out and Harvey Nicks is a hundred paces; turn right and Harrods is closer. If you want to eat somewhere fancy, try the Capital next door. It has a big reputation, is owned by the same family (the Levins), and Isabel will book you in. A very friendly, very pretty place.

rooms	12: 11 twins/doubles, 1 suite.
price	£200. Suite £215. Singles £175.
meals	Continental breakfast included; full English £6.50. Lunch & dinner £5-£20.
closed	Rarely.
directions	Tube: Knightsbridge. Bus: 14, 19, 22, 52, 74, 137, C1. Parking: £25 a day off-street.

Hotel

	Isabel Murphy
tel	020 7589 6286
fax	020 7823 7826
email	reservations@lhotel.co.uk
web	www.lhotel.co.uk

The Dorchester

Park Lane, Mayfair, London W1A 2HJ

Enter through revolving doors and be greeted by a battalion of liveried doormen, gliding effortlessly across marble floors under a gilded ceiling that defies overstatement. Keep going and you're in The Promenade, a stunningly beautiful room through which all Dorchester life flows. It is *the* place to linger – a window back in time to an England that once was – so come for afternoon tea or to sip champagne while the pianist plays. Bedrooms are what you'd expect: the crispest linen, the plushest fabrics, fabulous marble bathrooms, pure heaven. The Oliver Messel suite is considered one of the finest in the world (and comes with a price tag of £2,500 a night), but all rooms elate. Downstairs in the piano bar there's Liberace's mirrored piano, while in the Grill Room you can eat the best roast beef in the world. You also get spas, saunas and steam rooms, hi-tech gadgetry coming out of your ears, and a private dining room where you can watch the cooks at work. I've hardly scratched the surface, but if you're looking for the show-stopping best, then this is it. *Weekend rates from £315, full breakfast included.*

rooms	250: 170 doubles, 30 twins, 50 suites.
price	£395-£510. Suites from £650. Singles from £325.
meals	Breakfast £19.50-£23. Lunch & dinner from £30.
closed	Never.
directions	Tube: Green Park. Bus: 2, 10, 16, 36, 73, 74, 82, 137. Parking: Brick St car park £35 24 hrs.

Hotel

David Wilkinson

tel	020 7629 8888
fax	020 7409 0114
email	reservations@dorchesterhotel.com
web	www.dorchesterhotel.com

The Royal Park Hotel

3 Westbourne Terrace, Lancaster Gate, Hyde Park, London W2 3UL

Paddington is just round the corner – and Hyde Park a three-minute stroll – yet there is none of the sleaze that surrounds many railway stations. The houses here are dignified and handsome; in this case, three houses newly rolled into one in a grand gesture of solidarity – but so discreetly that you would hardly know there was a hotel here at all. It is easy to imagine the carriages trundling up to the door in Victorian times. Staff are attentive and kind – and charmingly multi-national. If you arrive at tea-time you will be served complimentary scones and jams in one of the two small drawing rooms, where you may pretend to be grander than you feel. (If the company is uninspiring, bury yourself in a newspaper or gaze studiously at the flickering gas fire.) Later, champagne and canapés will be served too, all 'on the house' – a lovely touch that encourages guests to chat. The bedrooms are serenely impeccable, generous with their beds, handmade mattresses, crisp sheets, woollen blankets, fat pillows and elegant bathrooms – and with almost every conceivable minor luxury.

rooms	48: 2 singles, 28 doubles, 5 twins, 2 four-posters, 11 suites.
price	£165-£285. Suite £285-£345. Singles £141-£180.
meals	Continental breakfast £9.95. Restaurants nearby.
closed	Rarely.
directions	5 minutes walk from Paddington or Lancaster Gate tube stations.

Hotel

Lina Stahl

tel	020 7479 6600
fax	0207 479 6601
email	info@theroyalpark.com
web	www.theroyalpark.com

Miller's

111a Westbourne Grove, London W2 4UW

This is Miller's, as in the antique guides, and the collectibles on show in the first-floor drawing room make it one of the loveliest rooms in this book. Breakfast is taken communally around a 1920s walnut table, while at night, cocktails are served on the house, a fire crackles in the carved-wood fireplace and a couple of hundred candles flicker around you. It is an aesthetic overdose, exquisitely bohemian, every wall stuffed with gilt-framed pictures. An eclectic collection of regulars include movie moguls, fashion photographers, rock stars, even a professional gambler. An opera singer once gave guests singing lessons at breakfast. Wander at will and find an altar of Tibetan deities (well, their statues), a 1750s old master's chair, busts and sculptures, globes, chandeliers, plinths, rugs and a three-legged chair stuffed on top of a Regency wardrobe. Things get moved around all the time, so expect the scene to change. Muralled walls in the hall were inspired by the Pope's palace at Avignon. Bedrooms upstairs are equally embellished, just a little less cluttered. Incredible, in oh-so-cool Notting Hill.

rooms	8: 6 doubles, 2 suites.
price	£175-£270.
meals	Continental breakfast only & open bar.
closed	Occasionally.
directions	Tube: Bayswater, Queensway, Notting Hill Gate. Bus: 7, 23, 28, 31, 70. Nearest car park, £25 for 24 hrs.

Hotel

	Verginie Le Rumeur
tel	020 7243 1024
fax	020 7243 1064
email	enquiries@millersuk.com
web	www.millersuk.com

Portobello Gold

95-97 Portobello Road, Notting Hill Gate, London W11 2QB

A quirky little place bang on the Portobello Road; Bill Clinton once stopped here for a pint, then left without paying. On Saturdays the market passes directly outside, but for the rest of the week you can sit out on the pavement and watch Portobello life pass by. A very easy-going place, a cheep and cheerful sleepery where you can stay for the London equivalent of next to nothing. Rooms are basic – bed, chair, desk, TV – so if you're after fancy hotel luxury, apply elsewhere. If, however, you want to bring out your inner hippy, you'll love it here (as does a certain Alastair Sawday); the backpacker room is amazingly cheap. There's a conservatory/jungle dining room at the back (book the cushioned hippy deck), tiled floors and open fires in the bar, and good art on the walls – the place doubles as a gallery. The cyber café is free to hotel guests, there are trappist ales, Belgian beers and the best wines available by the glass (Linda is a wine writer). Superb food – Thai moules, *sashimi*, Irish rock oysters, Sunday roasts – friendly natives, and the apartment has a roof terrace, so watch the Carnival pass in August.

rooms	7: 5 doubles; 1 backpacker twin with separate shower; 1 suite.
price	From £60. Backpacker from £40. Apt £180. Singles from £56.
meals	Continental breakfast included; full English £5.50. Bar meals from £6. Dinner £20-£25.
closed	Never.
directions	Tube: Notting Hill. Bus: 12, 27, 28, 31, 52, 328. Parking meters outside.

Restaurant with Rooms

	Michael Bell & Linda Johnson-Bell
tel	020 7460 4910
fax	020 7229 2278
email	reservations@portobellogold.com
web	www.portobellogold.com

Hotel "Le Deconstruction"

Somewhere Street, Downtown, London N01 Z35

Once the local planners had been to see Damien Hirst at the Tate there was no stopping them. All new buildings had to show their innards on their outtards – not unlike the Pompidou Centre in Paris. Developers learned to design in such a way that buildings appeared to have been sliced in two, pickled and then suspended. In the case of this particular redevelopment, the owners have succeeded magnificently, ensuring that the hotel is seen as one half of a whole, and that the other half is seen to have had its own existence. The effect is raw and direct, and you will either love it or hate it – probably the latter. To have achieved this effect with such an unpromising building is unusual. The 'Action' sign on the side is the developer's logo, and is as dynamic as their whole approach. Inside, rooms are done out in the new 'bleak' style: you enter with your personality intact and leave without it. Little, not even this text, will prepare you for the experience of staying here. We thought it worth including, if only to test the flexibility of our readers – famous for their uniquely open-minded approach.

rooms	112 multi-function spaces, with fresh air for insulation.
price	£1,500. Only the most moneyed can afford this level of discomfort.
meals	None - that would be pandering.
closed	Never, but often pretends to be.
directions	To be found on many modern tourist maps of London but may be missed when passing because the ruination effect is so convincing.

Other place

	The Management
tel	01 01 01 01 / 10
email	dis-info@action-against-comfort.no.uk
web	www.de-commodation.com.co.uk.com.not

Didsbury House

Didsbury Park, Didsbury Village, Manchester M20 5L

Stylish Eleven Didsbury Park made a name for itself on the 'boutique hotel' circuit; now along comes a bigger, more stylish version in a converted Victorian villa. Didsbury House seduces the moment you enter: beautiful inlaid parquet floors and an original carved wooden staircase that carries the eye upwards to a magnificent stained-glass window. Planners and building regulations may have thwarted Eamonn and Sally's wilder ambitions at their first hotel down the street but here in this 1840 merchant's house their ideas run rampant: the luxurious attic suite has separate his and her roll-top baths as well as his and her seats in a gigantic shower cubicle; in every gorgeous room, baths fit two. Two split level 'duplex' rooms add further intrigue; a walkway spans a central atrium above your head; a sitting room, with ostrich-egg-shaped lights and pewter bar, leads outside through French windows; a floor below are the gym and spa. Contemporary interior design and down-to-earth Mancunian humour. Superb.

rooms	26: 20 twins/doubles, 6 suites.
price	£81-£145. Suites £140-£350.
meals	Breakfast £10.95-£12.95.
closed	Rarely.
directions	From Manchester city centre, A34 south for 4 miles, then right on A5145 Wimslow Rd. Didsbury Park 4th on right; hotel on corner.

Hotel

	Eamonn & Sally O'Loughlin
tel	0161 448 2200
fax	0161 448 2525
email	enquiries@didsburyhouse.co.uk
web	www.didsburyhouse.co.uk

The Lifeboat Inn

Ship Lane, Thornham, Norfolk PE36 6LT

The Lifeboat Inn is ideal for some away-from-it-all, traditional, unpretentious good cheer – there's not enough of it about. It's been an ale house since the 16th century, they know how to serve a decent pint – Adnams, Greene King, Woodfordes – and use locally-sourced food whenever possible to good effect in both the beamy bar and the more formal, richly coloured restaurant. Try the bar for its staples – steaming cauldrons of Norfolk mussels and chips and real ale-battered fish – and the restaurant for dishes with a more sophisticated air. The bedrooms are pine-furnished, not huge but entirely functional and well-equipped; most have mind-clearing views over the marsh to the sea. North-west Norfolk is a great place for being outdoors; come when the wind blows and the hall fire flickers around damp dogs, while the odd stuffed animal looks on. Bask in the sheltered courtyard when it's sunny and let the children run. Staff are kind and unfussy, the atmosphere easy. We understand that there are other rooms nearby in the Old Coach House – do check when booking.

rooms	14: 1 double, 13 twins/doubles.
price	£78-£110. Half-board (minimum 2 nights) from £84 p.p. Singles £59-£75.
meals	Lunch from £8.95. Dinner £26.
closed	Rarely.
directions	From King's Lynn, A149 via Hunstanton to Thornham. In village, left into Staithe Road; follow road round to right. Inn on right.

Inn

	Angela Coker
tel	01485 512236
fax	01485 512323
email	reception@lifeboatinn.co.uk
web	www.lifeboatinn.co.uk

The Hoste Arms

The Green, Burnham Market, Norfolk PE31 8HD

The Burnhams comprises seven villages on the north Norfolk coast and Burnham Market is the loveliest. Paul Whittome reckons he and the Hoste Arms were made for each other. In its 300-year history the place has been a court house, a livestock market, an art gallery and a brothel. Paul has been a potato merchant, a property developer and a bouncer in a Chinese shanty pub in Australia; he has not shrunk since then, merely transformed himself from ejector to welcomer. Brilliantly, too, for The Hoste has won almost every prize going – *The Times* voted it their second favourite hotel in England, their 27th in the world, and gave it a 'Golden Pillow' award. The place has a genius of its own – brave and successful mixtures of bold colour, chairs to sink deep into, panelled walls, its own art gallery – and food to be eaten in rapture, anywhere and anytime. Every bedroom is different: a tartan four-poster here, a swagged half-tester there, a leather TV console in the state-of-the-art Zulu wing. There's no one to rush you, breakfast lasts as long as you like and the bar pulls in an intriguing array of regulars – spot the stars.

rooms	36: 12 twins/doubles, 5 singles, 1 family, 6 suites, 4 four-posters. Zulu wing: 5 doubles, 3 suites.
price	£108-£168. Singles £78-£164. Suites £136-£168.
meals	Lunch & dinner £4.25-£30.
closed	Rarely.
directions	From King's Lynn, A149 north; A148. 2 miles, left onto B1153. At Gt Bircham, branch right onto B1155 to B. Market.

Hotel

	Paul & Jeanne Whittome
tel	01328 738777
fax	01328 730103
email	reception@hostearms.co.uk
web	www.hostearms.co.uk

The Victoria at Holkham

Park Road, Wells-next-the-Sea, Norfolk NR23 1RG

Come for Rajasthan colour and the prettiest rooms on the north Norfolk coast. On the Holkham Hall estate, owned by the Earl of Leicester, Tom (Viscount Coke) and his wife Polly have taken on the old Vic and turned it into a heavenly hotel. Families and stressed city folk are drawn to the rare mix of escapism and boho chic... splashes of aubergine, lime-green and pink mingle with the old colonial feel, in homage to the pub's royal namesake. Stone flags and seagrass floors, velvet sofas and leather armchairs, huge bowls of lemons and limes, a buzzing bar, a feel of anticipation... not your usual retreat. In a dining room redolent with lilies, unobtrusive young staff ferry in crabs from Cromer, game from the estate and great steaming nursery puddings; children get their own two-course menu – and outdoor swings. Bedrooms vary in size and look but all are serene in their Indian garb, the quietest away from the bar; their views are to marshes and sea or walled garden with beached boat. Sands and skylarks are a stroll away – at their finest, and quietest, out of season. And the Big Hall is magnificent.

rooms	10 + 1: 9 doubles, 1 attic suite. 1 self-catering lodge.
price	£110-£200. Singles £90-£110. Lodge £160-£200 for up to 4. Children in parents' room £15.
meals	Lunch/dinner £25-£30.
closed	Rarely.
directions	On A149, 2 miles west of Wells-next-the-Sea.

Hotel

	Paul Brown
tel	01328 711008
fax	01328 711009
email	victoria@holkham.co.uk
web	www.victoriaatholkham.co.uk

Saracens Head

Wolterton , Erpingham, Norfolk NR11 7LX

Food, real ale, good wines, a delightful sheltered courtyard and walled garden, Norfolk's bleakly lovely coast – this is why people come here. But the food is the deepest seduction. Robert and his team cook up "some of Norfolk's most delicious wild and tame treats". Typical starters are Morston mussels with cider and cream, or fricassée of wild mushrooms. Expect pigeon, Cromer crab, venison. Then Robert works his own magic on old favourites such as bread and butter pudding... vegetarians are pampered too; try baked avocado with sweet pear and mozzarella. The bar is as convivial as a bar could be, a welcome antidote to garish pub bars with their fruit machines – Robert will have none of them. There's a parlour room for residents, with a big open-brick fireplace, deep red walls, colourful plastic tablecloths, candles in old wine bottles, a black leather banquette along two walls. Bedrooms are colourful, comfortable and in keeping with the quality of the food. The whole mood is of quirky, committed individuality – slightly arty, slightly unpredictable and in the middle of nowhere.

rooms	4: 3 doubles, 1 twin.
price	£75. Singles £45.
meals	Bar meals from £3.95. Dinner about £17.
closed	Christmas Day.
directions	From Norwich, A140 passed Aylsham, then left, for Erpingham. Through village to Calthorpe. Over x-roads. On right after 0.5 miles.

Inn

	Robert Dawson-Smith
tel	01263 768909
fax	01263 768993
web	www.saracenshead-norfolk.co.uk

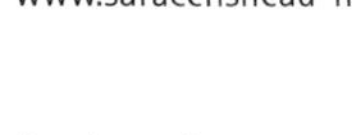

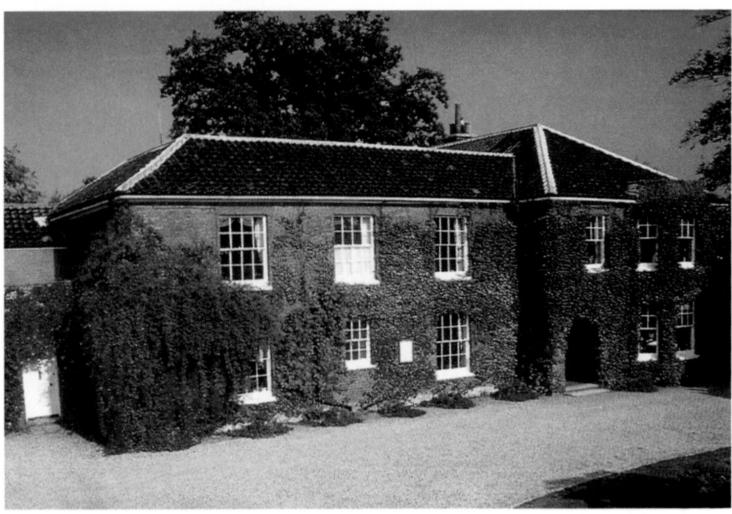

Beechwood Hotel

Cromer Road, North Walsham, Norfolk NR28 0HD

There's an old-fashioned perfectionism about the Beechwood – it is impeccable, professional and immensely well-mannered. Agatha Christie was a frequent guest when it was a private house and it is not difficult even now to imagine quiet conspiratorial conversations over dinner. The atmosphere is that of a traditional country-house hotel but with imaginative flourishes: bold black and white tiling in one bathroom, with a splendid, old roll-top bath painted black on the outside – the cistern is still, quite rightly, high on the wall, the down-pipe gleaming. Curtains in the dining room are richly pelmeted, the separate tables elegant and attractive. The food is British with a strong mediterranean influence: *fettucine* with a wild mushroom, stilton and tarragon sauce, roast Scottish salmon on a saffron risotto, haddock, prawn and chive cakes... all sound delicious. The bread is homemade and organic ingredients are used whenever possible. In the bedrooms, curtains match the bedspreads; in the smart sitting room, old leather sofas and armchairs demand to be wallowed in. Above all, there is space – and peace.

rooms	10: 8 doubles, 1 twin, 1 four-poster.
price	£90-£160. Half-board £60 p.p. Singles £68.
meals	Lunch £18. Dinner £30.
closed	Christmas.
directions	From Norwich, B1150 to North Walsham. Under railway bridge, then left at next traffic lights. Hotel 150 yds on left.

Hotel

	Lindsay Spalding & Don Birch
tel	01692 403231
fax	01692 407284
email	enquiries@beechwood-hotel.co.uk
web	www.beechwood-hotel.co.uk

The Norfolk Mead Hotel

Coltishall, Norwich, Norfolk NR12 7DN

The setting is enchanting and you can paddle your canoe from the bottom of the garden to the Broads. But make time for these eight acres – lawns, trees, walled garden, swimming pool, fish-stocked lake and dinghy for messing about on the river. The sugar planter's house was built in 1740 – big, gracious and beautifully proportioned. Come for the people, the food and the easy-going comforts of a country-house hotel. A coronet bedhead, a Victorian bath with brass fittings, a striped attic snug… each bedroom is individual, super-comfortable and full of special touches: be-ribboned sheaves of Norfolk lavender, a teddy on the pillows, a basket of primroses, scrumptuous linen. There are a fine entrance hall with sofas and log fire, a bar that opens to the garden, and menus from a creative young chef who loves his kitchen. Food is light, delicate and sophisticated – partridge from Norfolk, mussels from Morston, whisky and orange jelly with hazelnut tuiles, perfect cheese biscuits (homemade). Jill is lovely and full of ideas, daughter Nicky can massage or manicure you, and the barn owl may hoot you to sleep.

rooms	13: 7 doubles, 3 twins, 1 garden suite. Cottage suite: 1 double, 1 twin.
price	£85-£160. Singles £70-£95. Suites from £160. Half-board from £72 p.p.
meals	Dinner £31.50. Sunday lunch £16.75.
closed	Rarely.
directions	From Norwich, B1150 to Coltishall, over bridge; after 600 yds, bear right at petrol station, 1st right before church; down drive, signed.

Hotel

	Jill & Don Fleming
tel	01603 737531
fax	01603 737521
email	info@norfolkmead.co.uk
web	www.norfolkmead.co.uk

Strattons

4 Ash Close, Swaffham, Norfolk PE37 7NH

It's not just the feel of rural France, nor the spectacular interiors that make Strattons so special – it is also one of the most eco-friendly hotels in Britain. "Everything is homemade, recycled, bought locally, restored, renewed and rethought," says Vanessa. Enter a peaceful courtyard where Silky bantams strut – a minute's stroll from the market square – to charmingly informal gardens. Les and Vanessa met at art school, and have covered every square inch of this Queen Anne villa with mosaics, murals, marble busts, plump pillows, piles of books, bunches of dried roses, rugs on wooden floors – it feels like a wildly original French château. Bedrooms are exquisite: a carved four-poster, a tented bathroom, Indian brocade, stained glass, trompe l'œil panelling and sofas by a log fire; the two suites are heaven. Dine in the pure and simple lower-ground floor bistro, with white-painted brickwork, crisp linen, voile curtains and gilt-framed paintings. Vanessa's fresh and seasonal cooking style has won many awards. E M Forster dreamed of a "holy trinity of soil, soul and society" – this comes pretty close.

rooms	8: 3 doubles, 1 twin, 1 four-poster, 3 suites.
price	£100-£140. Singles from £80. Suites from £180.
meals	Dinner, 4 courses, £37.50.
closed	Christmas.
directions	Ash Close runs off north end of market place between W H Brown estate agents & fish and chip restaurant.

Hotel

	Vanessa & Les Scott
tel	01760 723845
fax	01760 720458
email	enquiries@strattonshotel.com
web	www.strattonshotel.com

Congham Hall

Grimston, King's Lynn, Norfolk PE32 1AH

The distant whinny of a horse, the hoot of an owl, the smack of leather on willow – this is as traditional as it gets. Sweep through the graceful Georgian portico into the sunshiney hall for Regency-striped sofas, tea by the fire and country-house living at its English best. Deep sash windows gaze onto 30 acres of parkland, lawns and aromatic gardens (bliss for a summer wedding); after a spot of tennis or a round of clock golf, retire to a chandeliered dining room for ballotine of poussin, a brandy at the bar and a sumptuous bed. There are apples in the orchard, artichokes in the kitchen garden, honey in the hives and over 50 different types of mint... cookery weekends are on the agenda and they smoke their own fish. Food and wines are taken seriously here, with vegetarians looked after as stylishly as the rest. Bedrooms have floral drapes and bedspreads, a sofa to sink into, pot pourri from the garden, a bathroom filled with towels. Cheerful, involved staff are the icing on the cake and the Queen is down the road: pop in to Sandringham on your way home and experience one more immaculate retreat.

rooms	14: 11 doubles, 2 suites, 1 single.
price	£195-£225. Suites £285-£300. Singles £115.
meals	Lunch £13.50-£17.50. Dinner £31.50-£39 (no children under 7).
closed	Rarely.
directions	6 miles east of King's Lynn on A148, 200 yards after r'bout, right tfor Grimston. Signed; hotel 2.5 miles on left. (Do not go to Congham.)

Hotel

	Julie Woodhouse
tel	01485 600250
fax	01485 601191
email	info@conghamhallhotel.co.uk
web	www.conghamhallhotel.co.uk

The Falcon Hotel

Castle Ashby, Nr Northampton, Northamptonshire NN7 1LF

Follow the example of Purdy, The Falcon's gorgeous black labrador, and live life at a contented plod when you stay here. Stone-built and originally a farmhouse dating back to 1594, the inn lies opposite the castle after which this pretty village is named. The Easticks came here after Michael decided he needed another change – he has already been a farmer and a racing driver, among other things. These days, he is quite happy being a hotelier, making sure the cellar bar is full of beer, the oils hang symmetrically, the fire crackles with huge logs and guests get well fed in the pretty stone-walled restaurant; much of the produce comes from their vegetable garden. In summer, eat outside and watch cows saunter up to the dairy as sheep graze beyond; the garden is full of flowers. Bedrooms are split between the inn and a cottage next-door-but-one; all received a makeover recently, with country cottage fabrics, bright yellows and blues, bathrobes, fresh flowers and gentle village views. Wander round the spectacular castle grounds or mooch in nearby craft shops... no need to hurry.

rooms	16: 13 twins/doubles, 3 singles.
price	£89.50-£139.50. Half-board from £69.50 p.p. Singles £69.50-£95.
meals	Lunch from £14.95. Dinner from £19.95 or à la carte.
closed	Rarely.
directions	From Northampton, A428 towards Bedford for about 6 miles, then left, for Castle Ashby. Inn in village.

Hotel

Michael & Jennifer Eastick
tel 01604 696200
email falcon.castleashby@oldenglishinns.co.uk

The Pheasant Inn

Stannersburn, Kielder Water, Northumberland NE48 1DD

A really super little inn, the kind you hope to chance upon: not grand, not scruffy, just right. The Kershaws run it with huge passion and an instinctive understanding of its traditions. The stone walls hold 100-year-old photos of the local community; from colliery to smithy, a vital record of their past heritage – special indeed. The bars are wonderful: brass beer taps glow, anything wooden – ceiling, beams, tables – has been polished to perfection and the clock above the fire keeps perfect time. The attention to detail is staggering. Robin and Irene cook with relish, again nothing fancy, but more than enough to keep a smile on your face – game pies, salmon and local lamb as well as wonderful Northumbrian cheeses. Bedrooms next door in the old hay barn are as you'd expect: simple and cosy, and great value for money. You are in the Northumberland National Park; hire bikes and cycle round the lake, sail on it or go horse-riding. No traffic jams, no rush and wonderful Northumbrian hospitality – they really are the nicest people.

rooms	8: 4 doubles, 3 twins, 1 family.
price	From £65. Half-board from £48 p.p. Singles from £40.
meals	Bar meals from £7.95. Dinner £16-£26.
closed	Mon & Tues November-March.
directions	From Bellingham, follow signs west to Kielder Water & Falstone for 7 miles. Hotel on left, 1 mile short of Kielder Water.

Inn

Walter, Irene & Robin Kershaw

tel 01434 240382

fax 01434 240382

email thepheasantinn@kielderwater.demon.co.uk

web www.thepheasantinn.com

The Hope & Anchor

44 Northumberland Street, Alnmouth, Northumberland NE66 2RA

Hard to believe little Alnmouth was once a bustling port: it used to export more corn than Newcastle. Then in 1806 its banks burst in a great storm, the river became a channel and the port went into rapid decline. Now it's the gentlest of seaside villages. The Hope & Anchor, three dwellings knitted into one, has been an inn for as long as anyone can remember. And Debbie has swept in with a squeaky-clean broom, replacing artex and swirly carpets with 21st-century fabric and colour. You step off the street and into the bar – a straightforward, no frills affair, with a fire for winter snuggery. Then up the stair to creamy-walled bedrooms with new pine, soft lights and comfy beds – spotless and cosy. Debbie's enthusiasm and warmth animates every room; she cooks well, too, and plans a dinner menu for the future. A great little place for families – there's Alnwick Castle round the corner (worth a detour for Harry Potter fans: it's Hogwarts in the film), the fabulous new Alnwick garden, Newcastle and Edinburgh are a train ride away, and mile upon mile of unspoilt beaches await buckets and spades.

rooms	8: 4 doubles, 1 twin, 3 family.
price	£72.
meals	Lunch from £5.95. Dinner from £19.
closed	Rarely.
directions	A1 to Alnwick. At r'bout follow sign for Alnmouth. 1st pub on left in village.

Hotel

Debbie Philipson
tel 01665 830363
email debbiephilipson@hopeandanchorholidays.fsnet
web www.hopeandanchorholidays.co.uk

Lace Market Hotel

29-31 High Pavement, Nottingham, Nottinghamshire NG1 1HE

Once 20,000 women toiled in these city-centre streets, making lace for an empire. Now trendy bars, restaurants, shops and clubs dominate the scene. Bang opposite the old court house is Lace Market Hotel, perfectly carved out of four Georgian houses, and with all its old world charm intact. Inside the feel is swish and contemporary but not minimalist, with wholesome French cooking in the brasserie, sensational cocktails in the bar, and distinctly modern service from cheery staff. At the helm is Mark, he is deeply non-corporate in his approach, loathes UHT milk and tea bags in bedrooms and doesn't approve of calling guests 'Sir' or 'Madam'. It works, and all very comfortably too: bedrooms are richly coloured – burgundy and olive – but light and airy with modern furniture and space to work or flop, beds are all Sealy Posturepedic and huge, bathrooms have pretty tiles and designer basins. Guests also get to use Holmes Place Health Club down the road – a stunning conversion of a Victorian railway station – as well as the hotel's traditional Victorian alehouse next door.

rooms	42: 33 doubles, 6 singles, 3 suites.
price	£110-£135. Singles from £90. Suites £169-£199.
meals	Set lunch 2-3 courses £11.95-£14.95 (Mon-Sat). Dinner, 3 courses à la carte, approx. £24.
closed	Rarely.
directions	From city centre follow brown information signs for Lace Market, Galleries of Justice & St Marys Church.

Hotel

	Mark Cox
tel	01158 523232
email	reservations@lacemarkethotel.co.uk
web	www.lacemarkethotel.co.uk

Langar Hall

Langar, Nottinghamshire NG13 9HG

Langar Hall is one of the most engaging and delightful places in this book – reason enough to come to Nottinghamshire. Imogen's exquisite style and natural joie de vivre make this a mecca for those in search of a warm, country-house atmosphere. The house sits at the top of a hardly noticeable hill in glorious parkland, bang next door to the church. Imo's family came here over 150 years ago. Much of what fills the house came here then and it's easy to feel intoxicated by beautiful things here; statues and busts, a pillared dining room, ancient tomes in overflowing bookshelves, a good collection of oil paintings. Bedrooms are wonderful, some resplendent with antiques, others with fabrics draped from beams or trompe l'œil panelling. Heavenly food, simply prepared for healthy eating, make this almost a restaurant with rooms so you'll need to book if you want to enjoy their own lamb, fish from Brixham, game from Belvoir Castle and garden-grown vegetables. In the grounds: medieval fishponds, canals, a den-like adventure play area and, once a year, Shakespeare on the lawn.

rooms	12: 7 doubles, 2 twins, 1 four-poster, 1 suite & 1 chalet for 2.
price	£90-£185. Singles £65-£100.
meals	Lunch £15. Dinner £30 and à la carte.
closed	Rarely.
directions	From Nottingham, A52 towards Grantham. Right, signed Cropwell Bishop, then straight on for 5 miles. House next to church on edge of village, signed.

B&B

	Imogen Skirving
tel	01949 860559
fax	01949 861045
email	langarhall-hotel@ndirect.co.uk
web	www.langarhall.co.uk

Falkland Arms

Great Tew, Chipping Norton, Oxfordshire OX7 4DB

In a perfect Cotswold village, the perfect English pub. Five hundred years on and the fire still roars in the stone-flagged bar under a low-slung timbered ceiling that drips with jugs, mugs and tankards. Here, the hop is treated with reverence; ales are changed weekly and old pump clips hang from the bar. Tradition runs deep; they stock endless tins of snuff with great names like Irish High Toast and Crumbs of Comfort. In summer, Morris Men jingle in the lane outside and life spills out onto the terrace at the front, and into the big garden behind. This lively pub is utterly down-to-earth and in very good hands. The dining room is tiny and intimate with beams and stone walls; every traditional dish is home-cooked. The bedrooms are snug and cosy, not grand, but fun. Brass beds and four-posters, maybe a heavy bit of oak and an uneven floor – you'll sleep well. The house remains blissfully free of modern trappings, nowhere more so than in the bar, where mobile phones meet with swift and decisive action.

rooms	5 doubles.
price	£75-£100.
meals	Lunch from £4. Dinner from £9. Open all day weekends during summer.
closed	Christmas & New Year. Inn open all year for food & drink.
directions	From Chipping Norton, A361, then right onto B4022, signed Great Tew. Inn by village green.

Inn

Paul Barlow-Heal
& Sarah-Jane Courage

tel 01608 683653
fax 01608 683656
email sjcourage@btconnect.com
web www.falklandarms.org.uk

The Kings Head Inn

The Green, Bledington, Oxfordshire OX7 6AQ

About as Doctor Dolittle-esque as it gets. Achingly pretty Cotswold stone cottages around a village green with quacking ducks, a pond and a perfect pub with a cobbled courtyard. Archie is young, affable and charming with locals and guests, but Nic is his greatest asset – a milliner, she has done up the bedrooms on a shoe string and they look fabulous. All are different, most have a stunning view, some family furniture mixed in with 'bits' she's picked up, painted wood, great colours and lush fabrics. The bar is lively – not with music but with talk – so choose rooms over the courtyard if you prefer a quiet evening. The flagstoned dining room with pale wood tables is elegant and food is cooked by a Swedish chef who is just as good with meat (local) as with fish (truly tasty mackerel and haddock fishcakes). Homemade puds, serious cheeses, lovely unpompous touches like jugs of cow parsley in the loo, tons of things to do (there's a music festival in June) could make this your favourite place to unwind and remember that life isn't all about work.

rooms	12: 10 doubles, 2 twins.
price	From £70. Singles £50.
meals	Lunch from £7.95. Dinner from £9.50.
closed	Christmas.
directions	A429 from Stow-on-the-Wold, left on A424. On right in village.

Inn

Archie & Nic Orr-Ewing

tel	01608 658365
fax	01608 658902
email	kingshead@orr-ewing.com
web	www.kingsheadinn.net

Burford House

99 High Street, Burford, Oxfordshire OX18 4QA

Burford House is a delight, intensely personal, full of elegant good taste, relaxing, and small; small enough for Simon and Jane to influence every corner, which they do with ease and good cheer. Classical music and the scent of fresh flowers drift through beautiful rooms; oak beams, leaded windows, good fabrics, antiques, simple colours, log fires, immaculate beds, roll-top baths and a little garden for afternoon teas… all in this pretty Cotswold town. And there's an honesty bar, with homemade sloe gin and cranberry vodka, to be sipped from cut-glass tumblers. Hand-written menus promise ravishing breakfasts and tempting lunches, and they will recommend the best places for dinner. Both are happy in the kitchen: Simon cooks and Jane bakes, and Cotswold suppliers provide honey, jams, smoked salmon and farmhouse cheeses. Jumble the cat is 'paws on', too. Unwind, then unwind a little more. Enchanting river walks start in either direction through classic English countryside. Guests return time after time. A perfect little find.

rooms	8: 3 doubles, 2 twins, 3 four-posters.
price	£105-£155. Singles from £85.
meals	Light lunch & afternoon tea (restaurant closed Sundays & Mondays). Dinner available in Burford & nearby villages.
closed	Rarely.
directions	In centre of Burford.

B&B

Jane & Simon Henty

tel	01993 823151
fax	01993 823240
email	stay@burfordhouse.co.uk
web	www.burfordhouse.co.uk

The Lamb Inn

Sheep Street, Burford, Oxfordshire OX18 4LR

Old inn – new owners. Bruno and Rachel haven't made any big changes and in many ways there's no need; the inn proper dates back to 1420 when it used to be a dormy house. In the old bar, the footsteps of monks and thirsty locals have worn a gentle groove into the original stone floor and there's a glorious smell of wood smoke. Make a grand tour and you'll come across four fires, two sitting rooms, rambling corridors, lots of polished brass and silver, thick rugs, mullioned windows, old parchments and a settle with a back high enough "to keep the draught off a giant's neck". Bedrooms are just as good, with plump-cushioned armchairs, heavy oak beams, brass beds with excellent mattresses and gorgeous antiques. Exciting changes though have been made in the kitchen under Head Chef Adrian Jones's direction; lunch and dinner menus make the best use of seasonal, local food, and you can choose to eat in the bar, lounges, dining room – or outside under a stylish parasol. The new wine list is remarkable with some real surprises, the beer is excellent. Lucky locals!

rooms	15: 11 doubles, 3 twins, 1 four-poster.
price	£125-£185. Singles from £80.
meals	Dinner, 2 or 3 courses, £25-£29.50.
closed	Rarely.
directions	From Oxford, A40 west to Burford. Sheep Street is 1st left down High Street.

Inn

Bruno & Rachel Cappuccini
tel 01993 823155
email info@lambinn-burford.co.uk
web www.lambinn-burford.co.uk

The Feathers Hotel

Market Street, Woodstock, Oxfordshire OX20 1SX

Once a draper's, then a butcher's, this serene English townhouse hotel has stayed true to its roots, with the finest fabrics and award-winning food its proud standard. Follow labyrinthine corridors under mind-your-head beams to the four original staircases that once led their separate ways before these four 17th-century houses became one: open fires, stone floors, oil paintings, beautiful antiques and an elegant upstairs sitting room point to a luxurious past. A pretty terraced bar, Johann the grey parrot and tumbling, colourful flowers at windows that frame the bustle of old Woodstock. The restaurant is part library, half-panelled with soft yellow walls and low ceilings. Bedrooms are beautiful; some are smaller than others, all have period furniture, towelling bathrobes, purified water and homemade shortbread; most have marble bathrooms and one suite has a steam room. Relax with backgammon in the study while devouring afternoon teas, take to the sky in a hot-air balloon, or drift down the Thames in a chauffeured punt – all can be arranged. And Blenheim Palace is on your doorstep.

rooms	20: 8 doubles, 8 twins, 4 suites.
price	£135-£185. Singles from £99. Suite £235-£290.
meals	Lunch from £17.50. Dinner about £38; menu gourmand, 6 courses with champagne & port, £65.
closed	Rarely.
directions	From Oxford, A44 north to Woodstock. In town, left after traffic lights. Hotel on left.

Hotel

	Gavin Thomson
tel	01993 812291
fax	01993 813158
email	enquiries@feathers.co.uk
web	www.feathers.co.uk

Old Parsonage Hotel

1 Banbury Road, Oxford, Oxfordshire OX2 6NN

It must have been a good year for cooks. Edward Selwood, master chef of nearby St John's College, completed his grand house in 1660 and the vast oak front door still hangs. Inside, sympathetic design details and use of materials have kept the old-house feel and the intimacy of a private club. The hall has glorious stone flags, huge original fireplace – log-stocked in winter – and urns of dried flowers. Bedrooms have fine florals and checks, some in the old house have magnificent fireplaces and panelling; all have gorgeous bathrooms. There's a first-floor roof garden, lush with plants, for tea or sundowner, and a snug sitting room downstairs for those seeking quiet. All roads seem to lead to the Parsonage bar/restaurant, the hub of the hotel; newspapers hang on poles, walls are heavy with pictures and people float in all day long for coffee, drinks and good food. First-class service from real people too – they'll do just about anything they can to help. Much comfort, not a whiff of pretension, and within strolling distance of the dreaming spires. Oscar Wilde reputedly had digs here.

rooms	30: 25 twins/doubles, 4 suites, 1 single.
price	£135-£170. Singles £125. Suites £195.
meals	Breakfast from £9. Lunch & dinner from £15. Gee's restaurant nearby.
closed	24-27 December.
directions	From A40 ring road, south at Banbury Road r'bout to Summertown city centre. On right next to St Giles Church.

Hotel

	Marie Jackson
tel	01865 310210
fax	01865 311262
email	info@oldparsonage-hotel.co.uk
web	www.oxford-hotels-restaurants.co.uk

Apartments in Oxford

St Thomas' Mews, 58 St Thomas' Street, Oxford, Oxfordshire OX1 1JP

Bang in the middle of the city, these stylish apartments are an excellent – and discreet – alternative to staying in a hotel. And great value! In the largest of the modern, mewshouse blocks, flats surround a pretty, central courtyard; the smaller block has a teak-tabled roof terrace *and* a garden. Each apartment is beautifully decorated in neutral colours with comfortable beds, feather duvets, perfect pelmets, immaculate bathrooms. Business folk will be thrilled with the PCs, internet access, scanner, printer, fax and customised e-mail address in each apartment; cooks will be charmed by the quality of the kitchen equipment and the white bone china. Those who simply want to let their hair down will make a bee-line for the sofas and welcome hamper. Continental breakfast is delivered to your door each morning, with a newspaper. There's free parking, too – a treat in Oxford, so leave your car while you explore. Theatres and restaurants can be booked by the lovely and unsnooty reception staff, and children are welcome, too. There's even a duck for the bath.

rooms	34 apartments for 2, 4 and 8.
price	From £90 (two-person apartment, low season).
meals	Available locally. Shopping or dinner party service available.
closed	Rarely.
directions	200 yards from Oxford railway & coach stations.

Serviced accommodation

tel	01865 254000
fax	01865 254001
email	roger@oxstay.co.uk
web	www.oxstay.co.uk

Phyllis Court Club Hotel

Marlow Road, Henley-on-Thames, Oxfordshire RG9 2HT

Classically English right down to the rose emblem, with the sort of protocol you'd expect from a private member's club, Phyllis Court is a class apart. Founded almost a century ago to create somewhere swish for bright young things from the city to zoom up to in their new motor cars, it still attracts the great and the good. It isn't hard to see why. Apart from the grandstand and its own Thames frontage with moorings – it's bang opposite the finishing line of the Royal Regatta – the house itself is a grandly self-effacing place: tweed, tennis and *The Telegraph* blend with a sense of fun. Members number some 3,000 today, and run the place with great pride – and grace. There *are* 'rules' but Muirfield it isn't! The club is named after the old English word for a red rose, 'fyllis'. Once moated, Phyllis Court was rebuilt in the 17th century, then again in the 18th and 19th. Bedrooms are easy on the eye and full of spoiling touches; the long drive sweeps past lawn and croquet 'courts'. There are river walks, and Henley buzzes with day-trippers just as it always has. *Teas & meals for residents only.*

rooms	17: 9 doubles, 8 twins/doubles.
price	£131-£161. Singles £112-£126.
meals	Dinner, 3 courses, à la carte, about £27.50. Table d'hôte £23.
closed	Rarely.
directions	From Henley-on-Thames, A4155 towards Marlow. Club on right.

Hotel

	Sue Gill
tel	01491 570500
fax	01491 570528
email	enquiries@phylliscourt.co.uk
web	www.phylliscourt.co.uk

Thamesmead House Hotel

Remenham Lane, Henley-on-Thames, Oxfordshire RG9 2LR

Patricia's eye for a news story has proved equally adept at creating a wonderful place to stay in the home of the Royal Regatta. The former arts correspondent has transformed a "seedy" 1960s Edwardian guesthouse into a chic getaway just a short amble from the centre of Henley-on-Thames; the walk over the famous three-arched bridge (1786) is easily the best introduction to this charming town. Soak up lazy, idyllic river views in both directions, then walk along towpaths or mess about in a rowing boat. Thamesmead is small but perfectly formed. Elegant bedrooms are decorated in a comfortably crisp Scandinavian style: mustard yellows, terracotta and soothing blues, big Oxford pillows to sink into, modern art on the walls, an extraordinary fossil fireplace in one, and painted wooden panelling in the bathrooms. The breakfast/tea room is relaxing, with Thompson furniture – spot the distinctive carved mouse motif – and French windows that let in lots of light, and maybe a gentle summer's breeze. Presiding over all is the erudite and fun-loving Patricia, a Dubliner to the core.

rooms	6: 4 doubles, 1 twin/double, 1 single.
price	£115-£140. Singles £95-£115.
meals	Afternoon tea. Restaurants in Henley.
closed	Rarely.
directions	From M4 junc. 8/9, A404 (M) to Burchett's Green; left on A4130, for Henley (5 miles). Before bridge, right after Little Angel pub. On left.

Hotel

	Patricia Thorburn-Muirhead
tel	01491 574745
fax	01491 579944
email	thamesmead@supanet.com
web	www.thamesmeadhousehotel.co.uk

Mr Underhill's at Dinham Weir

Dinham Bridge, Ludlow, Shropshire SY8 1EH

Chris and Judy moved Mr Underhill's from its Suffolk home after 16 years, to the foot of Ludlow Castle in 1998 – they regained their Michelin star in the first year. The setting of this restaurant with rooms is dreamy; in summer you can eat in the courtyard and watch the River Teme drift by. The dining room, too – long, light and airy, modern, warm and fun – has river views and masses of glass to draw it in. Bedrooms dazzle with natural fabrics, locally-woven carpet, cherry, maple and blond oak… big, comfy beds. Judy has designed the smaller rooms so they feel bigger; all are good and restful with stylish bathrooms. Fabulous new suites in the Miller's House have their own sitting rooms and look over the Green to Dinham Bridge, but the biggest 'wow' is saved for The Shed, a green oak building with an open-plan studio room: at the press of a button the curtains open to reveal breathtaking views up river. Good people with huge commitment – not forgetting Mungo and Toby, two British blues and heirs to Frodo's empire, after whose alias, as Tolkien fans will confirm, the restaurant is named.

rooms	8: 4 doubles, 2 twins/doubles, 2 suites.
price	£95-£150. Singles from £85. Suites £175-£220.
meals	Dinner £36. Not Tues & some Mon.
closed	Occasionally.
directions	Head to castle in Ludlow centre, take 'Dinham' Road to left of castle; down hill, right at bottom before crossing river. On left, signed.

B&B

Chris & Judy Bradley
tel 01584 874431
web www.mr-underhills.co.uk

Cleobury Court

Cleobury North, Shropshire WV16 6RW

It's been quite a spree since Bill and Christina took over this former dower house. Francophiles both, they've collected furniture, tapestries and prints on their French forays. There's also a hint of the East as Christina once ran a Balinese shop. The colour schemes are hers, such as the pale lemon sitting room carpet; fabrics, boldly floral, are dramatically swathed. She makes the curtains, and upholsters, too. Bill's more in charge of the food – good, local – and the garden. There are two suites: Ludlow, with its open country views, has a smart sitting room, a huge four-poster and a big, luxurious bathroom. The more intimate Garden suite has twin beds, set together under a super king-size half-tester, a charming Regency-striped sitting room, and a roll-top bath. The cosy double is blue and white in a French style. Be pampered in the manner of a private home rather than a hotel – Bill, who's Canadian, and Christina, a Londoner, are both extremely hospitable. Play the grand piano, or billiards, or stretch yourself in the gym. Ludlow is a short drive, or walk up Brown Clee from the back door.

rooms	3: 1 double, 2 suites.
price	£75. Singles from £60. Suites £90-£99.
meals	Available locally.
closed	Occasionally.
directions	From Bridgenorth, B4364 to Cleobury North. On right 0.5 miles from Cleobury North. Signed.

Hotel

Bill & Christina Mills
tel 01746 787005
fax 01746 787005
email cleoburycourt@aol.com

The Old Vicarage

Worfield, Bridgnorth, Shropshire WV15 5JZ

From the miniature bay trees by the porch to the bedroom decanters glowing with sherry, the Old Vicarage exudes comfort and distinction. David has not been here long yet has rung in many changes – the woodchip is going, the regeneration continues. Revealing a hotelier's skills tweaked at top London hotels, he combines professionalism with human warmth; his is a happy ship. Afternoon teas are splendid, lunches and dinners, served in three dining rooms, superb. Citrus salad topped with sautéed king scallops; vine-tomato and tapenade tart; thyme-marinated French quail… these are merely the starters. Bedrooms, warm and restful, come with real and repro antiques and an Edwardian feel in sympathy with the house; some have beams, others private patios, and bathrooms are freshly white. The largest bedrooms, replete with jacuzzis, are in the Coach House, some on the ground floor. The hotel is brilliant at organizing weddings, conferences and parties – pony-trekking, shooting, you name it – and equally good at looking after the romantic or family guest. Dreamy Shropshire lies at the door.

rooms	14: 8 doubles, 5 twins, 1 four-poster.
price	£99.50-£175. Singles £75-£110.
meals	Dinner, 3 courses, £35.
closed	Rarely.
directions	From Bridgnorth towards Wolverhampton A454; signposted on left after 2 miles.

Hotel

	David Blakstad
tel	01746 716497
fax	01746 716552
email	admin@the-old-vicarage.demon.co.uk
web	www.oldvicarageworfield.com

Pen-y-Dyffryn Country Hotel

Rhydycroesau, Oswestry, Shropshire SY10 7JD

Staggeringly beautiful scenery surrounds this old rectory, commissioned in 1845 by its first rector, Robert Williams, who compiled the first Celtic dictionary. He was said to be a stuffy character... the very opposite of Miles and Audrey, and their staff, whose relaxed and easy-going manner suffuses the house with comfort and joy. The entrance hall doubles as a bar; the bar itself an old *chiffonier* – "a posh sideboard," says Miles – with menus tucked away in the drawers. The bedrooms are 'comfy old house', with good fabrics and some with hand-painted furniture. One little double has its own flight of stairs, while the four rooms in the old stable are big and contemporary, with private terraces. Nearly every room has spectacular views. There's a sitting room with log fire to curl up in, a restaurant for all tastes serving wonderful food (breakfasts, too, are spot on), organic beers and wines and a front terrace on which to sip long drinks. The five green acres of Pen-y-Dyffryn start at the top of the hill and roll down to Wales, the river at the foot of the beautiful valley marks the natural border.

rooms	12: 6 doubles, 4 twins, 1 single, 1 family.
price	£98-£140. Singles £78.
meals	Dinner £28.
closed	Christmas & 1-14 January.
directions	From A5, head to Oswestry. Leave town on B4580, signed Llansilin. Hotel 3 miles on left just before Rhydycroesau.

Hotel

	Miles & Audrey Hunter
tel	01691 653700
fax	01691 650066
email	stay@peny.co.uk
web	www.peny.co.uk

Bellplot House Hotel

High Street, Chard, Somerset TA20 1QB

The original 1727 plot was, and still is, bell-shaped – hence the name. The listed, four-square Georgian house has had some interesting owners down the years, including a Malayan rubber planter and a clutch of spinster sisters; bedrooms Anne, Mary, Sarah and Lydia are named in their honour. Today an atmosphere of sunny bonhomie reigns, thanks to Betty, who does warm front of house, and son Thomas, who stars in the kitchen... with a little help from dad. Dennis also mans the bar, a sunny, south-facing room with an almost clubby feel (green walls, polished floors, a chesterfield). No tennis or pool, but a special arrangement enables you to stretch and pamper at the leisure club a short drive away. Then back to the elegant dining room and some seriously good home cooking that includes the catch of the day – and the occasional dinner devoted to 'Italian Specialities', 'Champagne' or, tantalizingly, 'Puddings'. Bedrooms are uncluttered and airy: modern pine, white duvets, navy curtains, impressive showers, rooftop views. A super bolthole for travellers, and in the centre of Chard.

rooms	7: 5 doubles, 1 single, 1 family.
price	£69.50. Singles £59.50.
meals	Breakfast £4.50-£9. Picnic lunch £12. Dinner, 3 courses £20-£25. Restaurant closed Sunday.
closed	Rarely.
directions	In centre of Chard, 500 yards from Guildhall.

Hotel

	Betty Jones
tel	01460 62600
fax	01460 62600
email	info@bellplothouse.co.uk
web	www.bellplothouse.co.uk

Greyhound Inn

Staple Fitzpaine, Taunton, Somerset TA3 5SP

A classic English country pub, walls bedecked with collages of pictures and fishing memorabilia that create an atmosphere of warmth and hospitality. Let the eye wander... while sitting at old, wooden tables, worn nicely from frequent use and decorated simply with vases of wild flowers. A roaring hearth in winter, a flagstoned bar busy with friendly locals – ask after Mr Flack and Mr Grabham – and a good meal, with fish delivered daily from Brixham and meat from within four miles. Then "retreat in good order", as one boxing print wisely suggests, to clean, comfortable bedrooms: more hotel than individual. Ivor and Lucy bought the inn after leaving careers in the pharmaceutical industry. "We still work long hours but we see each other now," says Ivor, a relaxed host, seemingly made for the job of community landlord. The Back Room restaurant serves a new fusion of fresh food. All this in deepest rural Somerset with walks through forestry to Castle Neroche and stunning views from the Blackdown Hills. Henry VIII's heart is said to be buried in the churchyard. *Children over 12 welcome.*

rooms	4: 2 doubles, 1 twin/double, 1 twin.
price	£75-£90. Singles £49.95.
meals	Lunch from £4. Dinner, à la carte, about £20.
closed	Rarely.
directions	M5, junc. 25, A358 towards Ilminster for 4 miles, then right, for Staple Fitzpaine. Left at T-junc. Village 1.5 miles further. Inn on right at x-roads.

Inn

	Ivor & Lucy Evans
tel	01823 480227
fax	01823 481117
email	stay@the-greyhoundinn.com
web	www.thegreyhoundinn.fsbusiness.co.uk

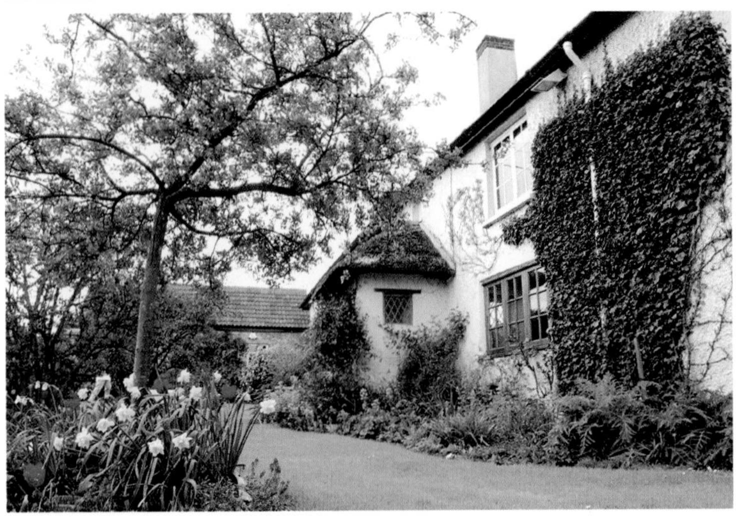

Orchards Restaurant at Wrexon Farmhouse

Dipford Road, Angersleigh, Taunton, Somerset TA3 7PA

The axiom that some people are made for each other surely applies to the immensely likeable owners of Orchards Restaurant. Norman and Julie have known each other for ever and this charming, established restaurant in an old Somerset crofter's cottage marks a lifetime of unswerving devotion. Relax with an aperitif by a wood stove in a cosy bar, or sit out in summer in a courtyard full of honeysuckle and rosemary. Herbs, salads, apples, damsons and plums grow on four acres for the table. Norman is a no-frills cook, preferring classic English methods to current trends: fish from Brixham, roast duckling, pavlovas, homemade ice creams and an excellent dessert trolley. In the restaurant, tables lit by candlelight fit snugly around gnarled beams and an elm trunk that seems to grow upstairs. You stay in huge comfort in a barn next door and breakfast arrives at the time of your choosing. As for the traffic, you'll be too busy enjoying yourself to notice the march of the nearby motorway. The cottage's thick walls insulate and the prevailing wind blows the sound in the other direction!

rooms	1 apartment for 2-3.
price	£71. Singles £55.
meals	Continental breakfast £6.95. Dinner, à la carte, about £28. Restaurant closed Sundays & Mondays.
closed	Rarely.
directions	From Taunton centre towards Trull; right after Queen's College, into Dipford Rd, for Angersleigh. 2 miles on right, just after bridge over M5.

Restaurant with Rooms

Norman & Julie White
tel 01823 275440
email mail@orchardsrestaurant.co.uk
web www.orchardsrestaurant.co.uk

Bindon Country House Hotel

Langford Budville, Wellington, Somerset TA21 0RU

An extraordinary, beautiful building, Bindon hides on the edge of woodland where rare wild flowers flourish. Seven years ago it was derelict, full of dust and cobwebs; now it's full of Mark and Lynn's enthusiasm. What strikes you most, entering through the large glass front door, is the crispness of it all: the tiled entrance hall, the stained glass, the wall tapestries, the plaster mouldings on the ceiling, the galleried staircase, the glass-domed roof... absolutely pristine. Keep going into the snug panelled bar, past the wrought-iron candlesticks, for coffee served with piping hot milk and delicious homemade biscuits. In summer, move outside through open hall doors and sit by a magnificent stone balustrade that looks over rose gardens down to an old dovecote. Bright bedrooms come in different sizes: two oval rooms at the front of the house are *huge*, with dusky pink furniture, patterned wallpaper depicting genteel garden scenes, a high brass bed and Victorian baths; the others are large and very comfortable. Add gorgeous food and a luxuriously heated pool for a hidden treasure.

rooms	12: 10 twins/doubles, 2 four-posters.
price	£115-£215. Half-board (min. 2 nights) from £67.50 p.p. Singles £95.
meals	Lunch £12.95. Dinner, 5 courses, £29.95.
closed	Rarely.
directions	From Wellington, B3187 for 1.5 miles; left at sharp S-bend for L. Budville; right in village for Wiveliscombe; 1st right; on right after 1.5 miles.

Hotel

Lynn & Mark Jaffa

tel 01823 400070
fax 01823 400071
email stay@bindon.com
web www.bindon.com

The Royal Oak Inn

Withypool, Somerset TA24 7QP

The drive to this oasis of luxury through twisting lanes shrouded in early morning mist leaves a magical impression of Exmoor which is impossible to shake. Look on any map and Withypool is the point at which all roads across the moor meet. A small, forgotten place made immune to outside cares by the barren embrace of stone and bog, and heather that blazes a resplendent purple in summer. The 300-year-old Royal Oak will indulge you completely. Gail has a background in producing adverts for television but she isn't exaggerating when she says her bedrooms are "the nicest on the moor". Full of style and simple good taste, they are divided between the main inn and two superb cottages across the courtyard, also let as holiday homes: toile de Jouy fabrics and wallpaper, tongue-and-groove-panelled bathrooms, maybe an antique half-tester, or an old slipper bath, and dyed sheepskin rugs to cosset tired feet. The food is excellent, the welcome warm and the bar bustles with country brio. Walk to Tarr Steps, but heed Jake the barman's advice: an Exmoor mile is longer than an ordinary mile.

rooms	8: 6 doubles, 2 twins/doubles.
price	£90-£110. Singles £60-£70.
meals	Lunch from £4.75. Dinner about £20.
closed	Rarely.
directions	M5, junc. 27. A4361 to Tiverton; right on A396, for Bampton & Dulverton. At Exbridge, left on B3222 to Dulverton & onto Withypool.

Inn

Gail Sloggett

tel	01643 831506/7
fax	01643 831659
email	enquiries@royaloakwithypool.co.uk
web	www.royaloakwithypool.co.uk

The Crown Hotel

Exford, Somerset TA24 7PP

Entering Hugo's mildly eccentric world in the middle of Exmoor is sure to be entertaining – you might find a horse propping up the bar! Hugo is a gentleman of the old school, impeccably dressed beneath a shock of white hair; a generous host with a knack of looking after you. He sharpens his wits playing bridge with seasoned oldies who "clout me over the head if I make a foolish bid". You're in wild, horsey country where laid-back locals downing pints in the spit 'n' sawdust bar draw just comparison with the easy-going outlook of rural Ireland. The building itself is Exmoor's oldest coaching inn, set in front of the village green, with a rambling garden and woodland walk to the rear. Inside, a carpeted dining room with a private table for shooting parties, and a smartly comfortable sitting area with log fire. The Jeune way is gradually transforming bedrooms and bathrooms into lighter, brighter ones, handsomely furnished, while good service and brilliant food is making a difference downstairs. Bring your dog; if you don't have one, black labs Samsox and PJ never say no to a run. *Minimum stay two nights.*

rooms	16: 9 doubles, 4 twins, 2 singles; 1 twin with separate bath.
price	£99-£130. Half-board £75-£92.50. Singles £65.
meals	Lunch, 3 courses, £18.50. Dinner £32.50. Bar meals from £3.95.
closed	Rarely.
directions	M5, junc. 25, A38 to Taunton, A358 for Minehead; B3224 to Exford, via Wheddon Cross; by village green.

Hotel

	Hugo Jeune
tel	01643 831554
fax	01643 831665
email	info@crownhotelexmoor.co.uk
web	www.crownhotelexmoor.co.uk

Porlock Vale House

Porlock Weir, Somerset TA24 8NY

Exmoor National Park runs into the sea here, tiny lanes ramble down into lush valleys while headlands rise to meet the waves. Saddle a horse and ride off into the sunset. Well, maybe not, but this is an exceptional riding school – all levels welcome. Or just sit out under the wisteria on the terrace and watch the deer eat the garden – or walk down across fields and paddle in Porlock Bay. Whatever you do, you'll enjoy coming back to this splendid country house with its comforting smells of polish, woodsmoke and fresh flowers. Good 'imaginative English' food – most of it local – in the oak-panelled, burgundy dining room, crackling log fires and leather sofas in the hall, deep sofas in the pretty sitting room, books and games, prints and pictures galore. Bedrooms, many newly-dressed and styled, are enticing – big and bright with sofas if there's room; most have sea views and the biggest are huge. Make sure you see the beautiful Edwardian stables… you may find the blacksmith at work. The horses couldn't be better looked after and you will be too – owners and staff are just great.

rooms	15: 10 doubles, 4 twins, 1 single.
price	£110-£150. Singles £60-£90. Half-board £60-£95 p.p.
meals	Lunch from £5. Dinner £24.50.
closed	Mid-week in January & early February.
directions	West passed Minehead on A39, right in Porlock, for Porlock Weir. Through West Porlock, signed right.

Hotel

Kim & Helen Youd

tel	01643 862338
fax	01643 863338
email	info@porlockvale.co.uk
web	www.porlockvale.co.uk

Glencot House

Glencot Lane, Wells, Somerset BA5 1BH

Jacobean elegance spills from this beautiful late-Victorian mansion into its 18-acre parkland setting. Inside, it's as you would expect: four-poster beds, carved ceilings, walnut panelling, hallways filled with ancient furniture and bric-a-brac, plants and flowers everywhere. The drawing room is the magnet of the house; you'll meet the other guests here, all admiring the carved ceiling and the inglenook fireplace with open chimney flue the size of a room; in winter the flames leap six feet high. Hard to believe it has all mod-cons, and a sauna and small indoor jet-stream pool – most welcome after a game of table tennis, snooker or croquet. Glencot was rescued from a state of dilapidation by Jenny and her husband; long hours of toil have brought it back to life. Don't miss the garden: a magnificent terrace with stone balustrade and wide, gracious steps which sweep you down to the River Axe. There are fountains, a waterfall (planned to provide hydro-electric power) and an old stone bridge to take you over to the cricket pitch where the village team plays. *Pets by arrangement.*

rooms	13: 2 doubles, 3 twins, 3 singles, 5 four-posters.
price	£94-£122. Singles £68-£85.
meals	Packed lunch from £3.50. Dinner from £26.50.
closed	Rarely.
directions	From Wells, follow signs to Wookey Hole. Sharp left at finger post, 100m after pink cottage. House on right in Glencot Lane.

B&B

	Jenny Attia
tel	01749 677160
fax	01749 670210
email	relax@glencothouse.co.uk
web	www.glencothouse.co.uk

Babington House

Babington, Frome, Somerset BA11 3RW

Many places imitate Babington; this is the real thing. Staying here is like being invited to the delightful Georgian house of a friend who has taste that glows and shows off in the sort of heavenly bedrooms and bathrooms you only dream about – so delicious they actually make you excited; food as sophisticated or as homely as you want, served when and where you want; a swooping lawn to a lake; indoor and outdoor swimming pools and a charmingly bovine-themed spa; a good-sized cinema and – this list is not exhaustive – seriously good spaces to park your children should you need. This obliging friend has also searched tirelessly for the right people to look after you: young, bright, easy and natural. Meals are whipped up by clever Barnaby Jones, using proper local ingredients and masses of home-grown veg and leaves from the walled garden – which also provides fruit and herbs for in-house smellies. Best of all, your friend leaves you entirely alone to enjoy it all. What fool would lose touch with a pal like that? Granted, you do have to pay a bill at the end, but it's worth every pound.

rooms	28.
price	From £235-£390.
meals	Breakfast £12.50. Lunch, 1 course, from £10-£15. Dinner, 3 courses, from £35.
closed	Rarely.
directions	Can be hard to find. Ask for map when booking.

Hotel

Stefanie Mason

tel	01373 812266
fax	01373 812112
email	enquiries@babingtonhouse.co.uk
web	www.babingtonhouse.co.uk

The Bell Inn

Ferry Road, Walberswick, Suffolk IP18 6TN

A tiny summer-soft, winter-bleak Suffolk fishing village, home in August to the International Crabbing Festival, and central to the 1920s Craft Movement: Charles Rennie Mackintosh used to drop by. The village is still a refuge for artists. The ferry across the tiny boat-tangled river has been rowed by the same family for five generations; swim, sail, fish for crabs, paint, walk the beach to Dunwich. The venerable Bell is 600 years old and has ancient beams and flagstones, wooden settles and open fires. Time has also given it a few nooks and crannies in which to hide out with a pint of Oyster Stout. The country-style bedrooms are on the small side but full of comfort and charm, and some have blissful views. In the candlelit restaurant, delicious flash-fried red snapper and bitter chocolate tart; outside, a large garden that looks out onto beach huts, dunes and the sea. Sue is welcoming and attractive and has poured huge amounts of energy into making it such a happy place. An absolute treat – for foodies, families, dogs, bird watchers (Minsmere is here) and East Anglian architecture buffs.

rooms	6: 4 doubles, 1 twin, 1 family.
price	From £70. Singles from £60.
meals	Lunch from £3.50. Dinner, Friday & Saturday, from £16.
closed	Never.
directions	From A12, B1387 to Walberswick. The Bell on right, at far end of village near river.

Inn

	Sue Ireland-Cutting
tel	01502 723109
email	bellinn@btinternet.com
web	www.blythweb.co.uk/bellinn

The Old Rectory

Campsea Ashe, Nr Woodbridge, Suffolk IP13 0PU

In summer you eat in the conservatory, gazing admiringly over the 2.5 acres of lawns, herb garden, shrubs and orchard. But the dining room is not to be missed; it has plum silk curtains, a wooden floor with rugs, white-clothed tables with candles and silver cutlery. Fresh flowers add colour to every room. The bedrooms have been lavishly cared for: one is Victorian, with period bath, basin, taps and fireplace; another is in the attic, up a spiral stair. It's a subtly, classily decorated place – modern country-house style with oriental touches. There's an honesty bar, a sitting room with deep sofas and garden views and a delightful, welcoming mood. Sally has run her own design shop and pours her heart into this; she cooks, too, and the menus are irresistible – Moroccan chicken, monkfish, hot smoked salmon salad, Italian trifle, local fish galore. Breakfasts are as homemade (sausages, bread and marmalade) and locally-sourced as possible. You are close to the best of Suffolk – Snape Maltings, Orford, Aldeburgh, Southwold, Woodbridge, Sutton Hoo – in an ungrand yet lovely house with owners fired up with enthusiasm.

rooms	7: 3 doubles, 2 twins, 2 four-posters.
price	£75-£105. Singles from £55.
meals	Dinner, 3 courses, £24. Not Sunday.
closed	Christmas.
directions	North from Ipswich on A12 for 15 miles, then right onto B1078. In village, over railway line; house on right just before church.

B&B

Michael & Sally Ball
tel 01728 746524
email mail@theoldrectorysuffolk.com
web www.theoldrectorysuffolk.com

Ounce House

Northgate Street, Bury St Edmunds, Suffolk IP33 1HP

An extremely handsome 1870 red-brick townhouse minutes from the heart of one of England's prettiest ancient towns. Bury St Edmunds has a rich history; the Romans were here, its Norman abbey attracted pilgrims by the cartload, and the wool trade made it rich in the 1700s. A gentle, one-hour stroll takes you past 650 years of architectural wonder – special indeed. Ounce House is pristine and full of fine antiques. Enjoy sumptuous breakfasts around a mighty-sized mahogany dining table and slump in leather armchairs around an ornate carved fireplace. Light floods in all day through the double doors between the drawing and dining rooms. Elsewhere, a snug library has an honesty bar, while three fine, homely bedrooms are packed with books, mahogany furniture, local art and piles of magazines; the one at the back of the house has a pretty view of the garden. The Potts can arrange tickets to the Theatre Royal, pick you up from the train station, or help you decide between the 35 restaurants within five minutes of the house.

rooms	3: 2 doubles, 1 twin.
price	£85-£95. Singles £60-£70.
meals	Restaurants in Bury St Edmunds.
closed	Rarely.
directions	A14 north, then central junction for Bury, following signs to historic centre. At 1st r'bout, left into Northgate St. On right at top of hill.

B&B

Simon & Jenny Pott

tel	01284 761779
fax	01284 768315
email	pott@globalnet.co.uk
web	www.ouncehouse.co.uk

Clarice House Hotel

Horringer Court, Horringer Road, Bury St Edmunds, Suffolk IP29 5PH

A place to come to firm up your pecs and get those split ends sorted out – a professional yet personal (family-run) hotel and spa. The big old hall is impressive in its 20 wooded acres – and there's a path that cuts through it for those who fancy a stroll. Behind the 1898 building is the annexe housing the cosseting bits: a 20m pool with a spanking new purification system, a spa bath, sauna, steam room and gym, a dance studio for aerobics, yoga and pilates... ayurvedic stone therapy and reiki to energize the sluggish, algae wraps and body polishes to excite the frivolous, facials for every conceivable skin. For those lucky enough to be dossing down here, 13 comfortable, smartly-dressed bedrooms await; the superior ones are the biggest and have separate showers in addition to baths. In the bar and the darkly panelled restaurant there's a fantastic range of dishes to dip into, from Newmarket sausages with wine and mushroom sauce to tofu and teriyaki. Stuart is young and full of plans, for bedroom makeovers and a new conservatory. Charming Bury St Edmunds is down the road, Cambridge not much further.

rooms	13 doubles.
price	From £110. Spa breaks from £135 p.p.
meals	Club menu from £4. Lunch from £14.95. Dinner from £17.95.
closed	Christmas & New Year.
directions	From Bury St Edmunds A143 for Horringer & Haverhill. Clarice House 1 mile from town centre.

Hotel

	Stuart King
tel	01284 705550
fax	01284 716120
email	enquiry@clarice-bury.fsnet.co.uk
web	www.clarice.co.uk

The Great House

Market Place, Lavenham, Suffolk CO10 9QZ

A little pocket of France in a pretty corner of England, the Great House pulls off that rare trick of being a hotel that feels like a home. Régis and Martine are charming, as are their French staff, whose Gallic charm extends to the youngest guests. The house is authentic, too, with an 18th-century front and a 15th-century interior that is utterly lovely and full of surprises. The bedrooms have antique desks and chests of drawers, fresh flowers and perfect bathrooms. One has a Jacobean four-poster, like an island in a sea of rugs; another, in the roof, huge beamed timbers. Most have their own private sitting area and some have views over this bustling, historic market town. It's simply impossible to escape the generosity and good taste of it all, and that's never more true than in the restaurant – essence of France in the middle of Suffolk. The sheer splendour of the food brings guests back again and again, and the cheese board alone is a work of art. Catch the early sun in the courtyard for breakfast, or eat supper alfresco on warm and lazy summer nights. *Leisure break prices available during the week.*

rooms	5 doubles.
price	£90-£150. Half-board from £68.95 p.p. Singles from £70.
meals	Lunch from £11. Dinner from £22.95. Not Sunday nights & Mondays.
closed	First 3 weeks in January.
directions	A1141 to Lavenham. At High street first right after The Swan. Up Lady St into Market Place.

B&B

	Régis & Martine Crépy
tel	01787 247431
fax	01787 248007
email	info@greathouse.co.uk
web	www.greathouse.co.uk

The White Hart Inn

High Street, Nayland, Colchester, Suffolk CO6 4JF

Michel Roux's 'other place' is exquisite on all counts; the way things are done here is second to none. The service is remarkable. Staff here do have a sense of pride in their work – something of a rarity in Britain these days (although not in this book, of course...). The inn dates from the 15th century and has kept its timber-framed walls and beams. Inside has been opened up a bit, not enough to lose its rambling feel, but just enough to make it light and airy, and the feel is smart country French – as it should be. Feast on "scrumptuous food", to quote an enraptured guest, and sup from a vast collection of New World wines. "People like to travel when they drink," says Michel. Bedrooms, which vary in size, have a striking yet simple country-style elegance: yellow walls and checked fabrics, crisp linen and thick blankets, angled beams (two rooms almost have vaulted ceilings), piles of cushions, sofas or armchairs, immaculate bathrooms and wonderful art; some have wildly sloping floors and one has original murals that may be the work of Constable's brother. It's perfect – right down to the breakfast toast.

rooms	6: 5 doubles, 1 twin.
price	£82-£95. Singles £69-£75.
meals	Lunch from £9.95. Dinner about £24.
closed	Rarely.
directions	Nayland signed right 6 miles north of Colchester on the A134 (no access from A12). In village centre.

Inn

	Michel Roux
tel	01206 263382
fax	01206 263638
email	nayhart@aol.com
web	www.whitehart-nayland.co.uk

The Royal Oak Inn

Pook Lane, East Lavant, Chichester, Sussex PO18 0AX

There's a comfortable, cheery, wine-bar feel to the Royal Oak; locals and young professionals come with their children, as often as not, and it's as rural as can be. Inside, a modern-rustic look with traditional touches prevails: stripped floors, exposed brickwork, dark leather sofas, open fires, racing pictures on the walls – the inn was once part of the Goodwood estate. The dining area is big, light and airy, with a conservatory, and you can spill out onto the front patio, warmed by outdoor lamps on summer nights; you face a road but this one goes nowhere. Five chefs conjure up delicious salmon and chorizo fishcakes, honey and clove roasted ham, fillet steak. Bedrooms have a contemporary feel. Two are in a nearby barn, the rest are at the back of the pub, up the stairs; ask for one with a view. All have CD players, plasma screens and top toiletries – the best of modern – along with excellent lighting, brown leather chairs and big comfy beds. Staff are attentive, breakfasts are good and fresh, a secret garden looks over the South Downs, and you couldn't be better placed for Chichester Theatre or Goodwood.

rooms 5 + 1: 4 doubles, 1 twin. 1 cottage for 4.
price £70-£110. Singles £60-£70.
meals Lunch & dinner, £13.50-£24.50, à la carte.
closed Christmas Day and Boxing Day.
directions From Chichester A286 for Midhurst. 1st right at 1st mini r'bout into E. Lavant. Down hill, pass village green, over bridge, pub 200 yds on left. Car park opp.

Inn

Nick Sutherland
tel 01243 527434
fax 01243 775062
email nickroyaloak@aol.com
web www.sussexlive.co.uk/royaloakinn

The Griffin Inn

Fletching, Uckfield, Sussex TN22 3SS

The sort of inn worth moving house to be near; perfect almost because of the occasional touch of scruffiness. The Pullan family run it with gentle passion as a true local: regulars were queuing up before opening time when we arrived on a chilly Tuesday in January. Inside, open fires, 500-year-old beams, oak panelling, settles, red carpets, black and white photos on the walls... this inn has been allowed to age. There's a small club room for racing on Saturdays and two cricket teams play in summer. Bedrooms are perfect, tremendous value for money and full of uncluttered country-inn elegance: uneven floors, lots of old furniture, soft coloured walls, free-standing Victorian baths, huge shower heads, crisp linen, fluffy bathrobes, handmade soaps. Rooms in the coach house, recently renovated, are quieter. The seasonal menu changes daily: ribollita soup maybe, turbot, lobster and pea risotto, roasted wood pigeon. In summer, a jazz duo play in the garden against the backdrop of a 10-mile view across Ashdown Forest to Sheffield Park... and on Sundays they lay on a spit-roast barbecue as well.

rooms	8: 1 twin, 7 four-posters.
price	£80-£130. Singles £60-£80 (not at weekends). Min 2 night stay bank holiday weekends.
meals	Bar lunch/dinner £10-£20. Restaurant £22-£30.
closed	Christmas Day.
directions	From East Grinstead, A22 south, right at Nutley for Fletching. On for 2 miles into village.

Inn

Bridget, Nigel & James Pullan

tel	01825 722890
fax	01825 722810
email	thegriffininn@hotmail.com
web	www.thegriffininn.co.uk

Stone House

Rushlake Green, Heathfield, Sussex TN21 9QJ

One of the bedrooms has a bathroom with enough room for a sofa and two chairs around the marble bath – but does that make it a suite? Jane thought not. The bedroom is big, too, has a beautiful four-poster, floods with light and, like all the rooms, has sumptuous furniture and seemingly ancient fabrics. All this is typical of the generosity of both house and owners. Stone House has been in the Dunn family for a mere 500 years and Peter and Jane have kept the feel of home. Downstairs, amid the splendour of the drawing room, there's still room for lots of old family photos; across the hall in the library, logs piled high wait to be tossed on the fire. Weave down a corridor to ancient oak panelling in the dining room for Jane's cooking; she's a Master Chef with her own (stunning) kitchen garden, and regularly runs cookery courses. Having eaten, walk out to the superb, half-acre walled kitchen garden and see where it's all grown – they're 99% self-sufficient in summer. There are 1,000 acres to explore and you can fish for carp. Indulgent picnic hampers for Glyndebourne, including chairs and tables, can be arranged.

rooms	6: 3 twins/doubles, 2 four-posters, 1 suite.
price	£115-£225. Singles £80-£115.
meals	Lunch, by arrangement, £24.95. Dinner £24.95.
closed	Christmas & New Year.
directions	From Heathfield, B2096; 4th right, signed Rushlake Green. 1st left by village green. House on left, signed.

Hotel

	Peter & Jane Dunn
tel	01435 830553
fax	01435 830726
web	www.stonehousesussex.co.uk

Little Hemingfold Hotel

Telham, Battle, Sussex TN33 0TT

The south-east of England is much underrated in terms of rural beauty; drive up the bumpy dirt track that leads to Little Hemingfold and you could be miles from the middle of nowhere. People who want to get away to the simplicity of deep country will like it here. It is pretty rustic, a little like renting a remote country cottage without having to cook or clean; open fires, old sofas and armchairs, books and games, lots of flowers and floods of light. Breakfast in the yellow dining room is under beams; at night the candles come out for delicious home-cooked dinners. The bedrooms are all over the place, some in the main house, others across the small, pretty courtyard. They are fairly earthy, four having woodburning stoves – again that feel of deep country – with the odd four-poster, maybe a sofa, glazed-brick walls and simple bathrooms. Outside, a two-acre lake to row and fish or swim in, a grass tennis court (the moles got the better of the croquet lawn), woodland to walk in and lots of peace and quiet. Bring the dogs!

rooms	12: 10 twins/doubles; 2 family with separate bath.
price	£92-£98. Half-board £64-£69.50 p.p. Singles £56-£66.
meals	Dinner, 4 courses, £27.50.
closed	January 2nd-February 10th 2005.
directions	From Battle, A2100 for Hastings for 1.5 miles. Hotel signed left by 'sharp left' road sign, 0.5 miles up bumpy farm track.

Hotel

	Allison & Paul Slater
tel	01424 774338
fax	01424 775351
email	littlehemingfoldhote@tiscali.co.uk
web	www.littlehemingfoldhotel.co.uk

Jeake's House

Mermaid Street, Rye, Sussex TN31 7ET

Rye, one of the Cinque Ports, is a perfect town for whiling away an afternoon; wander and discover the tidal river, old fishing boats, arts and crafts shops and galleries. Jeake's House is in the middle of old Rye on a steep, ancient cobbled street. The house has a colourful past as wool store, school and home of American poet Conrad Potter Aiken. The galleried dining room, once an old Baptist chapel, is now painted deep red and is full of busts, books, clocks and mirrors – perfect for those who like to make a grand entrance at breakfast! Jenny is engagingly easy-going and has created a lovely atmosphere. Rooms full of beams and timber frames are pretty, generously draped and excellent value. Some have stunning old chandeliers, others four-posters, cosy bathrooms have Bronnley soaps... and a mind-your-head stairway leads to a generous attic room with views over roof tops and chimneys. A small sitting room with honesty bar, books and papers is an ideal spot for a nightcap, the hearth is lit in winter and musicians will swoon at the working square piano. A super little hotel. *Children over 12 welcome.*

rooms	12: 8 doubles, 3 suites; 1 single, sharing bath.
price	£86-£118. Singles £39-£79.
meals	Restaurants in Rye.
closed	Rarely.
directions	From centre of Rye on A268, left off High St onto West St; 1st right into Mermaid St. House on left. Private car park, £3 a day for guests.

Hotel

	Jenny Hadfield
tel	01797 222828
fax	01797 222623
email	stay@jeakeshouse.com
web	www.jeakeshouse.com

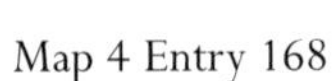

The Hare on the Hill

37 Coventry Road, Warwick, Warwickshire CV34 5HW

Come for organic food, flamboyant art, eccentricity and colour. And Prue – a warm and wonderful presence. She ensures you're well fed and watered, can plan your trips, gives you breakfast when you like it. She and her partner Mike have moved from a smaller Special Place to take on The Hare, a one time nurses' home on the Coventry road; the woodchip has gone, and funky furnishings and eco-friendly paints have taken its place. In the hall, an Edwardian Minton-tiled floor, Shakespearean carvings and stained glass; in the sitting room – large, light and cosy – fine watercolours and a deep gilded frieze. Two bedrooms are ample, the rest small; all are one-offs. You might have lilac doors and skirting, or a bright pink ceiling; an Australian dream painting or an English landscape; a stripy sofa or a fluffy bedspread. Breakfasts stand out and there's something different every day: haloumi pancakes, crunchy stuffed mushrooms, fruit platters. Great for carnivores too: sausages come from rare breed butchers, served with free-range eggs and spicy beans. Warwick Castle is a 10-minute stroll, Stratford not much further.

rooms	7: 3 twins/doubles, 4 doubles.
price	£80. Singles £60.
meals	Dinner by arrangement, £15-£25.
closed	Christmas & New Year.
directions	2-minute walk from the railway station.

B&B

Prue Hardwick

tel	01926 491366
email	prue@thehareonthepark.co.uk
web	www.thehareonthepark.co.uk

Fulready Manor

Ettington, Stratford-upon-Avon, Warwickshire CV37 7PE

A manor in 125 acres. From afar it's a 16th-century castle; close up, a brand-new, luxury home with all the character and none of the draughts. "Our slice of heaven," say the Spencers, who've been in the hospitality business for years and have come home to roost. Enter a stone-fireplaced hall, with floor-to-ceiling front window and Cretan chandelier. In the drawing room, paintings of children and pets, navy sofas piled high with matching cushions, hunting prints too (though the Spencers "hunt the clean boot", choosing to chase men not animals). The sense of fun extends to the bedrooms, 'themed' by daughter Verity and furnished with some magnificent antique pieces. One has midnight-blue fabric walls and faux wood panelling, a four-poster with gold-embroidered muslin and a shower for two; a second, a leather sleigh bed strewn with cushions and a bathroom in red; the third, a four-poster with lush, creamy hangings and a velvet chaise longue in palest pink. Old-fashioned comfort, soft bathrobes, no TV. Breakfasts are a feast, served on the patio on balmy mornings, surrounded by fields.

rooms	3: 2 four-posters, 1 double.
price	£90-£130.
meals	Dinner £25, by arrangement.
closed	Christmas.
directions	M40 junc. 11 for Stratford. A422 to Wroxton, B4451 for 0.25 miles; Fulready first driveway on left.

B&B

Michael & Mauveen Spencer

tel	01789 740152
fax	01789 740247
email	stay@fulreadymanor.co.uk
web	www.fulreadymanor.co.uk

The Howard Arms

Lower Green, Ilmington, Stratford-upon-Avon, Warwickshire CV36 4LT

Once upon a time Robert and Gill ran the Cotswold House Hotel in Chipping Campden with a mix of flair, quirkiness and professionalism. After a deserved sabbatical, they decided to cast their fairy-dust over this old inn. The Howard buzzes with good-humoured babble, as well-kept beer flows from the flagstoned, log-stocked bar, while a dining room at the far end has unexpected elegance, with great swathes of bold colour and some noble paintings. Gorgeous bedrooms are set discreetly apart from the joyful throng, mixing period style and modern luxury beautifully: the double oozes olde worlde charm; the twin is more folksy, with American art and patchwork quilts; the half-tester is almost a suite, full of antiques. All are individual, all huge by pub standards. The village is a surprise, too, literally tucked under a lone hill, with an unusual church surrounded by orchards and an extended village green. Round off an idyllic walk amid buzzing bees and fragrant wild flowers with a meal at the inn – folk come a long way to sample the food. Stratford and the theatre are close. *Bedrooms are no smoking.*

rooms	3: 2 doubles, 1 twin.
price	£90-105. Singles from £75.
meals	Lunch & dinner £9.50-£24.
closed	Christmas Day.
directions	From Stratford, south on A3400 for 4 miles, right to Wimpstone & Ilmington. Pub in village centre.

Inn

	Robert & Gill Greenstock
tel	01608 682226
fax	01608 682226
email	howard.arms@virgin.net
web	www.howardarms.com

Howard's House

Teffont Evias, Nr Salisbury, Wiltshire SP3 5RJ

Howard's has been a favourite of ours for years – luxurious without boasting, modest in its success, the sort of place where the sun shines, even in January. With one toe in deep country, this attractive 1623 stone house is the last building in a quiet village of soaring church spire and gently rising hills. Step inside the warm flagstoned entrance hall to beautiful mullioned windows of odd shapes and sizes, masses of space, flowers and bold colours everywhere. Mustard and red walls draw you into the sitting room to relax by a huge stone fireplace – you'll find *Tatler*, *The Economist* and *Classic Car* on the table. Strong yellows and blues lift the crisp, modern dining room, and pastel hues dominate faultless bedrooms with floral fabrics, fresh fruit, homemade biscuits, bathrobes and big towels. French windows lead to furnished patios. The quintessentially English garden has clipped hedges, croquet lawns, a fountain, a pond and vegetable and sensory herb patches; some of the produce ends up on your table; the modern British cooking is consistently good. Beautiful Wiltshire starts right outside.

rooms	9: 6 doubles, 1 twin/double, 1 family, 1 four-poster.
price	£145-£165. Singles from £95.
meals	Dinner, £23.95; à la carte about £27.
closed	Christmas.
directions	From Salisbury, A350, B3089 east to Teffont. There, right at sharp left-hand bend, following brown hotel sign. Entrance on right after 0.5 miles.

Hotel

	Noele Thompson
tel	01722 716392
fax	01722 716820
email	enq@howardshousehotel.co.uk
web	www.howardshousehotel.co.uk

The Compasses Inn

Lower Chicksgrove, Tisbury, Wiltshire SP3 6NB

The first impression on arriving at Compasses is of having found the perfect English pub; so is the second. In the middle of a lovely village of thatched and timber-framed cottages, this inn seems so content with its lot it could almost be a figment of your imagination. Over the years, 14th-century foundations have gradually sunk into the ground. Its thatched roof is like a sombrero, shielding bedroom windows that peer sleepily over the lawn. Duck instinctively into the sudden darkness of the bar and experience a wave of nostalgia as your eyes adjust to a long wooden room, with flagstones and cosy booths divided by farmyard salvage: a cartwheel here, some horse tack there; at one end is a piano, at the other, a brick hearth. The pub crackles with Alan's enthusiasm, and people come for the food as well: figs baked in red wine, topped with goat's cheese and chorizo, or grilled fish from the south coast. Bedrooms have the same effortless charm and the sweet serenity of Wiltshire lies just down the lane. Modest, ineffably pretty, and great value.

rooms	4: 2 doubles, 2 twins/doubles.
price	From £75. Singles £45.
meals	Lunch from £4. Dinner, à la carte, about £20.
closed	Mondays except Bank Holidays, then closed Tuesdays.
directions	From Salisbury, A30 west, 3rd right after Fovant, signed Lower Chicksgrove, then 1st left down single track lane to village.

Inn

Alan Stoneham & Susie Stoneham

tel	01722 714318
fax	01722 714318

Colwall Park

Colwall, Malvern, Worcestershire WR13 6QG

Actors stay here when treading the boards at the Malvern theatre down the road – rather famous ones, judging by the signed photos on the wall. The house is handsome Edwardian and its interiors are smart, but unintimidatingly so. Past the potted bay trees, beneath the flowered baskets, into green-carpeted reception, nicely kitted out with hunting photos, lilies and a ledger from 1907. Then up the stair to comfortable beds, matching wallpapers and bedspreads, white and chrome bathrooms, zappy showers, garden views and every extra, from baby listeners to satellite TV. Just-marrieds have a peach canopied bed with sofas to match and acres of space. The lounge has glass-topped tables and thick drapes, the bar real ales and cheery meals, and the dining room is the hub of the place: all oak panelling, white napery and sparkling glass, a sophisticated setting for some seriously good food. Iain and Sarah have been here four years and word has spread about the comfort and the smiles, the walks to the Malvern Hills – and the heavenly chocolate and amaretto crème brulée, with almond biscotti.

rooms	22: 17 doubles/twins, 3 singles, 1 suite, 1 family suite.
price	£80-£130. Singles £65. Suites £150.
meals	Lunch £15.95-£17.95. À la carte dinner approx. £30 for 3 courses.
closed	Rarely.
directions	M5 junc. 7 or M50 junc. 2. Colwall halfway between Ledbury & Malvern. Colwall Park in centre of village.

Hotel

Iain Nesbitt

tel 01684 540000

fax 01684 540847

email hotel@colwall.com

web www.colwall.com

The Cottage in the Wood

Holywell Road, Malvern Wells, Worcestershire WR14 4LG

Walk along a path through the woods, dappled with light, and emerge in a clearing in this very English jungle. There, The Cottage gazes across the wide, flat Severn Valley to the distant Cotswolds. Walk all the way to the breezy top of the Malvern Hills – England's oldest rock and much loved by Elgar. It is enough just to be here, but to find such an endearingly friendly, book-lined and log-fired country-house hotel is heart-warming. Furniture, curtains, carpets and wallpapers are polished, swagged, patterned and lined, and distinctly pre-modern. The service is magnificent, the sort you only get when a large and talented family is at the helm. Dominic's cooking is as good as his father's hotel-keeping, and his brother-in-law is front of house. Local produce is used in an eclectic, modern and imaginative way and portions are unusually generous: try poached pear with rocket and Cashel blue cheese, then baked salmon with a soft horseradish crust. Relax, drink in the views and John's well-chosen wines, play basketball from your bath. There's lots of humour as well as old-fashioned professionalism.

rooms	31: 21 doubles, 8 twins/doubles, 2 four-posters.
price	£99-£170. Half-board (min. 2 nights) £70-£117 p.p. Singles £79-£99.
meals	Lunch from £12.95. Packed lunch £8.50. Dinner, à la carte, £35.
closed	Rarely.
directions	M5 junc. 7; A449 through Gt Malvern. In M. Wells 3rd right after Railway Pub. Signposted.

Hotel

	John & Sue Pattin
tel	01684 575859
fax	01684 560662
email	reception@cottageinthewood.co.uk
web	www.cottageinthewood.co.uk

The Austwick Traddock

Austwick, via Lancaster, Yorkshire LA2 8BY

Friendly, unpretentious and full of traditional comfort, this family-run hotel is a terrific base for walkers – the Three Peaks of Whernside, Pen-y-Ghent and Ingleborough are at the door. The house is Georgian, with Victorian additions and its unusual name originates from the trading paddock, or horse-trading market, once held next door. Logs crackle in sitting room grates on winter days; deckchairs dot the garden in summer. Bruce and Jane are full of friendly enthusiasm and know how to look after you well. Bedrooms invite with soft carpets, antique dressing tables, quilted beds and Dales views; there are tins of shortbread, decanters of sherry, upmarket bathroom goodies and vases of flowers. Rooms vary in size, and those on the second floor have a cosy, attic feel. You eat well at the Traddock. Good British food combines the traditional and the contemporary and is generous – lamb shank with puy lentils, Spotted Dick. Breakfast, too, is a hearty affair, with a big-choice buffet. There's a cheerful, William Morris feel to it all, and the village, with two clapper bridges, is a gem.

rooms	10: 6 doubles, 1 twin/double, 1 family, 2 singles.
price	£100-£110. Singles £45-£50.
meals	Dinner £18-£23.
closed	Rarely.
directions	0.75 miles off the A65, midway between Kirkby Lonsdale & Skipton.

Hotel

Bruce Reynolds
tel 01524 251224
email info@austwicktraddock.co.uk
web www.austwicktraddock.co.uk

Simonstone Hall

Hawes, Yorkshire DL8 3LY

Drool over the picture of Simonstone, knowing it's just as good inside. This is a glorious country house, built in the 1770s as a shooting lodge for the Earl of Wharnecliffe. The drawing room is magnificent – gracious and elegant – with a wildly ornate fireplace, painted panelled walls and a flurry of antiques. Its triumph is the huge stone-mullioned window through which Wensleydale unravels – a place to stand rooted to the spot. Elsewhere are stone-flagged floors, stained-glass windows and old oils and trophies. There's a big warm traditional bar – almost an inn – with hanging fishing nets, clocks and mirrors, where you can eat well; or pull out all the stops and dine in the lovely, cream-panelled dining room on cream of celery soup, perhaps, and noisette of lamb. Bedrooms are superb. It's well worth splashing out and going for the grander ones – they indulge you completely: four-posters, mullioned windows, stone fireplaces, oils – the full aristocratic Monty. Breakfast on the terrace with those fabulous views, then stride off into the hills... preferably with a champagne picnic.

rooms	20: 9 doubles, 4 twins/doubles, 5 four-posters, 2 suites.
price	£120-£240. Singles from £60.
meals	Lunch from £5. Dinner about £35.
closed	Rarely.
directions	From Hawes, north for Muker for about 2 miles. Hotel on left, at foot of Buttertubs Pass.

Hotel

Jill Stott
tel 01969 667255
fax 01969 667741
email e-mail@simonstonehall.demon.co.uk
web www.simonstonehall.com

Waterford House

19 Kirkgate, Middleham, Yorkshire DL8 4PG

In a lively village dominated by Middleham Castle – northern stronghold of Richard III – is this comfortable Georgian-house hotel. Martin and Anne arrived here two years ago; they are exceptional hosts, easy and delightful. Settle into the sitting room where antiques and sofas jostle, chat by the Aga as Anne stirs a strawberry coulis. After canapés in the drawing room with guests, a memorable meal and ambrosial wines – the list is long. On summer evenings dine alfresco in the country garden with its trickling stream. Bedrooms, up narrow – in some parts steep – stairs have bags of old-fashioned comfort: wrought-iron beds, William Morris wallpaper, pictures, books, magazines, sherry, homemade cakes... the panelled four-poster with blue bedspread and bolsters is a treat. Middleham is a racing village and has 14 stable yards – horses clop by in the morning on their way to the gallops. Breakfast, served on fine china and white linen, is a feast of produce from Anne's parents' farm. Linger as long as you like – it's that sort of place; then pull on your hiking boots and unravel the Dales.

rooms	5: 2 doubles, 1 twin/double, 2 four-posters.
price	£80-£100. Singles £60-£65.
meals	Dinner from £29.
closed	Rarely.
directions	Southbound from A1 at Scotch Corner via Richmond & Leyburn. Northbound from A1 on B6267 via Masham. Hotel in right-hand corner of square.

Hotel

	Martin Cade & Anne Gardener
tel	01969 622090
fax	01969 624020
email	info@waterfordhousehotel.co.uk
web	www.waterfordhousehotel.co.uk

The Yorke Arms

Ramsgill-in-Nidderdale, Nr Harrogate, Yorkshire HG3 5RL

It takes a lot of nous to establish one of the best restaurants in Britain, let alone one up a small country lane in the middle of the Yorkshire Dales. The Yorke Arms is near perfection; exquisite food, wonderful rooms and beautiful countryside make it irresistible. The oldest part was built by monks in the 11th century, the rest added in 1750 when it became a coaching inn. The interior is charming, with polished flagstone floors, low oak beams, comfy armchairs, open fires and antique tables; in summer, eat under a pergola near a burbling beck. Classy rooms continue the theme; attention to detail is guaranteed. Bill, affable and considerate, is a natural host, while Frances scintillates the palette in the kitchen, using fish from the east and west coasts and meat and game from the Dales. Wander from the hamlet of Ramsgill to nearby Gouthwaite reservoir – formed during the Industrial Revolution to supply the city of Bradford with water – or work up an appetite visiting Brimham Rocks or Stump Cross Caverns. *Kennels £5 per night.*

rooms	14: 7 doubles, 3 twins/doubles, 3 singles.
price	Half-board only, £95-£170 p.p.
meals	Lunch £12-£14. Dinner included. Non-residents about £35-£40, not Sunday evenings.
closed	Rarely.
directions	From Ripley, B6165 to Pateley Bridge. Over bridge at bottom of High St; 1st right into Low Wath Road to Ramsgill (4 miles).

Inn

Bill & Frances Atkins

tel	01423 755243
fax	01423 755330
email	enquiries@yorke-arms.co.uk
web	www.yorke-arms.co.uk

The Boar's Head Hotel

Ripley Castle Estate, Harrogate, Yorkshire HG3 3AY

When the Ingilbys decided to reopen The Boar's Head, the attic at the castle got a shakedown and the spare furniture was sent round. The vicar even came to bless the beer taps – you'll find them in Boris's bar, his being the eponymous head. Elegant fun is the net result and there's something for everyone. Lady Ingilby has done a brilliant job with the décor. The sitting rooms and hall have crisp yellow Regency wallpaper, big old oils, roaring fires and gilt mirrors. The restaurant is a deep, moody crimson, candlelit at night, and you drink from blue glass. There are games to play, newspapers to peruse, menus to drool over and a parasoled garden where you can sip long summer drinks. Up the staircase, past more ancestors, to bright, smartly done bedrooms, with floral fabrics, antique furniture, fresh flowers, sofas, tumbling crowns above big beds and rag-rolled bathrooms; those in the coachman's loft in the courtyard have the odd beam and pretty pine panelling. Visit the castle gardens as a guest of the hotel; umbrellas and wellies are there for you on rainy days.

rooms	25: 4 doubles, 21 twins/doubles.
price	£120. Half-board (min. 2 nights) from £80 p.p. Singles £99-£120.
meals	Dinner, à la carte, £18.50-£30. Lunch & dinner in bistro from £9.95.
closed	Rarely.
directions	From Harrogate, A61 north for 3 miles, then left at r'bout, signed to Ripley & castle.

Hotel

	Sir Thomas & Lady Emma Ingilby
tel	01423 771888
fax	01423 771509
email	reservations@boarsheadripley.co.uk
web	www.boarsheadripley.co.uk

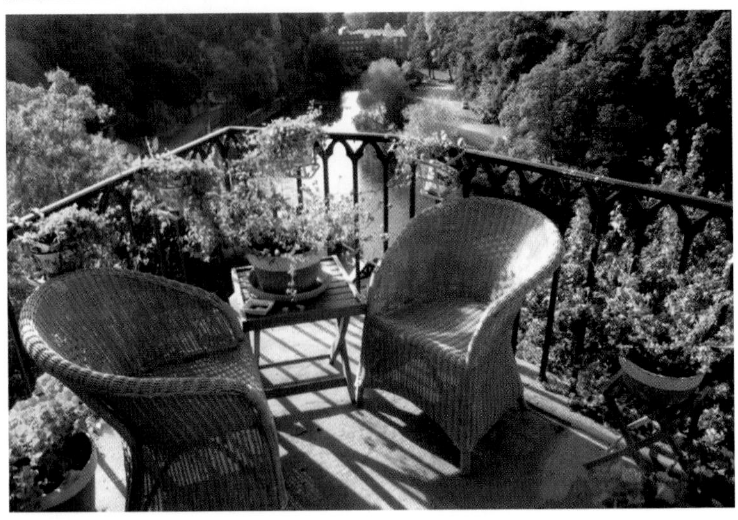

Gallon House

47 Kirkgate, Knaresborough, Yorkshire HG5 8BZ

The locals, poor things, used to transport bucketfuls of water from the river Nidd to the dwellings above – hence the Gallon's name. And as you sit on the south-facing veranda and pop another smoked salmon parcel into your mouth you will relish that spectacular view. Rick and Sue, who had another Special Place in Harrogate, fell in love with the eccentricities of this house and created an intimate hotel – and their natural enthusiasm for getting things right rubs off on a happy staff. The charming restaurant gives a sense of dining en famille: soup is brought to the shared table in a tureen, vegetables arrive in one bowl, and breakfasts are better than anything you'd get at home: organic eggs, Rick's breads and preserves, poached fruits, black pudding. Up narrow stairs to a sitting room with damask sofas and French windows; small, pretty bedrooms have deep mattresses, baskets of magazines, CDs, bottled water and Black Sheep ale and, bar one, window seats over the gorge. Loos are en suite, showers tucked into a corner, towels freshly white. Perfect. *Private dining for special occasions.*

rooms	3: 2 doubles, 1 twin.
price	£90. Singles £70.
meals	Lunch £12. Dinner, 3 courses, £18-£27, by arrangement.
closed	Rarely.
directions	3 miles from A1, in town centre, by railway station.

Hotel

Sue & Rick Hodgson

tel	01423 862102
email	gallon-house@ntlworld.com
web	www.gallon-house.co.uk

The Abbey Inn

Byland Abbey, Coxwold, Yorkshire YO61 4BD

The monks of Ampleforth who built this farmhouse would surely approve of its current devotion to good food; whether they'd be as accepting of its devotion to luxury is another matter. But one monk's frown is another man's path to righteousness. The Abbey Inn is a delightful oasis next to a ruined 12th-century abbey – lit up at night – that indulges the senses. They measure success in smiles up here; Jane loves to see the look on people's faces as they enter the Piggery restaurant, a big flagstoned space, lit by a skylight, full of Jacobean-style chairs and antique tables, that demands your joyful attention. Bedrooms are jaw-dropping, too. Abbot's Retreat has a huge four-poster while a bust of Julius Caesar in the gorgeous black and white tiled bathroom strikes a nice, decadent note – order a bottle of bubbly and jump in the double-ended bath. Priors Lynn has the best view – right down the aisle of the abbey; all have bathrobes, aromatherapy oils, fruit, homemade biscuits and a 'treasure chest' of wine. Come to revel in it all.

rooms	3 doubles.
price	£80-£120.
meals	Light lunch from £5. Dinner, à la carte, about £16. Not Sunday nights & Monday lunch.
closed	Rarely.
directions	From A1 junc. 49, A168 for Thirsk for 10 miles, A19 for York at r'bout. Left after 2 miles, for Coxwold. There left for B. Abbey. Opp. abbey.

Inn

Jane & Martin Nordli

tel	01347 868204
fax	01347 868678
email	jane@nordli.freeserve.co.uk
web	www.bylandabbeyinn.com

The Star Inn

Harome, Nr Helmsley, Yorkshire YO62 5JE

You know you've 'hit the jackpot' as soon as you walk into The Star – it ticks over with such modest ease and calm authority. Andrew and Jacquie arrived in 1996, baby daughters Daisy and Tilly not long after, and the Michelin star in 2002. It's been a formidable turnaround given this 14th-century inn had an iffy local reputation when they took over, yet there's no arrogance; the brochure simply says: "He cooks, and she looks after you"... and how! Andrew's food is rooted in Yorkshire tradition, refined with French flair and written in plain English on ever-changing menus: try dressed Whitby crab, beef from two miles away, Ryedale deer, or maybe Theakston ale cake. Fabulous bedrooms, all ultra-modern yet seriously rustic, are just a stroll away. Thatched and 15th-century, Black Eagle Cottage has three suites; the rest of the rooms are in Cross House Lodge, a breathtaking new barn conversion; the largest room has its own snooker table. There's also the Mousey Thompson bar, the roof mural, the deli and the Coffee Loft – just possibly the most enchanting attic in the world. Brilliant.

rooms	11: 6 doubles, 2 twins/doubles, 3 suites.
price	£120-£195.
meals	Lunch from £3.50. Dinner, à la carte, £25.
closed	Mondays inc. Bank Holiday Mondays. Christmas Day.
directions	From Thirsk, A170 towards Scarborough. Through Helmsley, right, signed Harome. Inn in village.

Inn

Andrew & Jacquie Pern

tel 01439 770397

fax 01439 771833

web www.thestaratharome.co.uk

The White Swan

Market Place, Pickering, Yorkshire YO18 7AA

Mix the boundless energy of a former futures trader with the magical beauty of the North Yorkshire Moors and amazing things can happen. Victor gave up a job in the City to take over this old coaching inn from his parents and it's obvious wandering round that he and Marion left the stress behind and brought a lot of style. They've refurbished the place throughout with simple good taste. Duck in through the front door to find cosy tap rooms that nicely contrast: the lounge with deep burgundy walls and open fire and the light dining room, with porthole mirrors and plaques from champagne cases on each table. Further on, the sitting room and formal restaurant add more indulgence. Bedrooms are elegantly clutter-free: good fabrics, Penhaligon smellies, antique beds, maybe a comfy armchair and a view of the pretty courtyard. The food is just as good – the head chef has been with the Buchanans for years; breakfast inspired one traveller to write a poem, now framed. Rievaulx Abbey is close, the steam railway even closer and a local pub has a tombstone in its roof. Full of surprises. *Pet surcharge, £7.50 per pet.*

rooms	12: 5 doubles, 5 twins/doubles, 2 suites.
price	From £120. Singles from £75. Suites from £140.
meals	Lunch about £15. Dinner about £25.
closed	Rarely.
directions	From North, A170 to Pickering. Entering town, left at traffic lights, then 1st right, Market Place. On left.

Inn

Victor & Marion Buchanan

tel	01751 472288
fax	01751 475554
email	welcome@white-swan.co.uk
web	www.white-swan.co.uk

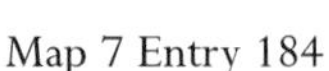

The Endeavour

1 High Street, Staithes, Yorkshire TS13 5BH

Named, like so many things along this stretch of coast, after Captain Cook's ship – built at nearby Whitby – the little fish restaurant with rooms has been successfully squeezed into four storeys of an old terraced house in the small fishing village of Staithes. Elegantly-laid tables occupy two floors, and look onto a narrow, cobbled street leading to the harbour. Bedrooms are comfortable and good value; one looks over the herb garden, one to the sea, another over rooftops to Cowbar's cliffs. The menu is stuffed full of fish dishes from today's catch and prepared by owners/chefs Charlotte and Brian: hake, crab, lobster, brill, turbot, mullet, halibut, shark, squid, wild salmon… some of the best seafood in Britain is landed here, and at Whitby. Meat and vegetarian dishes are also on the menu and puddings are an absolute treat. Walk to Cook's museum or round the exquisite, boat-bobbed harbour – waves crash, seagulls screech: little has changed since Cook gazed out to sea. Book well ahead – the secret is out! *Private parking spaces reserved for guests.*

rooms	3 doubles.
price	£65-£75. Half-board Tues-Thurs (min. 2 nights) £105-£115 p.p.
meals	Dinner, à la carte, £30 with wine. Not Sunday & Monday.
closed	Rarely.
directions	From Whitby, A174 for 8 miles, right for Staithes. Into old village. On right 100 yds before quayside.

Restaurant with Rooms

Charlotte Willoughby & Brian Kay
tel 01947 840825
email theendeavour@ntlworld.com
web www.endeavour-restaurant.co.uk

The Grange Hotel

1 Clifton, York, Yorkshire YO30 6AA

Half a mile from the city wall where the ancient Minster stands, this lovely hotel casts its spell immediately. The Grange is everything a big townhouse hotel should be: gracious, elegant, sumptuously grand, with a warmth that will unravel the tightest knot. Jeremy and Vivien rescued the Georgian building from years of municipal neglect. Effortless style runs throughout: stone floors, Doric columns and urns erupting with flowers greet you in the hall. Deep comfy sofas in the morning room ask to be worn in some more, and the gorgeous vaulted brasserie in the old cellars with red banquettes in snug corners is a treat. The formal dining room has a mural covering wall and ceiling showing a race scene through the open flaps of a blue-and-white-striped pavilion. The horse-racing link is apropos: York's course is considered one of the most exciting in Britain. The hotel is always full on race days – it's said the optimists meet here! Bedrooms are also full of flair: bold greens and reds, a silky purple four-poster, writing paper on the desks and rich fabrics. Those after history need only step outside.

rooms	30: 8 doubles, 16 twins/doubles, 3 singles, 2 four-posters, 1 suite.
price	£140-£200. Singles from £110. Suite £250.
meals	Lunch from £12.75. Dinner from £28.
closed	Rarely.
directions	From York ring road, A19 south into city centre. Hotel on right after 2 miles, 400 yds from city walls.

Hotel

	Jeremy & Vivien Cassel
tel	01904 644744
fax	01904 612453
email	info@grangehotel.co.uk
web	www.grangehotel.co.uk

Weaver's

15 West Lane, Haworth, Yorkshire BD22 8DU

If you don't know what a Clun or a Lonk is, use it as an excuse to make a trip to this unusual restaurant with rooms – the answer is somewhere on the walls. The rambling eccentricity here is superb; nothing has a place, yet everything is exactly where it should be. The front bar has the intimate feel of an old French café, with heavy wood, marble-topped tables, atmospheric lighting and comfy chairs, while the lively restaurant at the back seems in step with the Charleston era. None of this was intended, of course. Eat the best and most unpretentious food imaginable – smoked haddock soup, Pennine pie, homemade ice cream... even Yorkshire feta. It's outstanding value and people come back time and again. Bedrooms are full of surprises and understated originality: French beds, dashes of bright colour, the odd bust, antique furniture – everything is just right. Rooms at the back overlook the Brontë Parsonage. Colin runs front of house – from the kitchen – with true Yorkshire sass: straight-talking, down-to-earth, and blessed with a wicked sense of humour. Worth a long detour, for the organic breakfast alone.

rooms	3 twins/doubles, with separate bath.
price	£80. Singles £55.
meals	Dinner £12.50-£25; à la carte about £25; bar supper about £12.50. Lunch from £9.95. Dinner not Sun & Mon. Lunch not Mon, Tues & Sat.
closed	26 December-9 January.
directions	A6033 to Haworth, follow signs to Brontë Parsonage Museum. Use museum car park. Near passageway to High Street.

Restaurant with Rooms

Colin & Jane Rushworth

tel	01535 643822
fax	01535 644832
email	weaversinhaworth@aol.com
web	www.weaversmallhotel.co.uk

The Weavers Shed Restaurant with Rooms

Knowl Road, Golcar, Huddersfield, Yorkshire HD7 4AN

Stephen's reputation for producing sublime food goes from strength to strength at this restaurant with rooms, firmly fixed on the wish lists of foodies all over the country. His passion stretches as far as planting a one-acre kitchen garden; it now provides most of his vegetables, herbs and fruit. You may get warm mousse of scallops, Lunesdale duckling and rhubarb tartlet – the latter home-grown, of course – and edible flowers in the salad from Stephen's wildflower garden. The old mill owner's house sits at the top of the hill, with cobbles in the courtyard and a lamp by the door. Inside, whitewashed walls are speckled with menus from famous restaurants, a small garden basks beyond the windows and, at the bar, malts and eaux-de-vie stand behind a piece of wood that looks as if it came from an ancient church, but actually is from the Co-op. Earthy stone arches and plinths in the tiled restaurant give the feel of a Tuscan farmhouse. Elsewhere, gilt mirrors, comfy sofas and big, bright, brilliantly priced bedrooms that hit the spot with complimentary sherry, dried flowers, bathrobes and wicker chairs.

rooms	5: 3 doubles, 1 twin/double, 1 four-poster.
price	£65-£80. Singles £50-£65.
meals	Lunch from £11.50. Dinner about £30. Restaurant closed Saturday lunchtimes, Sundays & Mondays.
closed	Christmas & New Year.
directions	From Huddersfield A62 west for 2 miles, then right for Milnsbridge & Golcar. Left at Kwiksave; signed on right at top of hill.

Restaurant with Rooms

	Stephen & Tracy Jackson
tel	01484 654284
fax	01484 650980
email	info@weaversshed.co.uk
web	www.weaversshed.co.uk

Photography courtesy of Jersey Tourism, www.jersey.com

channel islands

La Sablonnerie

Little Sark, Via Guernsey, Channel Islands GY9 0SD

If you tell Elizabeth which ferry you're arriving on, she'll send down her horse and carriage to meet you. "Small, sweet world of wave-encompassed wonder," wrote Swinburne of Sark. The tiny community of 500 people lives under a spell, governed feudally and sharing this magic island with horses, sheep, cattle, carpets of wild flowers and birds. There are wild cliff walks, thick woodland, sandy coves, wonderful deep rock pools, aquamarine seas. No cars, only bikes, horse and carriage and the odd tractor. In the hotel – a 400-year-old farmhouse – there is no TV, no radio, no trouser press... just a dreamy peace, kindness, starched cotton sheets, woollen blankets and food to die for. Eat in the lovely dining-room or in the prettiest of well-tended gardens with gorgeous colourful borders. The Perrées still farm and, as a result, the hotel is almost self-sufficient; you also get home-baked bread and lobsters straight from the sea. Elizabeth is Sercquaise – her mother's family were part of the 1565 colonisation – and she knows her land well enough to point you to the island's secrets.

rooms	22: 5 doubles, 6 twins, 6 family, 1 suite; 2 doubles, 2 twins, sharing 2 baths.
price	£95-£155. Half-board £59.50-£75.50 p.p.
meals	Dinner, 5 courses, £30.
closed	2nd Monday in October-Wednesday before Easter.
directions	Take ferry to Sark & ask!

Hotel

	Elizabeth Perrée
tel	01481 832061
fax	01481 832408

The Golfer's Rest

On Course, St Bill, Jersey JOK 1NG

In a golf-obsessed age, it is encouraging to see that not all course-designers are so coarse after all. For here, on a bleak and windswept cliff on the magnificent islands, is a handsome place to which you and co-players may retire while halfway through a game. Slap bang beside a conveniently sited bunker – from which you may emerge, exhausted – is this little gem of a place, a jewel in the crown of the island's history. (The islands are a wee bit short on the sort of history that the rest of us know about.) Every stone has been dismantled, cleaned and re-assembled on this elevated spot, having survived a boat journey from another island. Nobody has a clue as to what shape the pile of old stones originally took – but a small, intimate hotel seemed an appropriate reconstruction. Your stay may prove perilous, for the put-happy locals take a rather perverse pleasure in chipping through one window and out through the other. Perfect for the adventurous and the open-hearted.

rooms	1 open-plan, large enough to fit a whole sky above it. BYO blankets.
price	Landlord will settle for a bit of your sleeve or an old sock.
meals	The landlord is the meal - though visitors have yet to persuade him of this.
closed	Rarely; always open to parachutists.
directions	Tee off, then pursue ball until The Golfer's Rest is in sight.

Other Place

	Mr William G Gruff
tel	Give him a bell...
email	billy@getmygoat.org.ba
web	www.getmygoat.org.ba

Atlantic Hotel

St Brelade, Jersey JE3 8HE

Perfect peace, perfect luxury – and sunsets across a golden sea will be your lasting memory of the Atlantic. It may look big, modern, almost brashly confident, but enter and you'll find the virtues we consider so important: warmth, personality and individual attention. Patrick has given the hotel built by his father in the early 70s an impressive makeover, creating the 21st-century equivalent of those grand old hotels of the Edwardian age. It is bold, beautifully run by loyal and friendly staff, irrepressibly comfortable, and understated. Classic and contemporary blend well, balancing antiques, urns, fountains, a wrought-iron staircase and specially commissioned furniture upholstered in warm, rich fabrics. The bedrooms are big, modern, pale and cool, with bathrooms of white marble, pale oak and polished chrome; many have sliding doors to balconies with ship-style balustrading and lovely sea views. Dine on smoked salmon parcels filled with fresh crab, tomato and saffron and then, perhaps, roast beef on potato rosti, wild mushrooms and shallot marmalade. Full of style – and the sound of the sea will hypnotise.

rooms	50: 48 twins/doubles, 2 suites.
price	£190-£275. Singles £145-£175. Suite £265-£455.
meals	Lunch £15. Dinner, 3 courses, £35; à la carte also available.
closed	2 January-4 February.
directions	From Jersey airport, B36 for St Brelade for 1.5 miles. Right at lights onto A13, for St Ouen's Bay, for 1 mile, right into La Rue De La Sergente. Hotel signed at top of hill.

Hotel

	Patrick Burke
tel	01534 744101
fax	01534 744102
email	info@theatlantichotel.com
web	www.theatlantichotel.com

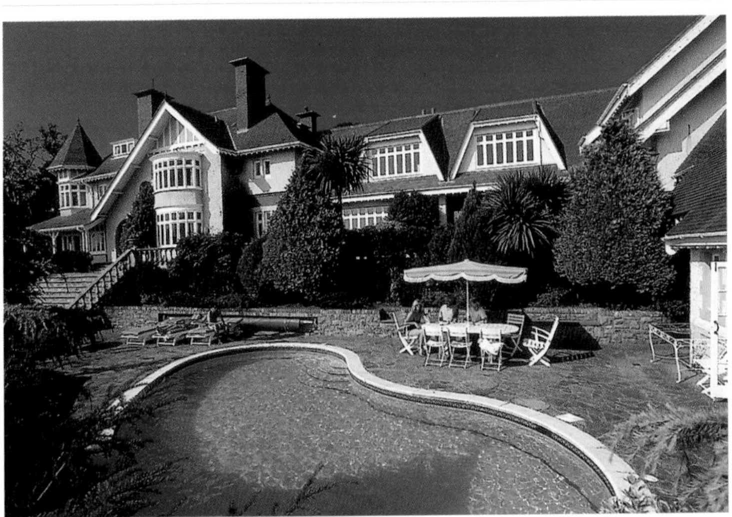

Eulah Country House

Mont Cochon, St Helier, Jersey JE2 3JA

Eulah Country House is a rare and wonderful treat, designed for hedonists, perfectionists, business people who can't put away the laptop, and for elegant weddings. Sink in, soak up and let this beautifully restored Edwardian house take the strain. Generous sofas tumble with cushions, flowers brim from vases, there's a curvaceous pool... of all the luxuries here, none is as engagingly self-mocking as the four-poster bath. Tables and chairs are attractive and chunky; the long, lovely sitting room has unexpected beams. Bedrooms are enormous, each carpeted with a meadow of rich, plain pile, each with its own breakfast 'nook'. Colours are bold and classic – swathes of material swoop up from behind headboards and over pillows to the ceiling. Few of us imagine having such impressive beds at home; the bathroom fittings are the ones you dare not buy for yourself. Long, lush views stretch across St Helier and St Aubin's Bay, and Penny runs the place with easy good humour. Whether you're in the sauna or the pool, you may wonder if it's a home or a hotel... in spite of the luxury, we found it hard to tell the difference.

rooms	9: 6 doubles, 3 twins/doubles.
price	£160-£230. Singles £125-£185.
meals	Restaurants locally.
closed	Rarely.
directions	From St Helier, A2 west, then right at lights on B27. Through next lights up Mont Cochon. Entrance 100 yds on right.

Hotel

	Penny Clarke
tel	01534 626626
fax	01534 626600
email	eulah@jerseymail.co.uk
web	www.eulah.co.uk

Photography by Jackie King

scotland

Raemoir House Hotel

Raemoir, Banchory, Aberdeenshire AB31 4ED

Grand it is – but not intimidating: the staff are lovely. The 1750 mansion, with east and west wings added, is built of granite and slate; the original House of Raemoir, known as the Ha' Hoose (Hall House), is older and makes a historically significant 'annexe'. (Mary Queen of Scots was a guest.) Raemoir is majestic on the outside, resplendent within. Vases burst with flowers, log fires glow, sofas tumble with cushions; stags' heads line the Morning Room and velvet brocade the dining room – an oval room, entirely lit by candles at night and with a fireplace big enough to take a small tree. Bedrooms are Old Scottish, or Italian, or Pine, the French Room is filled with Louis XV *ormolu*; each room is different, opulent, awash with modern comfort; the best look south to the hills. Splash in a large tub after a day's fishing, stalking or golf... bathrooms range from Edwardian to 21st-century spa. Food is modern classical – "Scottish with French flair" – and if you catch a fish they'll cook it. Acres of parkland and forest envelop you, the scenery is stunning, there are salmon in the River Dee and castles by the hatful.

rooms	21: 9 doubles, 6 twins, 3 singles, 3 suites.
price	£95-£117. Suites £138.
meals	Lunch from £4.75. Dinner from £26.50.
closed	Rarely.
directions	A597 into Banchory. Right at Raemoir Road junction. On for 3-4 miles to entrance across x-roads. Take care on crossing!

Hotel

	Peter Ferguson
tel	01330 824884
fax	01330 822171
email	relax@raemoir.com
web	www.raemoir.com

Darroch Learg

Braemar Road, Ballater, Aberdeenshire AB35 5UX

The Royal Family escapes to the fir district of Deeside in summer; the Franks family stays all year, welcoming those in search of genuine Scottish hospitality. They have been here 40 years and know how to run a good hotel; nothing is too much trouble. Darroch Learg is Gaelic for 'an oak copse on a sunny hillside' and this turreted 1888 granite building is in a raised position on the outskirts of the pretty village of Ballater. Views stretch across the Dee Valley to Lochnagar, snow-capped for much of the year. The main part of the hotel is a baronial Victorian manor house, with a twist of Scottish grandeur thrown in for good measure. Regency-style bedrooms are split between here and a next-door annexe: all are subtly different, with warm colours, local watercolours, fresh flowers, thick curtains and modern bathrooms with spoiling touches; most rooms have the view. An intimate conservatory-style dining room, with lamps at each table, draws in the view as well. Chef David Mutter's modern Scottish cooking has won various awards, supported by a good wine list. You'll feel good staying here.

rooms	17: 5 doubles, 10 twins/doubles, 2 four-posters.
price	£130-£160. Half-board (May to September) £97.50-£112.50 p.p.
meals	Dinner £37.50. Sunday lunch £21.
closed	Christmas week & last 3 weeks in January.
directions	From Perth, A93 north to Ballater. Entering village, hotel 1st building on left above road.

Hotel

Nigel & Fiona Franks
tel 01339 755443
fax 01339 755252
email nigel@darroch-learg.demon.co.uk

The Manor House

Gallanach Road, Oban, Argyll & Bute PA34 4LS

A 1780 dower house for the Dukes of Argyll – their cottage by the sea – built of local stone, high on the hill, with long views over Oban harbour to the Isle of Mull. A smart and proper place, not one to bow to the fads of fashion: sea views from the lawn, cherry trees in the courtyard garden, a fire roaring in the drawing room, a beautiful tiled floor in the entrance hall and an elegant bay window in the dining room that catches the eye. Compact bedrooms are pretty in blues, reds and greens, with fresh flowers, crisp linen sheets, radios, padded headboards and piles of towels in good bathrooms; those that look seaward have pairs of binoculars to scour the horizon. Sample Loch Fyne kippers for breakfast, sea bass for lunch and, if you've room, duck in redcurrant sauce for supper; try their home-baking, too. Ferries leave for the islands from the bottom of the hill – see them depart from the hotel garden – while at the top, overlooking Oban, watch the day's close from McCaig's Folly; sunsets here are really special. *Children over 11 welcome.*

rooms	11: 8 doubles, 3 twins.
price	Half-board only, £60-£90 p.p.
meals	Lunch £7-£13. Dinner, 5 courses, £29.50.
closed	Christmas.
directions	In Oban, follow signs to ferry. Hotel on right 0.5 miles after ferry turn-off, signed.

Hotel

	Gabriella Wijker
tel	01631 562087
fax	01631 563053
email	manorhouseoban@aol.com
web	www.manorhouseoban.com

Lerags House

Lerags, By Oban, Argyll & Bute PA34 4SE

An unexpected touch of city chic on the beautiful west coast, Lerags is a listed, solid-stone house with a stylish country-house interior. Charlie, ex sail-maker, and Bella, a cook, both originally from Australia, came for six months, stayed for nine years, and now own their place by the sea. They (and Fingal, the rescued greyhound) couldn't be nicer. Built in 1815, the house is large, with gardens that run down to tidal mud flats: enjoy watery views at high tide. Beautiful interiors mix neutrals and whites, with colour from checked blankets and paintings by Charlie. Bedrooms gaze serenely onto gardens or loch; beds are generous, comfortable and deliciously dressed, bathrooms fresh with Gilchrist & Soames. Charlie and Bella represent an emerging generation of Highland hoteliers: more style, less formality, good prices and remarkable food exquisitely presented – Barbreck rack of lamb with homemade mint relish, champagne jelly with strawberries in season. Walking sticks by the front door, a beach less than a mile away, and day trips to Mull, Crinan and Glencoe. Perfect.

rooms	7: 4 doubles, 1 double/twin, 1 single, 1 suite.
price	Half board only, £75 p.p.
meals	Dinner included. Packed lunch £6.
closed	Christmas.
directions	From Oban, south on A816 for 2 miles, then right, signed Lerags for 2.5 miles. Hotel on left, signed.

Hotel

Charlie & Bella Miller
tel 01631 563381
email stay@leragshouse.com
web www.leragshouse.com

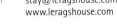

Ardanaiseig

Kilchrenan, By Taynuilt, Argyll & Bute PA35 1HE

The seduction begins the moment you leave the main road and set off on the twisting, 10-mile track. Such silence, and when you set eyes on the Ardanaiseig you think all is complete: a magical landscape of valley and snow-capped peaks embraces the 1834 baronial mansion that sits snug on the shores of Loch Awe. But there is more to come. From the big bay windows of the drawing room, watch the peat-burning steamboat pick up fellow guests from the end of the garden to transport them to fairytale castles. There's fun, too, from the art-collecting owner, to add a light touch... and comfortable bedrooms, each one different; 200 acres of woodland gardens with an amphitheatre for concerts; great food. Gary the chef who has been here for six years is "good at everything", creating wonders from scallops from Oban, venison from the woods, beef from Aberdeen. Peter, charming and gentle, is ever-present: all runs smoothly with him at the helm. Venture forth to the village, a three-mile ramble... feel the peace. People come for special occasions – to propose and to marry – but you should find any excuse.

rooms	16: 8 doubles, 8 twins/doubles.
price	£78-£250. Half-board (minimum 3 nights) £59-£148 p.p. Singles £69-£155.
meals	Light lunch from £3.75. Afternoon tea £2-£10. Gourmet menu, 7 courses, £42.
closed	January-mid-February.
directions	A85 to Taynuilt. Left, B845 for Kilchrenan. Then left at Kilchrenan pub; down track for 4 miles.

Hotel

Peter Webster

tel	01866 833333
fax	01866 833222
email	ardanaiseig@clara.net
web	www.ardanaiseig.com

The Royal at Tighnabruaich

Tighnabruaich, Argyll & Bute PA21 2BE

In that never-ending search for a tourist-free destination, Tighnabruaich is near the top of our list, an end-of-the-road village, lost to the world and without great need of it. The Royal is its relaxed and informal hub. Yachtsmen tie up to the moorings and drop in for lunch, the shinty team pops down for a pint after a game, and fishermen land fresh mussels and lobster straight from the sea for Roger and Claire to cook. Roger and Bea – ex-pat Scots – returned from London with an eye to "buying something run-down so they could…" run it up? Which is exactly what they've done: stripped wooden floors and a roaring fire in the brasserie, tartan carpets and leather sofas in the restaurant. Claire, their daughter, has joined the team, and is now chef. Food is a big pull: masses of fresh seafood, and local venison, as stalked by Winston Churchill of Dunoon. Big views of the Kyles of Bute seem bigger from the new conservatories. Bedrooms are stunning, with huge beds and fantastic views. Play tennis on a nearby tennis court where you can lose balls in the sea, or take a short ferry ride to Bute.

rooms	11: 9 doubles, 2 twins.
price	From £80-£150.
meals	Dinner, à la carte, 3 courses, about £30.
closed	Christmas.
directions	From Glasgow, A82 north, A83 west, A815 south, A886 south, A8003 south, then B8000 north into village. Hotel on seafront.

Hotel

	Roger & Bea McKie
tel	01700 811239
fax	01700 811300
email	info@royalhotel.org.uk
web	www.royalhotel.org.uk

Argyll Hotel

Isle of Iona PA76 6SJ

Iona doesn't need much selling – a ferry that stops at six in the morning, azure seas, golden beaches, gentle ridges, glorious walks, an abbey, a drop of history and nothing between you and America. It's been firmly fixed on the tourist trail ever since St Columba landed on the island in AD563. Scottish kings, Viking warlords and Celtic warriors have all visited, though given that the Argyll didn't open its doors until 1867, they must have had to rough it. It's a pretty place, with views over the water to Mull. Daniel and Claire have kept the old, cosy island feel alive: open fires, loads of books, pretty bedrooms and a delightful conservatory where you can watch Iona life pass by. The hotel is virtually self-sufficient for salads and vegetables and there's an impressive one-acre organic garden that provides much for your plate: expect seafood chowder, organic venison, homemade ice cream. Seals and dolphins pass through the Sound of Iona, and Mark, maintenance man, friend and sailor, will take you under sail around the island. Walk west a mile for astounding sunsets. You may see the Northern Lights.

rooms	16: 5 doubles, 2 twins, 1 family, 6 singles, 1 suite; 1 double with separate bath.
price	£44-£86. Half-board from £55 p.p. Singles £39-£48. Suite from £152.
meals	Dinner, à la carte, about £20.
closed	December-January.
directions	Oban ferry to Craignure on Mull; west to Fionnphort for Iona ferry. Cars can be left safely at Fionnphort.

Hotel

Claire Bachellerie & Daniel Morgan

tel	01681 700334
fax	01681 700510
email	reception@argyllhoteliona.co.uk
web	www.argyllhoteliona.co.uk

Tiroran House

Pennyghael, Isle of Mull PA69 6ES

The drive to Tiroran takes you through some of the wildest and most spectacular scenery in Scotland, single track roads connecting the island through a magical landscape of rugged mountains and stepped silhouettes. Tiroran lies on the north shore of Loch Scridain – and Iona is a ferry-ride away. A stirring burn tumbles past the house through an enchanting garden and down to the sea: it's the dreamiest of walks. Newcomers Laurence and Katie have enthuastically stepped into the previous owners' shoes; he first discovered Mull as a deep-sea diver 20 years ago and still dives for the odd lobster or clam; she, Cordon Bleu-trained, will tranform the catch into something delectable for dinner. Breakfasts are equally fine. During the school holidays their offspring may make friends with yours – families will love it here. Relax under the shade of a grape vine in the conservatory, nod off before a log fire in one of two lounges. Bedrooms are all different and most have garden views; binoculars are provided to spot grazing deer, or golden eagles. The isle is a vast playground for lovers of the outdoors.

rooms	6: 3 doubles, 3 twins.
price	£104-£110. Singles £55-£70.
meals	Dinner from £27.50
closed	Rarely.
directions	From Craignure or Fishnish car ferries, A849 for Bunessan & Iona car ferry, right on B8035 for Gruline for 4 miles. Left at converted church. House 1 mile further.

Laurence Mackay & Katie Munro

tel	01681 705232
fax	01681 705240
email	info@tiroran.freeserve.co.uk
web	www.tiroran.com

Highland Cottage

Breadalbane Street, Tobermory, Isle of Mull PA75 6PD

A double first for Highland Cottage; this is clearly the loveliest place to stay in Tobermory, and the tastiest place to eat. Expect to be plied with treats from the kitchen: gallons of fresh orange juice served in crystal glasses, piping-hot coffee and the full cooked works. On one table, guests spoke glowingly of supper the night before: haddock risotto, saddle of venison, hot raspberries and ice cream – Highland Cottage is emerging as one of the jewels of Scottish cooking. Elsewhere, nothing disappoints. Bedrooms are exceptional: regal fabrics, crushed-velvet cushions, silk bedspreads, tartan tiles in fine bathrooms, Cadell prints, huge porcelain lamps, a French sleigh bed, even the odd sea view. In the sitting room, Tobermory light floods in, CDs wait to be played, pot-boilers (or *Kidnapped* – it's set on the island) wait to be read. If you can tear yourselves away, head to Iona, Fingal's Cave, or just wander around Tobermory, the prettiest town in the Western Isles, with its Highland games, art festivals, yachting regattas, and the daily to and fro of islanders stocking up on supplies. Marvellous. *Children over ten welcome.*

rooms	6: 2 doubles, 2 twins, 2 four-posters.
price	£110-£135. Singles from £85.
meals	Dinner, 4 courses, £31.50.
closed	Mid-October-mid-November, & Christmas. Restricted opening January & February.
directions	From ferry, A848 to Tobermory. Across bridge at mini-r'bout, immed. right into Breadalbane St. On right opp. fire station.

Hotel

David & Jo Currie
tel 01688 302030
email davidandjo@highlandcottage.co.uk
web www.highlandcottage.co.uk

Calgary Hotel & Dovecote Restaurant

Calgary, Nr Dervaig, Isle of Mull PA75 6QW

Talk to Muilleachs about their island and they all tip you the wink on Calgary Bay – a place for picnics, for cricket on the huge beach, sea-angling off the rocks and wind surfing in the bay. It's a fantastic spot, lost to the rest of Mull, and if you walk on the beach after 8pm you'll probably have it all to yourself. You can stroll back to the hotel through Matthew's woodland walk, a natural art gallery of sorts that stops you in your tracks: standing stones, tree art, living sculpture... Back at the hotel, free-range children, a tearoom, a gallery, a sparkling restaurant in the old dovecote, delicious meals and a courtyard with a fountain. Calgary is a neat little homespun place that has an unmistakably mediterranean feel: family-run, no dress code, a slim rule book, a relaxed feel. Remarkably, Matthew renovated the whole place himself; walls were falling down, ceilings had disappeared. He also works in wood and much of what you see around the place is his workmanship. Bedrooms are farmhouse-cosy with country fabrics and whitewashed walls. Book for one night only and you'll kick yourself.

rooms	9: 4 doubles, 2 twins, 1 single, 2 family.
price	£60-£88. Singles £30-£44.
meals	Lunch from £5. Dinner £21.
closed	December-February. Open weekends November & March.
directions	From Dervaig, B8073 west for 5.5 miles. House signed right before Calgary Bay.

Hotel

Julia & Matthew Reade

tel 01688 400256

fax 01688 400256

email calgary.hotel@virgin.net

web www.calgary.co.uk

Culzean Castle

The National Trust for Scotland, Maybole, Ayrshire KA19 8LE

Few places to stay in the world come close to Culzean, pronounced 'Cullane' – Scotland's sixth most popular tourist destination defies overstatement. Built into solid rock a couple of hundred feet above crashing waves, the castle is considered to be architect Robert Adam's final masterpiece. It was presented to the Scottish people in 1945 by the 5th Marquess of Ailsa and the Kennedy family. General Eisenhower was given use of the top floor during his lifetime – Scotland's thank you for his contribution to the war effort. You stay on the same floor where every room is a delight; Ike's bed is always popular. The rest is awe-inspiring: hundreds of portraits, including one of Napoleon, the round drawing room that juts out over the sea, the central oval staircase with two galleries and 12 Corinthian columns, and the Armoury, with 713 flintlock pistols and 400 swords – a good reminder to pay the bill. Tour the castle before the tourists invade at 11am, take a stirring cliff walk in 560 acres of idyllic coastal scenery, and dine together country-house style. All guaranteed to exceed your wildest dreams.

rooms	6: 1 double, 3 twins/doubles, 1 four-poster; 1 twin with separate bath.
price	£225-£375. Singles from £140. Includes afternoon tea & evening drinks.
meals	Dinner, 3 courses with wine, £50, by arrangement.
closed	Rarely.
directions	From A77 in Maybole, A719 for 4 miles, signed.

B&B

David Heron
tel 01655 884455

Beechwood Country House Hotel

Harthope Place, Moffat, Dumfries & Galloway DG10 9HX

Once an adventure boarding school for young ladies, now an atmospheric country-house hotel. The whole place breathes an air of well-being, thanks to Stavros and Cheryl, so proud of their new venture and generous with treats: Penhaligon lotions in the bathroom, malt whiskies in the bar (Stavros's delight) and Loch Fyne kippers for breakfast. Beechwood walks – 12 acres of them – start from the door, and there are wellies in case you've forgotten yours. Even clean towels for muddy dogs: the attention to detail amazes. Sitting rooms have books, games and magazines, there's a smoking bar for cigars, hot cocoa for bed. The place hums with warmth and welcome: a cheerful mix of antiques and *objets* from far-flung places, family paintings on mellow yellow walls, kilims on polished pine, lilies from Edinburgh. Bedrooms are simply lovely, with white linen on big beds and wooden shutters to help you lie in. And in the dining room: fresh, colourful food from a singing chef, served on starched linen, and views over the gentle valley. Beyond, the spa town of Moffat bustles with restaurants, shops and bars.

rooms	7: 3 doubles, 3 twins, 1 family.
price	£96. Half-board £73 p.p. Singles £62.
meals	Packed lunch £12. Dinner £25.
closed	23 December-12 February.
directions	Exit M74 at junc. 15 for Moffat; through town centre, right between church & school. Hotel signed.

Hotel

Stavros & Cheryl Michaelides
tel 01683 220210
email enquiries@beechwoodcountryhousehotel.co.uk
web www.beechwoodcountryhousehotel.co.uk

Cavens Country House Hotel

Kirkbean, By Dumfries, Dumfries & Galloway DG2 8AA

Angus and Jane have painstakingly restored this 1752 house built by a tobacco baron whose estates stretched the length and breadth of South West Scotland. It's hard to appreciate the extent of their labours, but easy to enjoy the fruits – particularly in front of a roaring fire, wee dram in hand. The Fordyces are friendly professionals who put in a huge amount of effort to ensure guests will come back, and they do. Angus is chef and does superb home cooking with a Scottish-French twist, four courses that change every day. A highlight are the cheeses from Loch Arthur Farm – worth leaving home for. Jane does the décor and no two bedrooms are alike; all have comfort, elegance, rich colours, wide beds, padded bedsteads, chintz with swags and tails, books in glass-fronted cases. Views from the enormous drawing room sweep down the gardens to a temple at the far end. This neck of the woods is a wildlife heaven; go birdwatching in summer, shooting in winter, riding, walking or golfing. Or simply treat this as your place in the country and revel in doing absolutely nothing.

rooms	6: 4 doubles, 2 twins.
price	£80-£140. Singles from £95.
meals	Dinner, 3 courses, £30. Packed lunch available.
closed	Rarely.
directions	From Dumfries, A710 to Kirkbean (12 miles). Hotel signed in village.

Hotel

	Jane & Angus Fordyce
tel	01387 880234
fax	01387 880467
email	enquiries@cavens.com
web	www.cavens.com

Knockinaam Lodge

Portpatrick, Wigtownshire, Dumfries & Galloway DG9 9AD

The lawn runs down to the Irish sea, sunsets streak the sky red and roe deer amble down to eat the roses. An exceptional 1869 shooting lodge with unremitting luxuries: a Michelin star in the dining room, 150 malts in the bar, and a level of service that you don't expect in such far-flung corners of the realm. And history. Churchill once stayed and you can sleep in his big elegant room, where copies of his books wait to be read, and where you need steps to climb into an ancient bath. It remains very much a country house: plump cushions on a Queen Anne sofa in an immaculate morning room where the scent of fresh flowers mixes with the smell of burnt wood, invigorating cliff walks, curlews to lull you to sleep, nesting Peregrine falcons, and a rock pool where David keeps lobsters for the pot. In storms, waves crash all around – bracing stuff. Trees stand guard high on the hill, their branches buffeted by the wind. Remote, beguiling, utterly spoiling – Knockinaam is worth the detour. John Buchan knew the house and described it in *The Thirty-Nine Steps* as the house to which Hannay fled.

rooms	9: 7 doubles, 2 twins.
price	Half board only, £125-£180 p.p. Singles from £145.
meals	Lunch £3.50-£30. Dinner, 5 courses, included; non-residents £45.
closed	Rarely.
directions	From A77 or A75 follow signs for Portpatrick. 2 miles west of Lochans, left at smokehouse. Follow signs to Lodge for 3 miles.

Hotel

David & Sian Ibbotson

tel	01776 810471
fax	01776 810435
email	reservations@knockinaamlodge.com
web	www.knockinaamlodge.com

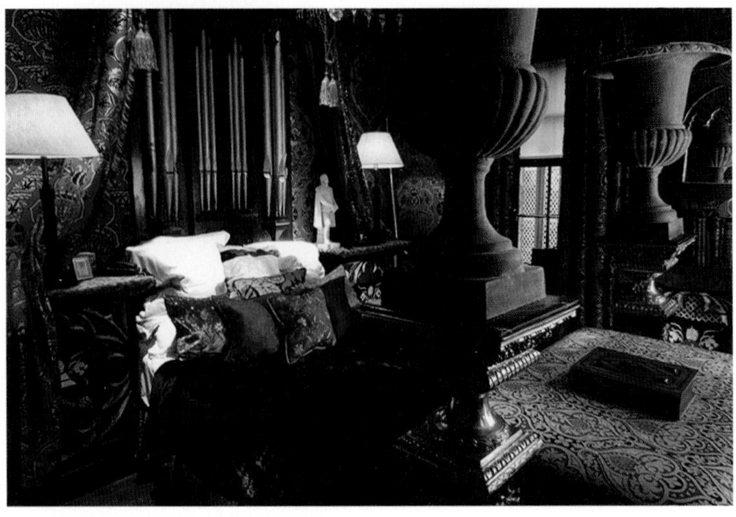

The Witchery by the Castle

Castlehill, Royal Mile, Edinburgh EH1 2NF

Ornately gothic in style and exuberant, this should really be a theatre. It's such a magical and passionate setting, it might best suit a Jacobean drama: there are enough drapes and alcoves to conceal a medium-sized cast of conspirators and lovers. The Witchery is the inspiration of the owner, James Thomson. He has trawled the flea-markets of Europe to fill two 16th-century tenements next to the gates of Edinburgh Castle with sumptuous architectural bric-a-brac, from the medieval to the quasi-Byzantine... the spiral staircase, the candles, the stone floors, the tapestries and even the shadows delight. The suites are incredible: the Inner Sanctum has one of Queen Victoria's chairs, the pillars in the Old Rectory came from London's Trocadero, the red, black and gold Vestry has a trompe l'œil swagged bathroom and all have Bose sound systems. A bottle of champagne is included, as is continental breakfast in bed – superb homemade pastries. The two restaurants excel – one is luminous, another gothic – and if you can drag yourself away, Edinburgh's not bad either.

rooms	7 suites.
price	From £250.
meals	Cooked breakfast from £10. Lunch £9.95. Dinner, à la carte, about £30.
closed	Christmas Day & Boxing Day.
directions	Find Edinburgh Castle. Witchery 20 yds from main castle gate.

Hotel

tel	0131 225 7800
fax	0131 220 4992
email	reservations@prestonfield.com
web	www.prestonfield.com

Royal Mile Residence

219 Royal Mile, Edinburgh, Edinburgh EH1 1PE

Textured wallpapers (very modern), painted shutters, Firth of Forth views... welcome to your serviced apartment. A private and roomy alternative to a hotel stay with daily maid service, free entry to the local health club for a swim or gym and breakfast hampers which can be arranged – leaving you free to do your own thing. It's spanking new and pretty darn swish, a fantastic spot, bang in the centre of one of Europe's grandest cities. The apartments at the front overlook pulsating, cobbled Royal Mile, those at the back, Princes Street Gardens and beyond. Originally the building was a maternity hospital, founded by Elsie Inglis (a sort of Scottish Florence Nightingale and Emily Pankhurst rolled into one); in this reincarnation a bold designer hand has been at work. Moody maroon sitting rooms with tartan blinds at sash windows, king-size beds with white linen, nut-brown walls, a flash of scarlet, kitchens in beech and granite with every mod con, bathrooms in cream and sand. A luxurious bolthole for business folk, romantics, escapists and families.

rooms	7 apartments for 2, 4 and 6.
price	£150-£300.
meals	Restaurants nearby.
closed	Rarely.
directions	On Royal Mile. Discounted secure parking. Five minute walk from Waverley station.

Serviced accommodation

tel	0131 226 5155
fax	0131 477 4636
email	info@royalmileresidence.com
web	www.royalmileresidence.com

Prestonfield

Priestfield Road, Edinburgh EH16 5UT

A long drive winds through parkland, highland cattle contentedly graze, peacocks shriek to announce your arrival. Strange, then, that you are just five minutes by car from the centre of Edinburgh. Prepare to be impressed and to marvel at wonderful architectural features: decorative, ornate plasterwork, a 300-year-old ceiling, a drawing room panelled with leather and marble floors. Owner, James Thomson has transformed the traditional country house to something altogether more 'wow'. Massive helpings of opulence: gilded tassel chandeliers, black and gilt regency banquettes, velvet upholstery, white marble, rich reds and the same wallpaper suppliers as the Lord Chancellor's! The 'destination restaurant' Rhubarb is a big draw and no less stylish with an ambitious menu. Sensuous bedrooms are a dream: a symphony of dark crushed velvet, textured wallpaper, low-level lighting, cushioned and bejewelled decadence; chocolate mousse and champagne by the bed, more treats in the bathroom. Thomson also owns The Witchery, another Edinburgh paradise. RIP the residents' dining room? Hurrah!

rooms	26: 24 twins/doubles, 2 suites.
price	From £150.
meals	Lunch from £13.95, 2 courses. Dinner, à la carte, about £30.
closed	Rarely.
directions	Dalkeith Road, passed the pool; left down Prestonfield Road; at end, on left.

Hotel

tel	0131 225 7800
fax	0131 220 4992
email	reservations@prestonfield.com
web	www.prestonfield.com

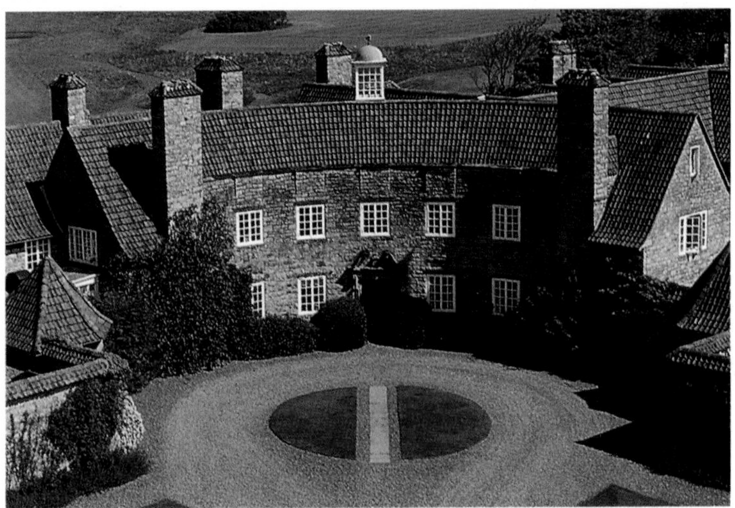

Greywalls

Muirfield, Gullane, East Lothian EH31 2EG

Gracious, stately and hugely impressive, yet you could curl up on a sofa and feel perfectly at home. Sir Edwin Lutyens built the house in 1901 for a golfer determined to be within a 'mashie niblick' shot of the 18th green; two gate lodges were added for staff, then a nursery wing. Now it's half hotel, half private home – held in equal affection by family and guests. Greywalls is discreet, peaceful, welcoming and unpompous – one guest said staying here was "like breathing silk". Enter a charmed world of log fires, French windows, family portraits, and views that sail over golf course to sea. There's a panelled library, a cosy bar, chintz in the bedrooms, jackets and ties for dinner and a dedicated team in the kitchen – the food is sublime. Bedrooms – four in the lodges, more in the house – have everything you could wish for, and there's the Colonel's House for private groups. The walled garden was designed by Gertrude Jekyll: a tapestry of arbours, arches, peonies, lavender and immaculate lawns. Sandy beaches, castles and Edinburgh by day; by night, the gentle click of backgammon and the crackle of the fire.

rooms	23: 19 twins/doubles, 4 singles.
price	£260. Singles £130.
meals	Dinner £45.
closed	Mid-October-mid-April.
directions	A198 from A1 & take last road at east end of Gullane village.

Hotel

	Giles Weaver
tel	01620 842144
email	hotel@greywalls.co.uk
web	www.greywalls.co.uk

The Inn at Lathones

Lathones, St Andrews, Fife KY9 1JE

Once upon a time in the Kingdom of Fife, two people fell in love, married and lived happily ever after in this old inn; beer flowed, food was plentiful, customers burst into song, even a dwarf highwayman dropped in after work. Legend says when the landlady died in 1736, the wedding stone above the fireplace in the lounge cracked, so strong was their love. Today, she and her horse haunt the wonderful Stables, the oldest part of the inn, with its garlands of hops and bottle-green ceiling – but in the friendliest way. Lathones could charm the most cantankerous ghost: superb food, the draw of an open fire, leather sofas to sink into, and a warm, Scottish welcome. Walk into the bar to find bottles of grappa and eau-de-vie asking to be sampled, while Marc Guibert's menu is mouthwatering: try local grilled sea bass followed by a clootie dumpling served with fresh strawberries. Comfortable, traditional-style bedrooms are split between a coach house and an old blacksmith's house either side of the inn. Historic St Andrews and the East Neuk of Fife fishing villages are close.

rooms	13 twins/doubles
price	£140-£200.
meals	Lunch £12.50. Packed lunch from £10. Dinner, à la carte, from £20.
closed	Christmas and 2 weeks in January.
directions	From Kirkcaldy, or St Andrews, A915 to Largoward. Inn 1 mile north on roadside.

Inn

	Nick White
tel	01334 840494
fax	01334 840694
email	lathones@theinn.co.uk
web	www.theinn.co.uk

Brunswick Merchant City Hotel

106-108 Brunswick Street, Glasgow G1 1TF

Stephen and Michael are simply gorgeous and bouncing with vim – indeed, they seem to create gentle mayhem wherever they go! The bar/brasserie is bold and clean with a black zebra stripe along the wall, graceful curved cream tiles and pretty lighting. A lift zooms you straight up to the bedrooms, all colour-themed in two tones and niftily designed so that only the white-cotton-sheeted beds stick out. Small rooms are not for partying (take the penthouse, with three bedrooms and sauna, instead) but if you want to sleep they're fine; bathrooms are tiled and lino'd in fun colours. At breakfast you might be sitting next to a famous actor, a local musician or a lorry driver, it's an egalitarian place – 'the boys' will be flitting hither and thither brewing up mind-blowing coffee and warming croissants, and the lovely Ellen, front of house, will be calming things down. Art galleries, museums, clubbing and shopping (Versace and Cruise a minute's walk) are on the doorstep if you want them, and when you've run out of funds, or your feet are killing you, limp back to a large G&T and a slice of TLC.

rooms	19: 18 doubles, 1 penthouse suite for 6.
price	£55-£95. Suite £395.
meals	Brasserie open noon-8pm. Main courses about £6.50. Closed Sunday.
closed	Rarely.
directions	10 minute walk from Queen Street or Central Station. Airport bus stop round the corner in George Square. Metred parking outside, NCP near.

Hotel

	Stephen Flannery & Michael Johnson
tel	01415 520001
email	enquiry@brunswickhotel.co.uk
web	www.brunswickhotel.co.uk

Saint Jude's

190 Bath Street, Glasgow G2 4HG

Hotel, restaurant and cocktail bar all rolled into one. If you dislike the corporate feel of many hotels but don't value the intimacy of a B&B then St Jude's is for you: an elegant, early Victorian townhouse on a wide street, intelligently converted into a fuss-free place to stay with no pomposity, great food and super staff. Luxurious bedrooms have good sound systems and access to other hi-tech joys, huge beds, bathrooms to linger in and fluffy blankets with designer spots. The restaurant is classic and contemporary, yet still cosy, with good lighting, gleaming floors, well-designed furniture and a modern, imaginative menu; each of Jenny's beautifully presented dishes is a work of art. The wide hall is dominated by a staircase illuminated by a vast glass cupola, the Club Room, with its skylit roof, is *the* space for private dinners and receptions, and the cocktail bar in the basement must be one of the city's most stylish. Shops, restaurants, galleries and museums are a short hop. But perhaps the best part of St Jude's are the people who work there – charming and self-confident.

rooms	6: 2 doubles, 3 twins/doubles, 1 suite.
price	£95. Suite £150.
meals	Lunch/supper, £14.50, 3 courses. Dinner £25 à la carte.
closed	Rarely.
directions	Exit 19 from M8 for city centre. 20 minutes from airport, 10 minutes from station.

Hotel

Jenny Burn & Walter Barrett

tel	0141 352 8800
fax	0141 352 8801
email	info@saintjudes.com
web	www.saintjudes.com

Rab Ha's

83 Hutcheson Street, Glasgow G1 1SH

Big, noisy, smoky and battered – that's the bar: a huge square room with stone walls, wooden floorboards, candles burning on rough wooden tables, a bright fire, nudes on the walls and the most eclectic mix of locals – students, housewives with buggies and some old fellas seriously staring into a pint, all rub shoulders with backpackers and businessmen in suits. You can eat old favourites like mince and tatties or cod and chips with mushy peas in the bar from lunch time till late or go a bit posher in the restaurant from 5.30pm: pan-seared Oban scallops, medallions of beef with red onion fondant, orange bread and butter pudding. They also do a mean Sunday roast. Bedrooms are modern and spruce – crisp white linen, yellow walls – with good bathrooms and claw-foot baths. Don't expect peace and quiet until late, hushed it is not! Continental breakfast can be delivered to your room or there's full Scottish in the bar. Extravagant, energetic Glasgow can be explored on foot: shops, museums, galleries, theatres, clubs, all are near – good transport too – but you may just want to stay and join in the fun.

rooms	4: 3 doubles, 1 twin.
price	£50-£75.
meals	Bar menu, 2 courses, from £10; lunch/dinner à la carte.
closed	Rarely.
directions	5-minute walk from Queen Street station.

Restaurant with Rooms

	Andy Young
tel	0141 572 0400
fax	1040 572 0402
email	e.management@rabhas.com
web	www.rabhas.5pm.co.uk

Tigh an Eilean

Shieldaig, Loch Torridon, Highland IV54 8XN

Tigh an Eilean is the Holy Grail of the west coast – when you arrive you realise it's what you've been looking for all these years. A perfect place in every respect, from its position by the sea in this very pretty village, to the magnificence of the Torridon mountains that rise all around… this area is one of the wonderlands of the world, an undisputed heavyweight champion of natural beauty. And Sheildaig itself is an exceptionally friendly village with a strong sense of community, the hub of which is the pub – like the shop, owned by the hotel – where locals come to sing their songs, play their fiddles, drink their whisky, and talk. Most surprising of all is the hotel. Christopher and Cathryn, two ex-London lawyers, now run an immaculate bolthole, airy and stylish, with tartan cushions on window seats, sensational views, homemade shortbread, and bedrooms that elate. No TVs, no telephones, but kind, gentle staff who chat and advise. Relax in sitting rooms with plump sofas, an honesty bar and an open fire. Dine – very well – on Hebridean scallops in the restaurant, or try the pub: fewer frills but lots of fun.

rooms	11: 4 doubles, 4 twins, 3 singles.
price	£120. Half-board from £60 p.p. Singles £55.
meals	Bar meals from £5. Dinner in restaurant from £32.50.
closed	November-March.
directions	On loch front in centre of Shieldaig.

Hotel

	Christopher & Cathryn Field
tel	01520 755251
fax	01520 755321
email	tighaneileanhotel@shieldaig.fsnet.co.uk

Glenelg Inn

Glenelg, By Kyle of Lochalsh, Highland IV40 8JR

Now they have their own boat to collect you from Kyle and Malloning – or you can take the road over Mam Ratagan from Loch Duich. Given that both routes are spectacular in their own right, it's not a bad idea to take one in, the other out; your reward is the view across the sea to the mountains of Skye. Inside, the bar is a Highland institution: an ancient fireplace, stone-flagged floors and piles of old fish boxes on which you sit (more comfortable than you'd imagine). There's music, too: pipers, fiddlers and folk musicians. If the bar is earthy, then the bedrooms are smart: rugs and books, old pine dressers, waffle blankets, soothing bathrooms. Light floods in, one room has two balconies, the suite its own garden, and most have sea views. In the restaurant, fresh, local crab, mussels, venison, lamb – cheerfully served in a bright room with great pictures. Residents have the run of a private drawing room (logs under window seats, a fender by the fire, cosy sofas). There are 10 Glenelgs around the world, all named after this one. Christopher will tell you why.

rooms	7: 3 doubles, 3 family, 1 suite.
price	Half-board only, £89-£99 p.p.
meals	Bar lunch from £8. Dinner, 4 courses, £29.
closed	Rarely.
directions	West off A87 at Sheil Bridge. Keep left into village & inn on right. Kylerhea ferry from Skye is a beautiful alternative.

Inn

	Christopher Main
tel	01599 522273
fax	01599 522283
email	christophermain7@glenelg-inn.com
web	www.glenelg-inn.com

The Dower House

Highfield, Muir of Ord, Highland IV6 7XN

A historic house in the cottage-*orné* style with excellent food and country-house comfort and style. Mena describes Robyn's eclectic brand of no-frills cooking as "gutsy and colourful" – which could just as well describe the chef himself, an instantly likeable presence with a tangible passion for food. Handfuls of herbs from the garden are used to great effect on local beef, lamb and venison and the warm raspberry soufflé bursts with home-grown fruit. They are a formidable team, cooking, decorating, waiting and doing the greeting themselves, not wanting to leave one moment of your enjoyment to chance. Décor – Mena's triumph – is impeccable and rooms are tastefully colourful with their well-chosen fabrics, some pretty, some striking. Bathrooms are just the place for a pre-dinner soak and a glass of wine. Dinner starts in a graceful dining room, with a piano at one end, and finishes with homemade truffles and coffee by an open fire in the very cosy sitting room. An absolute gem.

rooms	5: 2 doubles, 2 twins/doubles, 1 suite.
price	£110-£130. Singles £65-£85. Suite £150.
meals	Dinner £35.
closed	Rarely.
directions	A9 north of Inverness to Tore r'bout, then left on A832 for Muir of Ord. In village, A862, for Dingwall. Entrance 1 mile on left.

Hotel

	Robyn & Mena Aitchison
tel	01463 870090
fax	01463 870090
email	stay@thedowerhouse.co.uk
web	www.thedowerhouse.co.uk

The Boat Hotel

Boat of Garten, Inverness-shire PH24 3BH

A lounge with soft lights and swags, a bar full of bustle... the railway hotel has been pulling them in since 1865, a loved local institution. The immaculately carpeted corridors are lined with huntin', shootin' and fishin' prints; now people come for the skiing too, at Aviemore... the golf (next door), the hill-walking (the Speyside Way), the whisky trail, and the little steam railway that whistles by. The scenery is as spectacular as any in Scotland – all mist-hung mountains and deep cold lochs, the Cairngorms towering behind. How comforting, then, to return to fluffy white dressing gowns and slippers, stylish bathrooms stocked with Gilchrist & Soames, and big, traditional beds with matching curtains and covers. Food is Scottish with modern touches, served in a deep-blue dining room whose dark walls are emboldened by excellent copies of French Avant-Garde paintings. Intimate, smart, family-friendly – and they don't rest on their laurels: Shona is full of plans for little cottages with terraces and jacuzzis. A large garden sits at the back and, at the front, a pretty communal garden.

rooms	27: 13 doubles, 10 twins, 2 suites, 2 family.
price	£119-£135. Suites £165.
meals	Dinner table d'hôte, £32.50.
closed	Last three weeks of January.
directions	From A9 A95 towards Elgin. 4 miles from Aviemore right into Boat of Garten. After 1 mile hotel on corner in centre of village.

Hotel

	Shona Tatchell
tel	01479 831258
fax	01479 831414
email	info@boathotel.co.uk
web	www.boathotel.co.uk

The Cross

Tweed Mill Brae, Kingussie, Highland PH21 1LB

In his previous life David was a senior food inspector. So what did the poacher buy when he turned gamekeeper? One of his favourite restaurants, of course. The Cross, an old tweed mill, is a fusion of Scottish and Scandinavian styles. There are stone walls, old beams and whitewashed interiors downstairs, then clean lines, windows in the eaves and an open-plan sitting room one floor up. Bedrooms are stylishly simple, with Egyptian cotton linen, tongue and grooved bathrooms, halogen spotlighting and a clean crisp elegance. There are wicker chairs, canopied beds, a sofa if there's room, and you can fall asleep to the sound of the river in rooms that face south. Dinner is most important, with chef Becca Henderson at the helm. Expect the freshest local ingredients, perhaps scallops, cauliflower purée and basil oil, then rack of lamb, aubergine and dauphinoise potatoes, finally poached pear, chocolate sauce and caramel ice. There's also one of the best wine lists in Scotland. The river Gynack falls down a mountain right outside and a short circular walk crosses the river. *Children over eight welcome.*

rooms	8: 6 doubles, 2 twins.
price	£90-£160. Singles from £80. Half-board £80-£110 p.p.
meals	Dinner, 3 courses, included. Restaurant open Tuesday-Saturday. Dinner for non residents: 2-3 courses, £28.50-£33.50.
closed	Christmas & January.
directions	At the only traffic lights in Kingussie, right up hill (if coming from north); signed left.

Hotel

	Katie & David Young
tel	01540 661166
fax	01540 661080
email	relax@thecross.co.uk
web	www.thecross.co.uk

Ballachulish House

Ballachulish, Highland PH49 4JX

For today's traveller, seeing this charming Scottish laird's house come into view after a long day's trek in the mountains must surely be as special as it was for clansmen of yore – only for different reasons! Once a refuge from hostile neighbours, Ballachulish appears part fortress, part country house, tucked at the foot of mighty Glencoe mountain, scene of the 1692 massacre of the recalcitrant MacDonald clan. Flop into a comfortable chair by an open fire and savour the warm glow of more peaceful endeavours. The McLaughlins have altered little of the house's 18th-century origins, retaining its elegant simplicity. Bedrooms have comfortable beds, the odd combed plaster ceiling and little touches like fresh fruit. Most have mountain views across a part-walled garden of herb beds, stone fountain, orchard and specimen trees; two at the front have loch views over a croquet lawn. Raise a smile and your glass to 'Lang may your lum reek', inscribed on a tiled iron range in the dining room – the food is wonderful, the people are generous. *Children over 10 welcome.*

rooms	9: 4 doubles, 3 twins, 1 single, 1 family.
price	£125-£188. Singles £75. Family £218.
meals	Dinner, 5 courses, £44.
closed	Rarely.
directions	From Glasgow, A82, via Crianlarich & Glencoe, to Ballachulish; A828 at r'bout, signed Oban. Under Ballachulish Bridge. 100 yds further on left.

B&B

	Marie & Michael McLaughlin
tel	01855 811266
fax	01855 811498
email	mclaughlins@btconnect.com
web	www.ballachulishhouse.com

Tomdoun Sporting Lodge

Glengarry, Invergarry, Inverness-shire PH35 4HS

The single track road that passes outside follows its nose upstream for 20 miles to Kinloch Hourn, but as so little traffic passes, they play tennis on it. Down in the valley, the river Garry jumps from one loch to another, while across the water Glas Bheinn rises from Glengarry Forest. Tomdoun is a landmark for hikers heading for Knoydart (this is the only road in). It's a place for the last good meal, the last decent bed (occasionally you're joined at breakfast by ravenous folk who've spent days walking over mountains). It's stylishly unpretentious, with old leather trunks in the hall, a roaring fire in the grate – a place with loads of rugs and ramble, communal dining, great wines and food that puts a smile on your face. Bedrooms are homely, well-priced and spotlessly clean, and those at the front have Glengarry views. There's loads to do: clay-pigeon shooting, white-water rafting, water-skiing, abseiling, mountain-biking, fishing and some of the best walking in Scotland. There's also 'green' stalking: you shoot with film, not bullets.

rooms	10: 3 doubles, 2 family; 1 double, 1 single, 3 twins sharing 2 baths.
price	£70-£100. Singles from £45.
meals	Packed lunch £5.95. Bar meals from £7. Dinner, 3 courses, from £18.95.
closed	24-25 December.
directions	A82 north from Fort William, then A87 west from Invergarry. After 5 miles, left for Glengarry. Hotel 6 miles up on right.

Hotel

	Michael & Sheila Pearson
tel	01809 511218
email	enquiries@tomdoun-sporting-lodge.com
web	www.tomdoun-sporting-lodge.com

Kinloch Lodge

Sleat, Isle of Skye IV43 8QY

Skye is Scotland at its softest and the Sleat peninsula is positively velvety. Shimmering waters, lochs giving onto the Sounds of Sleat and Cullin, boats bobbing and drifting... Kinloch Lodge sits in Clan Donald territory; Godfrey is the High Chief and ancestors look down from the regal green walls. The family-run hotel feels just the right size – big enough to find a quiet corner and be private and small enough to feel personal – and Lady Macdonald's daughter, Isabella, and son-in-law Tom take day-to-day care of the hotel with a charming exuberance. Rooms are very comfy: chintzes and tartans, bathrobes and smellies; they vary in size and outlook – this was built as a shooting lodge, not a hotel – but dig deeper and grab yourself a dreamy view of Loch Na Dal, the lighthouse and Knoydart or the Cullins. At dinner, Tom glides between tables helping with wine choices and the chef trips out Skye crab tart with crisp mustard pastry, maybe salmon with sautéed fennel. Portions are generous; afterwards take a slow walk to a fireside seat in one of the three drawing rooms for coffee and homemade fudge.

rooms	15 twins/doubles.
price	Half-board only, £95-£140 p.p. Singles by arrangement.
meals	Dinner for non-residents, £35.
closed	30 December-7 February.
directions	From Bridge of Skye follow signs south on A851 to Armadale-Mallaig ferry. Lodge signed on left down forestry road, approx 20 minutes from bridge.

Hotel

	Lady Claire MacDonald
tel	01471 833333
fax	01471 833277
email	bookings@kinloch-lodge.co.uk
web	www.kinloch-lodge.co.uk

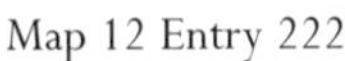

Doune

Knoydart, Mallaig, Inverness-shire PH41 4PL

Ever imagined taking a boat from a tiny Scottish fishing village and landing in paradise? Doune might persuade you if you haven't. The boat collects you at Mallaig, then crosses Loch Nevis, with the mighty mountains of Knoydart rising to the east… and lands in a sacred place, with no roads, a friendly community and a glorious view of Skye and the Cullins across the Sound of Sleat. Straining an ear confirms your first thought – the only sounds you can hear are natural: water lapping, the call of a bird, a whistling wind… and the whoops of joy of other guests as the combination of solitude, beauty, comfort and hospitality triggers an overpowering happiness. Hike and see no one all day, dive and find your own supper, or stroll over to Inverie and the pub – a couple of hours' walk. For at least one day, though, we recommend you do absolutely nothing. Food is exceptional – maybe something from the sea in front, or from the hills behind – and the kindest people look after you. Lodge bedrooms are perfect: wood, windows and cathedral roofs. Hard to find better value anywhere in Britain.

rooms	3: 2 doubles, 1 twin. Lodge sleeps 12.
price	Full board for 3 or 4 nights: £60 p.p. per night. 7 nights £360 p.p. Singles from £70.
meals	Dinner & packed lunch included.
closed	October-Easter.
directions	Park in Mallaig; the boat will collect you at an agreed time.

B&B

Martin & Jane Davies

tel	01687 462667
fax	08700 940428
email	martin@doune-knoydart.co.uk
web	www.doune-knoydart.co.uk

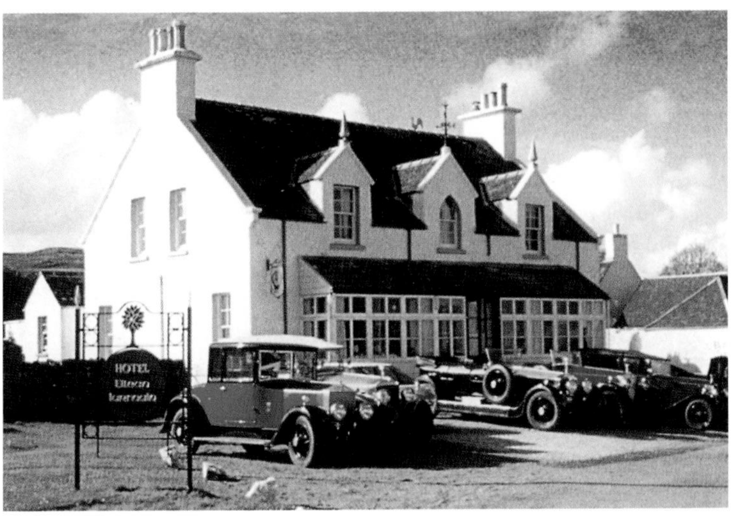

Hotel Eilean Iarmain

Eilean Iarmain, Sleat, Isle of Skye IV43 8QR

One of the prettiest spots on Skye – a whitewashed hamlet at the end of the road, with a pier. The Sound of Sleat wraps itself around the place and fishermen still land their catch 30 paces from the front door. Across the water Robert Louis Stevenson's lighthouse paddles in the shallows, while beyond the mountains of the mainland rise. Inside, the Hebrides of old survives, part shooting lodge, part gentlemen's club: tartan carpets, hessian on the walls, the papers by the fire in the morning room and a new Smuggler's Den where Gaelic whiskies can be savoured. Bedrooms, country-style, are split between the main house, the garden house and the stables, where sparkling two-storey suites sport crisp fabrics and new pine. Next door in the bar, the occasional ceilidh breaks loose and fiddles fly, but there's also a touch of refined culture in the art gallery round the corner. Sir Iain – born in Berlin, christened in Rome and schooled in Shanghai – is Skye through and through, and deeply involved in regenerating the woodland terrain to the south of the island. He'll teach you the odd word of Gaelic, too. Bring your kilt.

rooms	15: 6 doubles, 6 twins, 4 suites.
price	£120-£160. Singles £85. Suites £200-£220.
meals	Bar meals from £7. Dinner, 4 courses, £31.
closed	Rarely.
directions	A87 over Skye Bridge (toll £5.50), then left after 7 miles onto A851, signed Armdale. Hotel on left after 8 miles, signed.

Hotel

	Sir Iain & Lady Noble
tel	01471 833332
fax	01471 833275
email	hotel@eilean-iarmain.co.uk
web	www.eileaniarmain.co.uk

Stein Inn

Stein, Waternish, Isle of Skye IV55 8GA

The drive here is a treat and you sense that you'll find something special at the end of the gently undulating road. Waternish is a gem – Skye at its softest – and the Stein Inn sits snugly on the quay alongside bobbing boats; dating from 1790, it's the oldest on the island. Angus stocks over 100 single malts, thirst-quenching ales and seasoned opinion in the little wooden-clad bar. In good weather, sit out by the shore of the sea loch: across the water, the headland rises; to the north, low-slung islands lie scattered. Lose yourself with a pint watching locals potter about in their boats against a setting sun, then step inside to the simple little dining room with a fire and pine tables. The menu – mainly pub standards such as pork stroganoff, curry, breaded garlic mushrooms and homemade crumble – always has a couple of fresh fish specials and local cheeses. The rooms are neat with bright blue carpets, pine furniture and jolly quilts. There's a pool room, a play area and a place for afternoon tea and the affable Angus and Teresa are refreshingly child-friendly.

rooms	5: 2 doubles, 2 family, 1 single.
price	£51-£66. Singles £25.50-£33.
meals	Bar lunch from £5. Dinner, 3-courses, about £13.
closed	Christmas Day & New Year's Day.
directions	From Isle of Skye bridge, A850 to Portree. Follow sign to Uig for 4 miles, left on A850 for Dunvegan for 14 miles. Hard right turn to Waternish on B886. Stein 4.5 miles along loch side.

Inn

Angus & Teresa McGhie

tel	01470 592362
fax	01470 592362
email	angus.teresa@steininn.co.uk
web	www.steininn.co.uk

Viewfield House

Portree, Isle of Skye, Highland IV51 9EU

A former factor's house with a relaxed country-house feel, Viewfield blends grandeur with odd touches of humour brilliantly. A family friend once placed notes by various of the house's belongings, detailing their history, all of which were fictional; one survives today. It's a fine ancestral seat, built in 1790, with huge windows in the sitting room, roaring fires, piles of wood, rugs on stripped wooden floors and some 100-year-old wallpapers upstairs. At 7.30 each evening a gong summons guests to dinner – Hugh and Linda take it in turns to cook. Food is seasonal and delicious, bit it crab and tomato tart, fillet of pork with apricot and coriander or hazelnut cake with mascarpone cream. Each night Hugh dons a kilt in the family tartan, while Linda, a Californian, remains delightfully unfazed by the splendour of the surroundings: ancestors on the walls – their portraits, that is – and beautiful period furniture. Bedrooms are exquisite: luxurious beds, pretty fabrics, crisp cotton linen... even polished stair rods on the way up. Outside, climb through woods to Fingal's Seat for 360° views, or swim in a loch.

rooms	12: 4 doubles, 3 twins/doubles, 2 twins, 1 single; 1 double, 1 single sharing bath & shower.
price	£80-£100. Half-board £65-£75 p.p. Singles £40-£60.
meals	Packed lunch £4.80. Dinner, 4 courses, £25.
closed	Mid October-mid April.
directions	On A850, coming from south, drive entrance on left just before Portree, opposite BP garage.

B&B

Hugh & Linda Macdonald

tel 01478 612217

fax 01478 613517

email info@viewfieldhouse.com

web www.viewfieldhouse.com

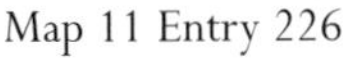

Applecross Inn

Shore Street, Applecross, Wester Ross IV54 8LR

No Highland fling would be quite complete without a visit to this simple little inn looking across the sands of Applecross; they extend about half a mile at low tide, and views go on for miles, to Rassay, then Skye beyond. Weather permitting, arrive by Bealach-Na-Ba, the highest mountain pass in Britain. The view at the top is magical, a 50-mile sweep of Hebridean heaven, of sea and mountain, of island and sky. Down at the inn, Judith continues to win rave reviews for her rooms and for her food. More renovation and redecoration will bring bright and breezy blues and yellows to the walls, and bathrooms to every room; all are great value. And so to the food: expect the freshest seafood, scooped from the water out front and cooked simply. The inn has become a magnet for foodies, a place of pilgrimage for those in search of dressed crab, squat lobster, queen scallops, or half a pint of fat prawns. Eat outside in good weather, but the down-to-earth bar is just as good; locals and visitors mix easily. As one guest wrote: "To be Applecrossed; a rare and wonderful experience." Don't miss it.

rooms	7: 1 double, 2 twins, 2 singles, 2 family.
price	£60-£70. Singles £25.
meals	Bar meals from £5. Packed lunch £5. Dinner about £25.
closed	New Year's Day.
directions	From Loch Carron, A896 north for 5 miles; left over Bealach Na Ba pass for 11 miles. Inn on left. Use road via Kenmore when snow closes pass.

Inn

Judith Fish
tel 01520 744262
fax 01520 744400

The Albannach

Baddidaroch, Lochinver, Highland IV27 4LP

Colin and Lesley would be anarchists if they took life seriously, which luckily they don't. Instead, they prefer to chew the cud, drink good wine, cook fine food and live with just a little irreverence and a lot of laughter. Half a mile from the fishing village of Lochinver, the Victorian house, built around the shell of an older cottage, stands in an elevated spot, but is sheltered by walled grounds. Colin and Lesley spend their days hatching new plans for the table; Gillian, a friend, crofts the veg and shellfishermen are also friends. Five-course dinners are fabulously fresh: come for the best wild and free-range fish and game to match the seasons. They've done the whole place themselves, brilliantly of course – renovated, extended, panelled, designed the conservatory, built the patio – and added a heater. Sink into white sofas amid rugs and erupting greenery and gaze out across water to Suilven rising majestically in the distance; climb it as well. Bedrooms have heaps of comfort – beds are king-size, pocket-sprung Rolls Royces – but it's the indefatigable spirit that makes it so special.

rooms	5: 3 doubles, 1 twin, 1 four-poster.
price	Half-board only, £102-£117 p.p.
meals	Dinner, 5 courses, included; non-residents £42.
closed	On Mondays and in between November and March.
directions	From Ullapool into Lochinver & right over bridge. Follow bay for 0.5 miles, cross cattle grid after Highland Stoneware Pottery; 1st left.

Hotel

	Colin Craig & Lesley Crosfield
tel	01571 844407
email	the.albannach@virgin.net

2 Quail Restaurant & Rooms

Castle Street, Dornoch, Sutherland IV25 3SN

The Royal Burgh of Dornoch feels prosperous and assured. It has a world-class golf course, sandy beach and a pretty, shop-lined high street; Madonna christening her child in the cathedral did nothing to harm visitor numbers. Such a town deserves a smart restaurant and 2 Quail is it. It's central, sparkling and atmospheric and upholds with ease its reputation as one of Scotland's best eating places. You step into an instantly welcoming atmosphere and the hard-working Michael and Kerensa look after you impeccably; their standards are high and they employ no staff, preferring to run the show themselves. Michael, a gifted chef, employs a light touch with the freshest ingredients – potted langoustine with tomato confit and a truffle salad, halibut with an orange crust, loin of roe deer, caramelised raspberry tart – while Kerensa really knows her wines. The rooms upstairs are the icing on the cake: spotlessly clean and stylish, with excellent bathrooms and a generous supply of first class bubbles and shampoos. Perfect.

rooms	3: 1 double, 1 twin, 1 twin/double.
price	£75-£95.
meals	Dinner, 4 courses, £35.50.
closed	Christmas, February and March.
directions	From Inverness, A9 north for 44 miles, then right on A949, for Dornoch. Restaurant on left before Cathedral.

Restaurant with Rooms

	Michael & Kerensa Carr
tel	01862 811811
email	stay@2quail.com
web	www.2quail.com

Culdearn House

Woodlands Terrace, Grantown on Spey, Moray PH26 3JU

Not for jet setters, but for those who thrive on excellent service, fine food (prime Highland beef, fish from the west coast, local cheeses, home herbs) and cosy tradition. Your hosts, friendly and generous, are enthusiastic about this venture. William, a Highlander, knows his whisky and masterminds distillery trips and tastings, Sonia worked for Constance Spry and is hatching plans for floristry breaks. Their small hotel in the once-fashionable spa is a Victorian Scottish villa whose original barley-twist panelling, moulded ceilings and marble fireplaces glow with care. Grates blaze with peat and logs in winter. Bedrooms, individual and spotless, come in pale greens, yellows and blues; a padded headboard here, a striped wall there, an antique rattan sofa, orchids and fine soaps; the suite has a luxurious bathroom. Dinners, served on crisp linen, are four-course delights; 'fine dining' plaques dot the walls. Come for Highland games and gatherings, fishing on the Spey, Cawdor Castle, romantically linked with *Macbeth*, walking in the National Park, golf courses by the dozen.

rooms	7: 3 doubles, 3 twins, 1 suite.
price	From £110. Half board £170. Singles £55.
meals	Dinner, £30.
closed	January & February.
directions	From south west enter Grantown. At 30 mph sign left & house faces opposite.

Hotel

	Sonia & William Marshall
tel	01479 872106
email	enquiries@culdearn.com
web	www.culdearn.com

The Pines

Woodside Avenue, Grantown-on-Spey, Moray PH26 3JR

Such a delight, the Pines, with its woodland garden, exceptional art, warm good taste, and owners who are a pleasure to meet. He is debonair, she is quiet and charming, and the King Charles Cavaliers are full of bounce. It feels like a house that's been in the family for ever, such is the softly ancestral feel. Gwen cooks – beautifully; Michael is 'mine host' with a passion for art. The jewels of his collection are paintings by David Foggie, the celebrated Dundee artist who taught his great uncle. Living rooms are soothing and sumptuous, bedrooms have great beds, fresh flowers, books, more art, and food is a harmony of traditional and modern – venison from a local estate, gravadlax from Strathaird, eggs free-range, bread homemade. Lap up the summer sunshine with drinks on the patio, wander the landscaped and woodland gardens, fringed with pines and rich with wildlife: red squirrels, roe deer, tree-creepers, ducks. Enter woodland and you reach the Spey within minutes; hikes, silver salmon (hire ghillie and tackle) and the odd whisky distillery may tempt you further. A laid-back yet civilised place.

rooms	8: 4 doubles, 3 twins/doubles, 1 single.
price	£90-£120. Half-board £75-£90 p.p. Singles from £50.
meals	Dinner, 4 courses, £30. Packed lunch available.
closed	November-February.
directions	A95 north to Grantown. Right at 1st traffic lights; A939 for Tomintoul, 1st right into Woodside Ave. 500 yds on left.

Hotel

	Michael & Gwen Stewart
tel	01479 872092
fax	01479 872092
email	info@thepinesgrantown.co.uk
web	www.thepinesgrantown.co.uk

Minmore House

Glenlivet, Banffshire AB37 9DB

Driving up from Balmoral in the late afternoon sun, you could be forgiven for thinking the colour green was created here. The east of Scotland often plays second fiddle to its 'other half' in the west, but this lush cattle-grazing land is every inch as beautiful. Amid it all is Minmore, a great wee pad run with breezy good cheer by Victor and Lynne. They used to run a restaurant in South Africa and once cooked for Prince Philip; their food continues to win rave reviews. Their kingdom stretches to 9 spotless bedrooms and a suite that Lynne describes as "very zoosh". Guests swap highland tales in a pretty sitting room or, best of all, in a carved wooden bar, half-panelled, with scarlet chairs, the odd trophy and 104 malts. The garden is a birdwatcher's paradise, with lapwing, curlew and a rare colony of oyster-catchers; free-range chickens, source of your breakfast eggs, roam. Visit the famous Glenlivet distillery nearby, or cycle deep into the Ladder Hills where buzzard, falcon and even eagles soar; then back to Lynne's irresistible chocolate whisky and yogurt cake and a blazing fire.

rooms	10: 3 doubles, 4 twins, 2 singles, 1 suite.
price	£100-£110. Singles from £50. Suite £140-£160. Half-board from £88 p.p.
meals	Light lunch £12-£15. Full picnic £10. Dinner, 4 courses, £35.
closed	February; two weeks in November.
directions	From Aviemore, A95 north to Bridge of Avon; south on B9008 to Glenlivet. At top of hill, 400 yds before distillery.

Hotel

Victor & Lynne Janssen

tel	01807 590378
fax	01807 590472
email	minmorehouse@ukonline.co.uk
web	www.minmorehousehotel.com

Cleaton House

Westray, Orkney KW17 2DB

The lamb has lived on a diet of seaweed, on the little island of North Ronaldsay. So when it appears on your plate, on a parsnip crumble with red wine sauce, you are in for a treat. The salmon comes from one of the best organic salmon farms in Scotland, where the current is strong, the fish robust and the cages are out there in the straits, between Westray and Papa Westray. Such is your food: local, fresh and delicious – and beautifully prepared. The big, old-fashioned bedrooms are astonishingly comfortable for a hotel so distant and remote – straightforward and traditional. The bar is cheerful and popular, with a touch of Scandinavian about it, whereas the dining room and sitting room are snug and 'country house' – even a bit formal. The views cannot be avoided, north, south, east and west: to the other islands, to the gently rolling island interior, to the tiny 'capital', to the sea in all its vastness. You wear the silence like a blanket. Westray is special: it has plans to be the country's first energy self-sufficient community. From here there are all those other islands to conquer.

rooms	6: 5 doubles, 1 suite.
price	From £72. Singles, £49.
meals	Dinner, 4 courses, £24.50.
closed	November.
directions	5 miles from either ferry terminal or airfield. Signposted at ferry terminal. Hotel can collect from point of arrival.

Hotel

Malcolm Stout
tel 01857 677508
fax 01857 677442
email cleaton@orkney.com
web www.cleaton

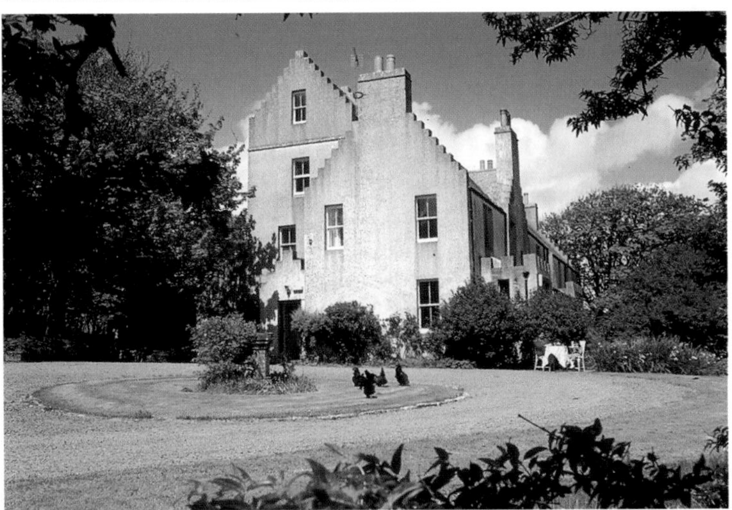

Woodwick House

Evie, Orkney KW17 2PQ

Trees are in short supply on Orkney but Woodwick sits in a sycamore wood fed by a burn that tumbles down to a seaweedy bay overlooking the Island of Gairsay; walk through wild flowers and hanging lichen to the sound of rushing water and babbling crows – magical. Woodwick promotes "care, creativity and conservation", so come here to think, free of distraction. Manager James and his young staff are quietly charming, and the house is nothing fancy, just nicely old-fashioned and homely. Built in 1912, it stands on the site of a larger building destroyed during the Jacobite rebellion – a remarkable 'doocot' remains. There's a wisteria-filled conservatory, a hushed dining room (food is delicious, much of it organic), two sitting rooms, an open fire, a piano, books and lots of good old films. Outside, a half-wild garden, clucking hens, distant sheep, and a pathway down to the small bay where seals nose about. A nearby ferry takes you to some of the smaller islands, while the Italian Chapel and numerous ancient sites are an absolute must. *Pets £7 for duration of stay.*

rooms	8: 2 doubles, 2 twins; 2 doubles, 1 twin, 1 single, all with basins, sharing 1 bath. Cots available.
price	£64-£92. Singles £32-£60..
meals	Lunch & packed lunch by arrangement. Dinner £24.
closed	Rarely.
directions	From Kirkwall, A965 to Finstown; A966 for Evie. Right after 7 miles; past Tingwall ferry turning, left down track to house.

B&B

	Ann Herdman
tel	01856 751330
fax	01856 751383
email	mail@woodwickhouse.co.uk
web	www.woodwickhouse.co.uk

Killiecrankie Hotel

Pass of Killiecrankie, By Pitlochry, Perth & Kinross PH16 5LG

You're well-positioned here for all things Highland: the games at Braemar, fishing, walking, castles, golf... and whisky, about which Tim, once a big shaker in the wine trade, knows a thing or two. He and Maillie have come north of the border to cook great food, to serve good wines and to provide the sort of comfortable indulgence that caps a hard day's pleasure with rod, club or map. Food is top of the list, with an ever-changing menu of fresh, local produce, reasonably priced wine by the glass to complement each course, and a vegetarian menu that could convert the most ardent carnivore... for an evening at least; meat is available, too. Much is home-grown, thanks to a dedicated effort to bring the kitchen garden back to life: soft fruits, potatoes, asparagus, leeks, mangetout... and there are more edible plans for the future. Bedrooms are a good size, cosy and warm, with lashings of hot water and views down the Garry Valley. There's a small bar, a snug sitting room with books and games, and an RSPB sanctuary near the house that's home to buzzards. Set out with the binoculars.

rooms	10: 4 doubles, 4 twins/doubles, 2 singles.
price	Half-board only, £79-£99 p.p.
meals	Lunch from £2.95. Dinner, 4 courses, included; non-residents £33.
closed	January-mid-February.
directions	A9 north of Pitlochry, then B8079, signed Killiecrankie. Straight ahead for 2 miles. Hotel on right, signed.

Hotel

	Tim & Maillie Waters
tel	01796 473220
fax	01796 472451
email	enquiries@killiecrankiehotel.co.uk
web	www.killiecrankiehotel.co.uk

Loch Tummel Inn

Strathtummel, By Pitlochry, Perth & Kinross PH16 5RP

A great little place for summer. "When you get here, look, listen, smell and let it all seep in." Michael's wise sentiments sum up the simple pleasures in store at this lovely old coaching inn on a remote stretch of road overlooking Loch Tummel. He and Liz, warm, funny and interesting, are in their element here. He's very much the consummate host orchestrating proceedings from behind the bar, and a firm believer in preserving the art of conversation; there's no piped music, your mobile won't connect, and televisions are only provided on request. Idiosyncratic bedrooms have rustic charm, with checked bedspreads, china and good bathrooms; soak in a bath of soft hill water in one room next to a log fire. All but one of the rooms have fantastic loch views. There's also a sweet bothy room, with an open fire, where guests can retreat for some privacy. Breakfast is served in a converted hayloft with views, the bar does a mean shepherd's pie, and the restaurant has a great chef; don't miss Michael's home-smoked salmon. Pitlochry has the best rep theatre outside London, and Perthshire is stunning.

rooms	7: 3 doubles, 2 family; 1 double, 1 single, both with separate bath.
price	£75-£100. Singles £50.
meals	Bar meals from £3.95. Dinner £25-£30; book ahead.
closed	November-Easter.
directions	From Perth, A9 north, turn off after Pitlochry, for Killicrankie. Left onto B8019 for Tummel Bridge & Kinloch Rannoch; inn 8 miles on right.

Inn

Liz & Michael Marsden
tel 01882 634272
fax 01882 634272

Creagan House

Strathyre, Callander, Perth & Kinross FK18 8ND

We search high and low for little places like Creagan; it brings to life all the ingredients that make a place special. Run with huge skill and passion by Gordon and Cherry, it is decorated not by numbers, nor by fashion, but by enthusiasm, evolving slowly and naturally. The welcome is second to none and the food magnificent – local Scottish produce, carefully sourced and cooked with great flair by Gordon. There are some nice surprises, too, such as a small treatise entitled *The Iconography of the Creagan Toast Rack*; worth reading while waiting for eggs and bacon at a slab of polished oak in the baronial dining room. A small bar is stocked with 45 malt whiskies, with a guide to help choose; one of its ceiling beams was 'acquired' from the Oban railway line. No airs and graces, just the sort of attention you get in small, owner-run places. Bedrooms in the eaves have Sanderson wallpaper, old furniture and no TVs. "You don't come to Creagan to watch a box," says Cherry. Bag a munro instead – walking sticks at the door will help you up Beinn An T-Sidhein.

rooms	5: 4 doubles, 1 twin.
price	£100. Singles £60.
meals	Dinner £26.50.
closed	February.
directions	From Stirling, A84 north through Callander to Strathyre. Hotel 0.25 miles north of village on right.

Hotel

	Gordon & Cherry Gunn
tel	01877 384638
fax	01877 384319
email	eatandstay@creaganhouse.co.uk
web	www.creaganhouse.co.uk

Monachyle Mhor

Balquhidder, Lochearnhead, Perth & Kinross FK19 8PQ

The position here is fabulous, with Loch Voil at the bottom of the hill, mountains rising all around you, and cars that pass at the rate of one an hour; the twisty road ends two miles up the track. Monachyle is a great place to be, far prettier than it first seems, with a rambling old farmhouse feel spruced up into a funky factory of fun: bold colours, dynamic people and brilliant food cooked by Tom. The freshest that Scotland has to offer is what sparks his imagination: game, fish, wild berries, artichokes from the organic garden, mushrooms foraged the day before... sensational. They started here as farmers – and still are – then began doing B&B, and now, that has evolved too... Various members of the family are involved, the place is extremely relaxed, and standards are kept high – a special combination. The restaurant is intimate, the panelled bar with its wood fire wonderfully snug. Bedrooms are split between the house, barns and coach house. All make bold use of space and contemporary colour, and are fabulous. Locals fill the place at weekends. And you pass Rob Roy's grave on the way in.

rooms	11: 3 doubles, 1 twin, 7 suites.
price	£95-£180. Singles from £65. Suites £125-£185.
meals	Dinner £37. Sunday lunch £22.50.
closed	January.
directions	M9, junc. 10, onto A84 17 miles North of Callander; left at Kings House Hotel for Balquhidder. 6 miles along road. Along Loch Voil. Hotel on right up drive, signed.

Hotel

	Rob, Jean, Tom & Angela Lewis
tel	01877 384622
fax	01877 384305
email	info@monachylemhor.com
web	www.monachylemhor.com

Glenmorangie, The Highland Home at Cadboll

Fearn, By Tain, Ross-shire IV20 1XP

Glenmorangie – glen of tranquillity – and so it is; this is heaven. Owned by the eponymous distillery, this 1700s farmhouse of thick walls and immaculate interiors stands in glorious country, with a tree-lined path down to the beach; see your supper landed by fishermen, or search for driftwood instead. A perfect place and a real find, with levels of service to surpass most others, where staff are attentive, yet unobtrusive, and where the comforts seem unending. Bedrooms are exceptional: decanters of whisky, *fleur de lys* wallpaper, tartan blankets and country views. Rooms flood with light, there are bathrobes and piles of towels, the best linen and blankets. Downstairs, the portrait of the Sheriff of Cromarty hangs on the wall, a fire crackles between plump sofas in the drawing room, and views of the garden – apple-blossom white, cherry-blossom pink – draw you out. Here you find a half-acre walled garden, both beautiful and productive, with much for your plate. Fields all around, absolute peace, delicious food, golf at Royal Dornoch, Tain and Brora. Exceptional.

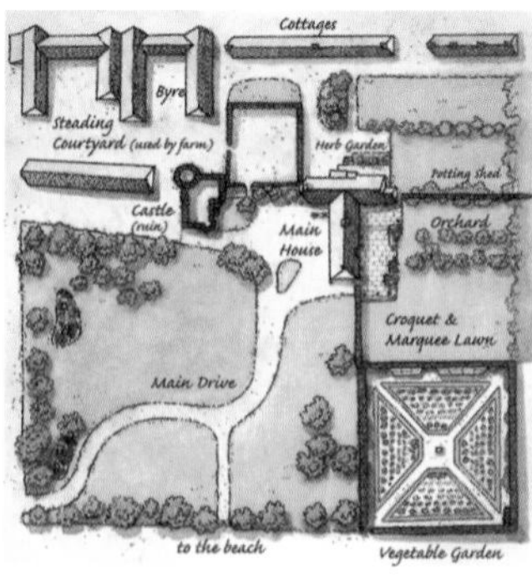

rooms	9: 6 twins/doubles, 3 cottage suites.
price	Half-board only, £120-£185 p.p.
meals	Light lunch from £5. Dinner, 4 courses, included; non-residents £38.50 with wine.
closed	3-23 January.
directions	A9 north from Inverness for 33 miles to Nigg r'bout. Right on B9175, for Nigg, over r'way crossing for 1.5 miles, then left, following signs.

Hotel

	Helen McKenzie-Smith
tel	01862 871671
fax	01862 871625
email	relax@glenmorangieplc.co.uk
web	www.glenmorangie.com

The Old Mill Highland Lodge

Talladale, Loch Maree, Ross-shire IV22 2HL

Chris and Jo are a remarkable pair providing the sort of effortless hospitality that few hotels can match. Old Mill isn't plush, but it doesn't pretend to be, and it's great value. Here are delightful home comforts, relaxing company and extremely good nosh. We sent along two self-confessed foodies who can be highly critical. They found Chris's food fresh, flavoursome and imaginative. Praise indeed! Jo, a keen photographer, is good on detail, and names. Both are great travellers and the comfy living room is full of travel books, novels and photo albums charting the fortunes of this 1840 horse-driven mill since its rebuild in the 1970s. The best bedroom is upstairs; those downstairs are pet-friendly. The Honeysuckle room is gorgeous, with a sumptuous duvet, giant pillows and garden views – watch the tame pine marten being fed, and fall asleep to the sound of burns hurrying through two acres of garden to Loch Maree, regarded as one of, if not *the* best loch in Scotland. It's wider than most, with islands in the middle and Caledonian pine forests at the foot of Beinn Eighe. Bring walking boots.

rooms	6: 2 doubles, 3 twins; 1 double with bath.
price	Half-board £75 p.p.
meals	Packed lunch £4. Dinner included.
closed	20 October-20 March.
directions	Hotel on A832, 10 miles north of Kinlochewe & 10 miles south of Gairloch, signed.

Hotel

	Chris & Jo Powell
tel	01445 760271
email	jo.powell@bosinternet.com
web	www.theoldmillhighlandlodge.co.uk

Churches

Albert Road, Eyemouth, Berwickshire TD14 5DB

As an introduction to hospitality north of the border, this fabulous restaurant with rooms is anything but traditional and we applaud it for that. Sure, Scotland wouldn't be Scotland without its tartan and thistles but it's always a pleasure to celebrate anywhere that's trying to be a little different. Marcus and Rosalind are a young couple doing just that. He's the exceptional chef, with experience in America and Europe and she, with a degree in law, manages front of house superbly. As for the setting, it couldn't be better: an old manse, overlooking the pretty harbour at Eyemouth – the name alone should be enough to tempt you. The place looks good and you'll eat well. Watch the catch unloaded, then eat it later: local monkfish with Chinese leaves, Berwickshire crab with a sweet chilli dressing and fresh North Sea lobster. Meat is special too; Northumbrian lamb and fresh game in season. Inside, the hotel has a classy, modern feel, with lots of style, wooden floors, wrought-iron beds, the odd luxurious four-poster… there's even a moongate in the garden.

rooms	6: 3 doubles, 1 twin, 1 family, 1 four-poster.
price	£80-£125. Singles £60-£90.
meals	Dinner, à la carte, £30.
closed	Rarely.
directions	From Berwick, A1 north for 7 miles, then right, signed Eyemouth. Follow brown signs to hotel.

Restaurant with Rooms

	Marcus Lamb & Rosalind Dryden
tel	01890 750401
fax	01890 750747
email	info@churcheshotel.co.uk
web	www.churcheshotel.co.uk

Scarista House

Isle of Harris, Western Isles HS3 3HX

All you need to know is this: Harris is one of the most beautiful places anywhere in the world. Beaches of white sand that stretch for a mile or two are not uncommon. If you bump into another soul, it will be a delightful coincidence, but you should not count on it. The water is turquoise, and coconuts sometimes wash up on the beach. The view from Scarista is simple and magnificent: field, ridge, beach, water, sky. Patricia and Tim are the kindest people, quietly inspiring. Their home is island heaven: coal fires, rugs on painted wooden floors, books everywhere, old oak furniture, a first-floor drawing room, fresh flowers and fabulous Harris light. The golf club has left a set of clubs by the front door in case you wish to play (the view from the first tee is one of the best in the game). A corncrake occasionally visits the garden. There are walking sticks and Wellington boots to help you up the odd hill. Kind local staff may speak Gaelic. And the food is exceptional, maybe twice-baked cheese soufflé, hand-dived Harris scallops, tarte tatin and cinnamon ice cream. A perfect place.

rooms	5: 3 doubles, 2 twins.
price	£150. Singles from £85.
meals	Packed lunch £5.50. Dinner, 4 courses, £45.
closed	Occasionally in winter.
directions	From Tarbert, A859, for Rodel. Scarista 15 miles on left, after golf course.

Patricia & Tim Martin
tel 01859 550238
fax 01859 550277
email timandpatricia@scaristahouse.com
web www.scaristahouse.com

Photography by John Coe

wales

SACO Serviced Apartments

76 Cathedral Road, Cardiff CF11 9LN

Folk intent on corporate lets, house-hunting, student-offspring-visiting or away for a family celebration are discovering the advantages of serviced-apartment independence. Kick off your shoes, pour yourself a glass of wine and settle down on a spotless burgundy sofa to satellite TV – it's like home, only neater. The immaculate apartment, whose Victorian sash windows overlook pleasant, wide, tree-lined Cathedral Road, is yours for the week (or three nights), with bedrooms quietly at the back. You get oatmeal carpeting, padded dining chairs, a spotlit kitchen, a smart little bathroom (and extra shower room in the apartments for four) all mod cons and a friendly local rep. Beds are king-size, with white duvets and fat pillows, bedroom furniture is attractively colour-washed, cots and broadband are on request. It's a neutral, contemporary and functional open-plan space that is, frankly, hard to fault. Best of all, you are a short walk from Cardiff Castle, the Millenium Stadium and the pedestrianised shopping centre. *Long-stay rates available. Minimum stay 3 nights*

rooms	15 apartments for 2 and 4.
price	£70-£110 + VAT.
meals	Plenty of restaurants within walking distance.
closed	Rarely.
directions	5-minute taxi ride from railway station.

Serviced accommodation

	Jo Redman
tel	0845 122 0405
email	info@sacoapartments.co.uk
web	www.sacoapartments.co.uk

The Big Sleep Hotel

Bute Terrace, Cardiff CF10 2FE

Cheap but sure damn groovy, this novel and gutsy designer hotel is a good launch-pad from which to discover a regenerated Welsh capital. Retro 1970s style and 1990s minimalism co-join inside a 10-storey former office block opposite Cardiff Intenational Arena. The building was converted to a hotel by a previous owner and then resurrected as The Big Sleep by two innovators with flair and a friend in the actor John Malkovich, who helped back the project. To keep costs down, Cosmo supplied the formica from his Bath-based factory – the first in Britain to bend the material – and Lulu sourced the fake teddy-bear fur to make full-length curtains and to carpet the fun penthouse suite. Cool blues and stark white walls were inspired by 1950s architect Gio Ponti. Most rooms have glittering city views at night. Pay extra for a bigger room or one of the two suites on the tenth floor. Elsewhere, modular seating re-upholstered in white PVC, an 'ironing station', a colourful lobby, and deep red 1960s wallpaper in the busy bar. Great value for a city hotel, and breakfasts are self-serve.

rooms	81: 42 doubles, 30 twins, 7 family, 2 suites.
price	£45-£135.
meals	Continental breakfast only.
closed	Christmas Day & Boxing Day.
directions	M4, junc. 29, A48, for Cardiff East. 3rd junc., A4232 to centre. At 1st r'bout, 2nd exit, 1 mile past Lloyds TSB, left at lights on A4160. Right at 3rd lights, under bridge. On left.

Hotel

	Cosmo Fry & Lulu Anderson
tel	02920 636363
fax	02920 636364
email	bookings.cardiff@thebigsleephotel.com
web	www.thebigsleephotel.com

Ty Mawr Country Hotel

Brechfa, Carmarthenshire SA32 7RA

Ty Mawr translates as 'big house' and this is a classic 15th-century Welsh building, with exposed stone, low beams, log fires and handsome sash windows. The house has been in the book for some time, but now has new owners; Steve and Annabel have worked in the business for years, then took time off to go travelling before settling on this peaceful part of the Brechfa forest to show off their skills. Steve is in charge of the kitchen and his philosophy about food is simple: use the best local and seasonal ingredients and you don't need to tamper with it much. And there are excellent local suppliers: organic Welsh Black beef from the neighbouring farm, fruit and veg, mostly organic, from another farm that also provides honey from their bees and homemade jams and pickles. Fish and shellfish come from a fisherman in Carigan who has a license to coracle fish on the River Teifi and also has lobster and crab pots out in Cardigan Bay. Friendly Annabel does 'front of house' and has enjoyed giving the bedrooms a makeover with light colours, pale pine furniture and claw-foot baths. Simple and good value.

rooms	6: 2 doubles, 1 twin, 1 family, 1 four-poster; 1 double with separate bath.
price	£82-£106. Half-board (for 2 nights) £130 p.p. Singles £55-£65.
meals	Sunday lunch £13.50. Packed lunch from £5. Dinner, 5 courses, £26.
closed	Rarely.
directions	M4 west onto A48, then B4310 exit, for National Botanic Gardens, north to Brechfa. In village centre.

Hotel

Steve & Annabel Viney
tel 01267 202332
fax 01267 202437
email info@tymawrhotel.co.uk
web www.wales-country-hotel.co.uk

Hurst House

East Marsh, Laugharne, Carmarthenshire SA33 4RS

Arriving at Hurst House is like falling off the end of the world onto a pillow of unadulterated style. This pocket of sophistication is miles from anywhere, isolated by windswept marshland that spreads endlessly in all directions; from a distance, the hotel looks half-crushed by the weight of the sky. The building is Georgian and older, with parquet floors, sash windows, stone fireplaces and exposed beams, but the interiors couldn't be more contemporary... bold colours, chic furniture, seductive lighting, pristine bathrooms and Bang & Olufsen televisions and DVD players in every room, all carefully designed with you in mind. Matt is young, friendly and believes in good food, generous service and great parties – there's no stuffy pretension here. (And no need to keep quiet for the neighbours: they own 69 acres of marsh towards the coast.) A pond created near the house is fantastic at night, lit by underwater fibre optics; a spa is planned for derelict barns. Dion the chef is young, talented and changes the menu according to what's local and in season. Fabulous for party people and the young at heart.

rooms	7 doubles.
price	From £125. Deluxe double £200.
meals	Lunch £11.95. Dinner £22.95; à la carte, about £26.
closed	Rarely.
directions	From St Clears, A4066 for Pendine, through villages of Laugharne & Broadway. 0.5 miles passed 2nd village, left down track towards marshes, signed. Follow signs.

Hotel

	Matt Roberts & Neil Morrissey
tel	01994 427417
fax	01994 427730
email	info@hurst-house.co.uk
web	www.hurst-house.co.uk

West Arms Hotel

Llanarmon Dyffryn Ceiriog, Denbighshire LL20 7LD

Come here if you dream of a traditional place in a gorgeous village where the road ends and the real country begins. The smell of fresh bread may greet you, perhaps the scent of fresh flowers, or a crackling fire. Hear the sound of the River Cleriog through the open front door; sit in the half-glow of the dimly-lit bar, warm and cosy. It's as a 16th-century inn should be, of flagstone, beam, and leaded window. Décor is simple, the layout higgledy-piggledy, with old Welsh colours, traditional furniture, a few antiques and an inglenook. Bedrooms are clean and modest, on different levels, some with oak beams and low ceilings; plainer ones at the back have pastoral views. The river runs through the peaceful garden, with the rolling Berwyn Hills beyond – for walks, wildlife and the Pistyll Rhaeder waterfall. Geoff and Gill are laid-back but dedicated, thoroughly at one with what they're doing. The chef is Welsh and superb – a local TV celebrity no less! – and backed by two other gourmet chefs. All manner of country pursuits can be arranged, from painting to shooting, and sheepdog trials are held in the village.

rooms	15: 2 doubles, 2 twins, 9 twins/doubles, 2 suites.
price	£95-£138. Singles £52.50-£74.
meals	Bar lunch from £4.25. Packed lunch from £7.95. Dinner £27.95.
closed	Rarely.
directions	From Shrewsbury, A5 north to Chirk. Left at r'bout on B4500, signed Ceiriog Valley, for 11 miles to Llanarmon DC. Hotel in centre.

Hotel

	Geoff & Gill Leigh-Ford
tel	01691 600665
fax	01691 600622
email	gowestarms@aol.com
web	www.thewestarms.co.uk

Tyddyn Llan

Llandrillo, Corwen, Denbighshire LL21 0ST

Everything is orchestrated superbly here. Your entry is into a smart country home – there's no reception desk – where owners Bryan and Susan Webb greet you with the promise of deep comfort and excellent modern cooking. There are three sitting rooms, a log fire, carefully chosen antiques and a dining room almost colonial in feel, with blue-painted wooden panelling and yellow floral curtains. Eat at white-clothed tables on fresh, locally sourced produce lovingly cooked: grilled scallops, Welsh black fillet of beef au poivre, calves' sweetbreads with pancetta, whimberry creme brulée. Bedrooms vary in size but all are cosy and well-designed in a traditional style with quiet colours, CD players and every indulging extra. Treat yourself to tea on the veranda after a game of croquet on the lawn... or walk the Berwin Ridge which rises to 2,000 feet. Or come with rod and wellies to fish trout and grayling on the River Dee. Great comfort and fine food in an astonishingly beautiful Welsh valley.

rooms	13: 8 doubles, 4 twins, 1 garden suite.
price	£130-£210. Singles from £65. Half-board £95-£120 p.p.
meals	Lunch, 2-3 courses, £17.50-£23. Dinner £29.50-£40.
closed	Rarely.
directions	From A5 west of Corwen, left on B4401 to Llandrillo. Through village, entrance on right after tight bend.

Hotel

	Bryan & Susan Webb
tel	01490 440264
fax	01490 440414
email	tyddynllan@compuserve.com
web	www.tyddynllan.co.uk

Penmaenuchaf Hall

Penmaenpool, Dolgellau, Gwynedd LL40 1YB

A long, windy road leads to the hall and it's worth taking for the views over the Mawddach estuary. You can stand at the front of the house, on the Victorian stone balustrade, and gaze down on the tidal ebb and flow, or walk around to the back to blazing banks of rhododendrons, azaleas and camellias, and a rising forest behind. Pass through the front door – all is equally delightful within. The house is pristine: rugs, wooden floors and oak panelling, flowers erupting from jugs and bowls, leather sofas and armchairs, open fires and seagrass matting and, everywhere, those views. Upstairs, bedrooms – more views, of course – come in different shapes and sizes, the big being *huge*, the small being warm and cosy. One room up in the eaves has a fine *bergère* bed. In the dining room, stiff white napery, a dress code and the best of modern British cooking. Fish in the hotel's 13 miles of river; back in the garden, they grow as much as they can. You'll warm to Mark's sense of humour, too. *Children over six welcome. Pets by arrangement.*

rooms	14: 7 doubles, 5 twins, 1 family, 1 four-poster.
price	£120-£180. Singles £75-£135.
meals	Lunch £3.50-£15.95. Afternoon tea from £4.95. Dinner, 4 courses, £32.50; à la carte also available.
closed	Rarely.
directions	From Dolgellau, A493 west for about 1.5 miles. Entrance on left.

B&B

Mark Watson & Lorraine Fielding

tel	01341 422129
fax	01341 422787
email	relax@penhall.co.uk
web	www.penhall.co.uk

Plas Bodegroes

Pwllheli, Gwynedd LL53 5TH

Close to the end of the world and worth every single second it takes to get here. Chris and Gunna are inspirational, their home a temple of cool elegance, the food possibly the best in Wales. Fronted by an avenue of 200-year-old beech trees, this Georgian manor house is wrapped in climbing roses, wildly roaming wisteria and ferns. The veranda circles the house, as do the long French windows that lighten every room; open one up, grab a chair and sit out reading a book. Not a formal place – come to relax and be yourself. Bedrooms are wonderful, the courtyard rooms especially good; exposed wooden ceilings and a crisp clean style give the feel of a smart Scandinavian forest hideaway. Best of all is the dining room, almost a work of art in itself, cool and crisp with modern art and Venetian carnival masks on the walls – a great place to eat Chris's Michelin-starred food. If you can tear yourself away, explore the Lleyn peninsula: sandy beaches, towering sea cliffs, country walks. Snowdon is also close, and Gunna and Chris will direct you.

rooms	11: 7 doubles, 2 twins, 1 single, 1 four-poster.
price	£80-£150. Singles £40-£80. Half-board from £70 p.p.
meals	Dinner £35. Sunday lunch £16.50.
closed	December-February & Sunday/Monday.
directions	From Pwllheli, A497 towards Nefyn. House on left after 1 mile, signed.

Hotel

	Chris & Gunna Chown
tel	01758 612363
fax	01758 701247
email	gunna@bodegroes.co.uk
web	www.bodegroes.co.uk

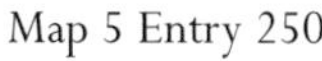

The Bell at Skenfrith

Skenfrith, Monmouthshire NP7 8UH

Indulge the senses at this classy 17th-century coaching inn on the banks of the Monnow. Follow remote country lanes to a blissful village setting, with a ruined Norman castle and an ancient humpback bridge. Inside is immaculately done but informal, and run with warmth – Janet treats young staff like members of the family. Expect the best of everything: coffee from a proper cappuccino machine, food mostly organic, wine and cognacs superb – there's even an organic menu for children (Mash Bang Wallop etc). Bedrooms, all different, are understatedly elegant with Farrow & Ball colours and beds dressed in cotton piqué and Welsh wool; you get homemade biscuits, Cath Collins toiletries and a hi-tech console by the bed so you can listen to music in your bath. After an energetic day out on the hills or the river, settle down to Usk Valley lamb and tarte tatin in the restaurant overlooking the terrace. Toast the occasion with local cider or champagne from a great list, then flop into one of the big sofas next to a roaring fire. Fine indeed.

rooms	8: 3 doubles, 1 twin/double, 2 four-posters, 2 attic suites.
price	£95-£170. Singles from £70 (not at weekends).
meals	Bar lunch from £15; Sunday lunch £18.50. Dinner £27-£32.50.
closed	Mondays November-Easter.
directions	From Monmouth, B4233 to Rockfield; B4347 for 5 miles; right on B4521, for Ross-on-Wye. Skenfrith 1 mile.

Inn

	William & Janet Hutchings
tel	01600 750235
fax	01600 750525
email	enquiries@skenfrith.co.uk
web	www.skenfrith.co.uk

Lake Vyrnwy Hotel

Llanwddyn, Montgomeryshire SY10 OLY

Lake Vyrnwy lives in a blissfully remote pocket of Wales, surrounded by pine forests and ancient grazing land. Both lake and hotel are man-made: the lake was completed in 1891 to provide Liverpool's water, taking two years to fill; the hotel was built shortly afterwards to allow civic dignitaries from the city to come and ogle the dam – they also came to fish the 400,000 trout that were released into the water. The view *is* stupendous, the lake stretching five miles into the distance, home to rolling mists and dramatic bursts of sunshine. Walk, or cycle around it, canoe, sail or fish here – all can be arranged; there's tennis and clay pigeon shooting, and birdwatchers will be in heaven. Once inside, a sense of old style splendour envelopes. The Bisikers have done a wonderful job of restoring the hotel, with wooden floors, a grand piano, heavy oak furniture, even a postbox in the entrance hall. Bedrooms are excellent and most have lake views, as do the award-winning restaurant, the yellow drawing room, the leather-chaired library, the new conservatory and the terraced bar. A place to return to again and again.

rooms	35: 32 twins/doubles, 2 four-posters, 1 suite.
price	£120-£190. Half-board £77.50-£110 p.p. Singles from £90.
meals	Bar meals from £8. Dinner £32.50.
closed	Rarely.
directions	A490 from Welshpool; B4393 to Lake Vyrnwy. Brown signs from A5 at Shrewsbury as well.

Hotel

	The Bisiker Family
tel	01691 870692
fax	01691 870259
email	res@lakevyrnwy.com
web	www.lakevyrnwy.com

Penally Abbey

Penally, Tenby, Pembrokeshire SA70 7PY

It's not often a hotel exceeds your expectations, but then there aren't many places like Penally. It's not a grand hotel and doesn't pretend to be. It just does well the simple things that make a stay memorable. Steve's gentle, unflappable manner suits front of house: chatting to guests one minute, taking orders and mixing a drink at a small bar the next – he makes it look so easy. There's an unhurried charm about the whole place; you won't feel rushed into doing anything. The building is a former 1790s abbey; there's also a ruined 13th-century church called St Diniel's – lit up at night – suggesting even earlier roots. A beautiful garden looks across Carmarthen Bay. The beach is a 10-minute walk and great for pebble collectors; beautiful coastal walks lead from here. Bedrooms are all different: most in the main house have gorgeous four-posters and antiques, while those in the Tuscan-style coach house are more cottagey. Elleen cooks in the French style, much of it picked up in the kitchen of a château many years back. The Tenby sea bass was exquisite.

rooms	12: 3 doubles, 1 twin, 8 four-posters.
price	£126-£148. Singles £98. Half-board £90-£104 p.p.
meals	Dinner £30. Lunch by arrangement.
closed	Rarely.
directions	From Tenby, A4139 for Pembroke. Right into Penally after 1.5 miles. Hotel signed at village green. Train station 5 mins walk.

Hotel

Steve & Elleen Warren
tel 01834 843033
fax 01834 844714
email info@penally-abbey.com
web www.penally-abbey.com

Twr-y-Felin

St David's, Pembrokeshire SA62 6QS

In this great, spiritual centre of Europe, lots of adrenaline is pumping for planet earth… and you're welcome to jump off a cliff and join in. Andy runs adventure holidays with a green slant from an old windmill that's been converted into a hotel. There's nothing preachy about his approach; he prefers to reverse widespread indifference to the environment by setting hearts racing: kayak, rock climb, sail, surf… even 'coasteer' with a wetsuit over cliff and rock – all overseen by qualified instructors. Pembrokeshire's rugged coastline and crashing surf is just as good to walk; or gaze out to sea past Ramsey Island from the top of the windmill. The hotel neutralises its carbon emissions (as does Alastair Sawday Publishing), planting trees to offset the pollution it causes – you're charged a £1 tax for driving here! Andy is at the forefront of a local campaign to make St David's the first – and smallest – sustainable city in the world. Most of the food served is organic and locally produced. Bedrooms are clean with good linen and life downstairs is laid back. Hands on, no frills, friendly: worth a modern day pilgrimage.

rooms	12: 1 double, 2 twins, 2 singles, 1 family, 1 bunk; 1 single, 2 twins/doubles, 2 family with separate bathroom.
price	£55-£68. Singles £30-£34.
meals	Lunch £5-£9. Dinner £19.50.
closed	Rarely.
directions	From Haverfordwest, A487 to St David's. Entering city, 1st left after flagpoles, signed, then next left down lane. Entrance on right.

Hotel

	Andy Middleton
tel	01437 721678
fax	01437 721838
email	stay@tyf.com
web	www.tyf.com

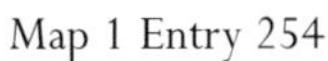

Cnapan

East Street, Newport, Nr Fishguard, Pembrokeshire SA42 0SY

Come for country comfort tucked into the village, good food and the sea down the hill. Cnapan is in the middle of Newport – "a together little town" – and locals drop by. It's a bar, a restaurant with rooms, and a family affair; mother and daughter slave (happily) in the kitchen, John is on breakfast duty and Michael front of house. Bright little rooms have a homey feel: pine settles in the bar, a woodburner in the sitting room, lacy cloths on the tables, horse-brasses on the wall. Upstairs, past a rogues' gallery of family and friends, are bedrooms with sea or hill views, knick-knacks and garden flowers, comfy sofas and books, and showers not baths. (Seek out the 'walkers' bathroom' for soaking weary limbs.) Arty Newport, home to candle-makers, wood-turners and potters, is on the edge of the Pembrokeshire National Park. Walks to hill, moor and cliff start from the door and you can be on Parrog beach inside 10 minutes; buses bring you back to the tastiest food around. Don't miss out on hazelnut meringue, raspberry and almond tart and 'Piggy's Delight': puddings are Judith's passion.

rooms	5: 1 double, 3 twins, 1 family. Extra bath available.
price	£70. Singles £42.
meals	Lunch from £6.50. Dinner from £24. Restaurant closed Tuesday evenings from Easter to October.
closed	Christmas, January & February.
directions	From Cardigan, A487 to Newport. 1st pink house on right.

Restaurant with Rooms

John & Eluned Lloyd
& Michael & Judith Cooper

tel	01239 820575
fax	01239 820878
email	cnapan@online-holidays.net
web	www.online-holidays.net/cnapan

Gliffaes Country House Hotel

Crickhowell, Powys NP8 1RH

Gliffaes is matchless: grandly comfortable but as casual and warm as home. It's a house for all seasons – not even driving rain could mask its beauty. Stroll along the rhododendron-flanked drive and wander the 33 acres of stunning gardens and woodland, or bask in the sun on the high, buttressed terrace as the River Usk cuts through the valley 150 feet below. In winter, curl up by fires burning in extravagantly ornate fireplaces – one looks like the Acropolis. Tea is a feast of scones and cakes laid out on a long table at one end of a sitting room of polished floors and panelled walls. The house could be a garden shed and you'd still love it – as long as the Suters remained at the helm, just as Susie's parents did. The clan has been welcoming guests for over 55 years – the fourth generation are ready for some rope-learning, while the first generation, the "granny patrol", is still seen walking her dog; go and have a chat – she's amazing. Bedrooms are excellent, the cooking modern, and membership of the Slow Food movement means local and seasonal food is used. Fisherfolk can cast to their heart's content.

rooms	22: 3 doubles, 13 twins/doubles, 6 singles.
price	£71.50-£180. Singles from £65.
meals	Light lunch from £3.50. Dinner £29.50.
closed	First 2 weeks in January.
directions	From Crickhowell, A40 west for 2.5 miles. Entrance on left, signed. Hotel 1 mile up windy hill.

Hotel

	James & Susie Suter
tel	01874 730371
fax	01874 730463
email	calls@gliffaeshotel.com
web	www.gliffaeshotel.com

The Felin Fach Griffin

Felin Fach, Brecon, Powys LD3 0UB

Stylish but cosy, fresh but not fussy. This bold venture mixes the buzz of a smart city bistro with the easy-going pace of Welsh country living, and it's hugely popular. Full of bright elegance, downstairs fans out from the bar into several eating and sitting areas, with stripped pine and old oak furniture. Make for three giant leather sofas around a raised hearth and settle in – or opt for the rustic charm of the chatty backroom bar. A Dutch chef stars in the kitchen, conjuring up simple but sensational dishes for smartly laid tables: Black Mountain smoked salmon, wild mushroom tagliatelli, braised ox cheeks with mash, vanilla creme brulée. Breakfast is served around one table in the morning room. Wallow with the papers and make your own toast on the Aga, as you like it – or have it as it comes. Bedrooms are in a modern style, clean and simple, with a few designer touches; tulips in a vase, muslin round the four-posters. Charles hosts with aplomb and is young and ambitious, as are smiley staff who genuinely seem to be enjoying themselves. Who wouldn't love this place? *Dogs welcome by arrangement.*

rooms	7: 2 doubles, 2 twins/doubles, 3 four-posters.
price	£92.50-£115. Singles from £67.50
meals	Lunch about £15. Dinner about £20. Restaurant closed Monday lunchtimes.
closed	Christmas Day, New Year's Day & occasionally.
directions	From Brecon, A470 for Builth Wells to Felin Fach (4.5 miles). On left.

Inn

Charles Inkin

tel	01874 620111
fax	01874 620120
email	enquiries@eatdrinksleep.ltd.uk
web	www.eatdrinksleep.ltd.uk

Llangoed Hall

Llyswen, Brecon, Powys LD3 0YP

One of the most refined hotels in Britain, Llangoed Hall rests in the valley of the Wye with glorious views to the Black Mountains and Brecon Beacons. It was Sir Bernard's dream to do up this Clough Williams-Ellis house, and the magnificent Edwardian manor has risen like a phoenix. The restaurant is one of the reason's for staying here: decorated in Elanbach blue and white, it's a sumptuous match for the food. Liveried butlers, cut-glass decanters, a million deep sofas, crackling logs and remarkable artefacts from around the world, from old Penguin editions to rare Whistler lithographs, are brought together with magnificent style. Sweep up the carved stair to big bedrooms – some with those views. Outside, clipped hedges, giant Wellingtonia, a maze big enough to get lost in and a private path to the River Wye for fishing and picnics on a private beach. Hushed afternoon tea served on a silver tray is sheer indulgence – as is Welsh black fillet steak for dinner, followed by dark chocolate fondant. It's all done in house-party style, and you're invited.

rooms	23: 20 twins/doubles, 3 suites.
price	£180-£315. Half-board £250-£410. Suite £340-£360.
meals	Lunch from £4.50. Afternoon tea £7.50-£14.50. Dinner from £43.
closed	Rarely.
directions	From Brecon, A470 for Builth Wells for about 6 miles; left on A470 to Llyswen. Left in village at T-junc. Entrance 1.5 miles further on right.

Hotel

	Sir Bernard Ashley
tel	01874 754525
fax	01874 754545
email	enquiries@llangoedhall.com
web	www.llangoedhall.com

Pwll-y-Faedda

Erwood, Builth Wells, Powys LD2 3YS

Anyone would want to live here, on the salmon river. The big, elegant, 1920s fishing lodge, set beneath plunging hills and moorland, has been given a new lease of life; sit back and let the river tumble past your window. There's a soft-carpeted, country-house glow here, with English antiques and a dash of oriental spice: rooms are full of interest, and rugs and paintings from far-flung travels. The entrance hall and library are quintessential, wood-panelled 'hunting lodge' – minus antlers on the walls. First-floor bedrooms have fine proportions and a light, harmonious feel; creamy carpets, rich wall-hangings, generous beds and (bar one) waterside views. Those that look downriver are as big as suites. Yolande has an eye for every little extra, gives you breakfast when you like and is a terrific cook; don't miss the sticky toffee pudding. If you're an angler like your host, there are 800 yards of double-bank salmon and trout fishing to cast your line in – and 27 acres of grounds. Pwll-y-Faedda runs on oiled wheels and is great for weddings and house parties. *Fishing by advance booking. Children seven and over welcome.*

rooms	6: 5 doubles; 1 twin.
price	£70-£90. Singles £50.
meals	Dinner, 3 courses, £28.
closed	Rarely.
directions	From Abergavenny towards Crickhowell; right, through Talgarth, towards Builth Wells. After Erwood look for lay-by & discreet sign on right which is entrance to drive.

Hotel

	Jeremy & Yolande Jaquet
tel	01982 560202
email	info@pwllyfaedda.co.uk
web	www.pwllyfaedda.co.uk

The Lake Country House

Llangammarch Wells, Powys LD4 4BS

Grand but not stuffy, and so cosseting, Lake House is the genuine article – a real country house. Afternoon tea is served in the drawing room where seven beautiful rugs warm a brightly polished wooden floor and five chandeliers hang from the ceiling. The hotel opened over 100 years ago and the leather-bound fishing logs and visitors' books go back to 1894. A feel of the 1920s lingers. Fires come to life in front of your eyes, seemingly unaided, walking sticks, grand pianos, antiques and grandfather clocks lie about the place and snooker balls clack in the distance. Dress for dinner: the food and wines demand it. The same grandeur marks the bedrooms, many of which have been updated; most are suites: trompe l'œil wallpaper, rich fabrics, good lighting, stacks of antiques, crowns above the beds, a turndown service – the works. Jean-Pierre runs his home with charm, happy to share his knowledge of this deeply rural slice of Wales. The grounds hold a lake to fish – you can hire rods – a nine-hole golf course, the River Ifron where kingfishers swoop, and acres of peace and quiet. Riding can also be arranged.

rooms	18: 8 twins/doubles, 10 suites.
price	£140-£200. Singles £105-£170. Suites £200-£240.
meals	Lunch, 3 courses, £23.50. Dinner £37.50.
closed	Rarely.
directions	From Builth Wells, A483 west for 7 miles to Garth. Signed from village.

Hotel

	Cheryl Hinksman
tel	01769 560501
fax	01769 560770
email	rest@northcotemanor.co.uk
web	www.northcotemanor.co.uk

Carlton House

Dolycoed Road, Llanwrtyd Wells, Powys LD5 4RA

A Welsh spa town – Wales's prettiest – with one of the most talented chefs in Britain. Mary Ann joined the cooking elite in 2002, winning a Michelin star; high time, said her legion of fans. They've been coming to this marvellously eccentric restaurant with rooms for years. Victorians flocked to Llanwrtyd Wells in the 1800s, drawn in the belief that the natural springs could cure everything from a troubled soul to a wart on the toe. This 1900 townhouse is all about food, the modest but, in places, bravely colourful rooms just somewhere to rest your sated self. The Gilchrists are old pros, and great company. Alan, an ever-engaging and unflappable host, orchestrates all in the ground-floor restaurant, full of madly colourful modern furniture and screened off by book shelves. Mary Ann is entirely self-taught and cooks with instinctive brilliance... scallops with crisped Carmarthen ham, fruit sorbets with Earl Grey syrup; she decides what to cook only hours before she puts on her apron. Pony-trekkers, cyclists and walkers fill the town in summer; Carlton suits all year.

rooms	6: 4 doubles, 2 twins/doubles.
price	£60-£80. Half-board (min. 2 nights) from £58. p.p. Singles £45.
meals	Lunch Tues-Fri by arrangement. Dinner £19.95-£40.
closed	Last 2 weeks December (open for New Year).
directions	From Builth Wells, A483 to Llanwrtyd Wells. 1st right in town. House 50 yds on right.

Restaurant with Rooms

	Alan & Mary Ann Gilchrist
tel	01591 610248
fax	01591 610242
email	info@carltonrestaurant.co.uk
web	www.carltonrestaurant.co.uk

Milebrook House Hotel

Milebrook, Knighton, Powys LD7 1LT

Your arrival at Milebrook is peculiarly comforting and understated, with no hidden surprises. The parquet floor in the hall smells of lavender floor wax, the clock ticks quietly, the flowers are fresh and Beryl is likely to come out of the kitchen in her apron to greet you. Fabrics are blended rather than matched; the furniture comfortable rather than remarkable; and the service is attentive and unobtrusive. Chickens that produce the eggs for your breakfast cluck contentedly in the walled kitchen garden where flowers and vegetables are grown for the table – a table to reckon with, for their chef trained in France and is eager to win recognition. He mixes classic French with the best of English, ably assisted by that garden. There's wild terrain, too, devoted to a mature arboretum and a wildlife pond. Elsewhere, terracing, a gazebo, a pergola with roses growing over obelisks, and still room for a croquet lawn. The River Teme runs along the bottom of the garden where you can fly-fish and the countryside belongs to a portion of Britain – sadly decreasing – that can still be called 'tranquil'. Come to rest completely.

rooms	10: 5 doubles, 4 twins, 1 family.
price	£89-£95. Half-board, 2 nights, £120-£130 p.p. Singles £58-£62.
meals	Dinner £24.50; à la carte about £30.50. Restaurant closed Monday lunchtimes.
closed	Rarely.
directions	From Ludlow, A49 north, then left at Bromfield on A4113 towards Knighton for 7 miles. Hotel on right.

Hotel

Rodney & Beryl Marsden

tel	01547 528632
fax	01547 520509
email	hotel@milebrook.kc3ltd.co.uk
web	www.milebrookhouse.co.uk

Bedtime stories

Some tales from the world of 'hospitality' to help you drift off:

"Smile and agree to everything" was the way one hotel owner described perfect hospitality to me. But what if you were asked to turn the river down outside because it was too noisy, or to switch a lighthouse off? These bizarre requests are true, according to a survey that recently landed on my desk. And one hotelier near Truro was even asked on a Sunday morning if he could turn the cathedral bells down!

Unusual behaviour and weird requests litter the list: a couple who shunned the lovely double bed in their room and chose instead to pluck ivy from the wall outside their bedroom, making a little nest on the floor with it, a twee two-some who brought their entire family of stuffed toys on holiday with them, and a chap who left an extremely generous tip and then returned a week later to ask for it back because he was hard up!

The survey goes on to describe a German couple who entered the dining room early one morning, ate generous bowls of decorative pasta and beans from a glass jar, then complained that the breakfast cereal was stale – and a rude man who stood in the bath to spray polish on his shoes, leaving a perfect imprint of his size 9's.

The meanest tips were three pence on a £105 bill and a group of 20 stingy doctors who had a huge meal with wine and left a tip between them of £1. But the most generous were a businessman who gave a car to a member of staff because his initials matched the number plate and a group of Arabs who left a £5,000 tip in a London hotel.

The survey goes on to describe our hotel habits: 50% of us turn the TV on before we go to sleep but only 14% of us read a book, and a meagre 13% say their prayers. 8% obviously don't trust a wake up call from reception because they bring their own alarm clocks, 15% of men sleep naked while only 4% of women shun their pyjamas or a nightie. It seems that we are almost all creatures of habit as a remarkable 70% of us sleep on the same side of the bed when in a hotel as we do at home.

An extensive list of things that are left behind in hotels makes alarming reading. Apart from the obvious - pairs of spectacles, books and toothbrushes that might be easy to overlook - a false leg was once found in a lift (and never claimed). (One wonders whether the poor owner is still walking around in circles somewhere.) And false teeth, hearing aids, crutches, wigs, a glass eye and even a budgie in a cage

(found in the shower) are among items waiting for collection. Poor budgie! Sex aids are mentioned as common lingerers but I think the story of the sex partner still tied, marooned to a bed and then left, is probably a tall tale. At least I hope so. A red-faced 13% of folk surveyed confessed that they were too ashamed to collect things that they had forgotten to pack.

Locating the owner of things left behind is not without risk for the beleaguered hotelier either. A friend of mine who had been away for a weekend received a beautifully laundered and packed nightie through the post from the hotel. Only trouble was, it wasn't hers...

Photo John Coe

Then there are items that are not left behind. And not the obvious things like towels and smellies and hangers. In one hotel a grand piano disappeared entirely from the lobby without anybody noticing, which just goes to show that if you do something, even a terrible thing, with a large dollop of chutzpah, you will probably get away with it. An Indian carpet that was so large it had to be rolled up and carried by two, television sets, lavatory seats, a medieval sword, the owners dog and a four-foot wooden bear are among things that have mysteriously 'walked' out of hotels.

The Most Revolting Fact was the germ count. It is not those peanuts in the bowl on the bar that contain the most bacteria, apparently, but that innocent looking TV remote on the bed which is the only thing that never gets cleaned. I feel some rubber gloves coming on next time I go to stay in a hotel – but then I might leave them behind and people may think all sorts of terrible things.

On a less worrying note the survey recounts some funny and unintentional misuses in the English language spotted at hotels abroad. A Paris hotel urged guests to "leave their values" at the front desk, while the Japanese asked them to make sure to take advantage of the chambermaid. An Austrian ski-resort hotel put a notice up asking people "not to perambulate the corridors in the hours of repose in the boots of ascension." Pregnant ladies might feel insecure in a certain Norwegian hotel where "Ladies are requested not to have children in the bar" and in Acapulco apparently "the manager has passed all the water served here". My absolute favourite though was from a Polish hotel menu, assuring guests that should they choose to eat the trout "you will be singing its praise to your grandchildren as you lie on your deathbed".

We cannot finish this without a shocker – only it's more of a slow creeper: the story of the disappearing hotel room. The legend has it that just before the opening of the Great Exposition in Paris in 1889 a distraught young English woman rushed into the British Embassy and reported both her mother - and the hotel room she had left her in as missing. The story has been told many times through fact, fantasy and fiction ever since. This is the one I like best.

The girl and her mother were on their way home from India and had to spend a few nights in Paris. The mother chooses room 43 which is elaborately decorated with rose-strewn wallpaper and plum-coloured velvet curtains, and the daughter has the adjoining room, 42, which is rather plainer. In the middle of the night the daughter hears the mother moaning and goes in to see what is wrong. It's obvious that the mother is seriously ill and so the daughter asks the hotel manager if there is a doctor who could come and see her. After examining the unconscious mother and talking excitedly to the hotel manager in French, the doctor pronounces that the mother is seriously ill and must have some medicine. The only trouble is that the proper medication can only be found in his office on the other side of the city. The doctor says that he must stay with the patient and the daughter must go in his carriage and carry a note to the doctor's wife who would hand her the drugs.

What should have been a short journey ends up taking hours and hours. The carriage seems to travel in slow circles in spite of the daughter urging the driver to hurry

Photo Quentin Craven

and then the doctor's wife takes an age to find the right medicine.

Finally, the frustrated daughter arrives back at the hotel to find all queries about her mother met with blank stares. The manager says that she arrived alone, the doctor says he doesn't know of any sick woman. The daughter demands to see the register and doesn't recognise the signature next to room 43. She pushes past the doctor and manager to rush up the stairs and into her mother's room, but it is decorated completely differently and there is no sign of the rose-strewn wallpaper or the plum coloured velvet curtains. At this point she flees to the Embassy where she is received with sympathy but general disbelief. Trapped in a hideous nightmare the daughter goes home and ends her days in a mental hospital.

Sometimes the location for the story varies, but it is usually set in Paris and always during a busy time (hence the slow cab journey and the delays). In some versions the daughter has difficulty speaking to the manager and the doctor because of a language barrier, on rare occasions the searcher and the one sought after are not mother and daughter but young men. In one telling, when the daughter gets back to the hotel, the manager and the doctor are two completely different people.

Photo Creatas.co.uk

In nearly all versions the story ends when the daughter gives up and rushes to the Embassy, but some have her doggedly sniffing out the truth. Usually it is that the mother has contracted the plague and the hotel (and the city) conspire to get the mother's body out of the way and mislead the daughter before anybody finds out and there is a mass panic. In this story the cab driver is obviously in on the conspiracy, deliberately going slowly and getting 'lost' so the doctor and the manager have time to refurbish the room.

Versions of this story have appeared in the following novels: Belloc Lowndes' 1913 *The End of Her Honeymoon*, Lawrence Rising's 1920 *She Who Was Helena Cass*, Sir Basil Thomson's 1925 *The Vanishing of Mrs Fraser* and Ernest Hemingway's 1926 *The Torrent Of Spring.* It has also turned up in the films *The Midnight Warning* (1932) and *So Long At The Fair* (1950).

The National Cycle Network

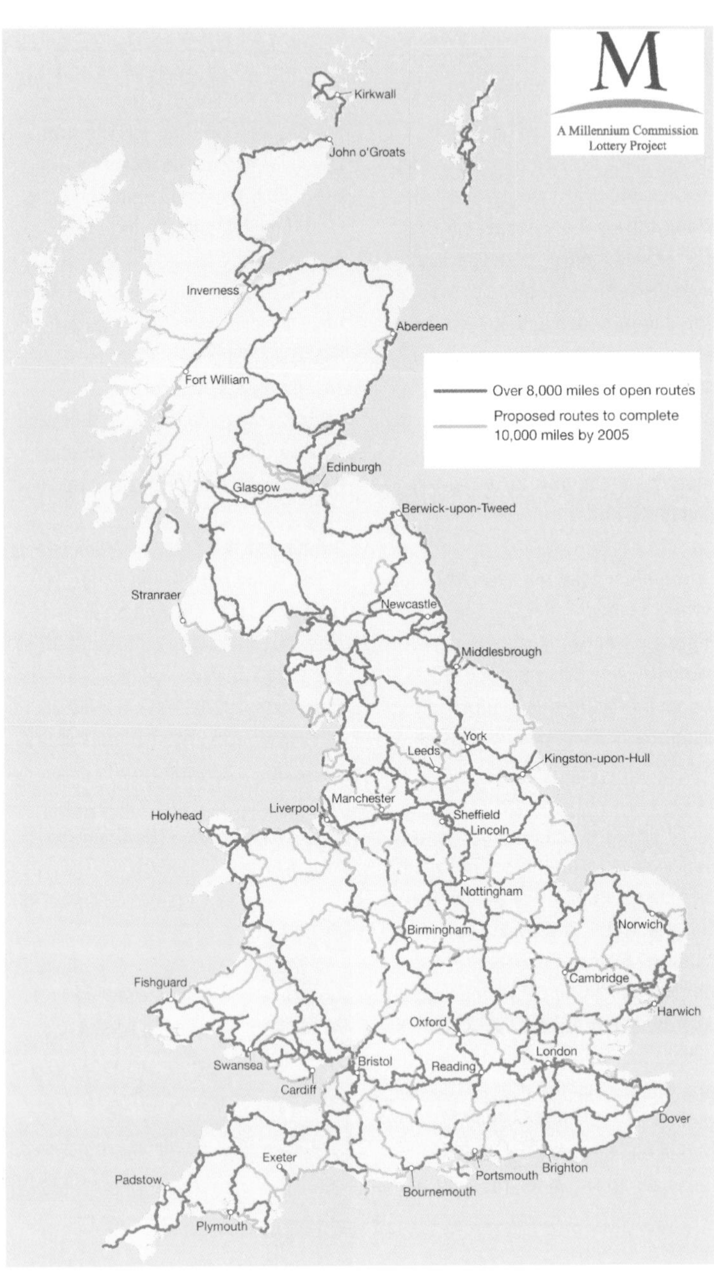

Places near the National Cycle Network

These Special Places are within 2 miles of the National Cycle Network.

England
Bath & N.E. Somerset 1 • 2 • 3 • 4 • 5
Berkshire 6 • 7
Brighton & Hove 8 • 9 • 10 • 11
Bristol 12 • 13
Cambridgeshire 14
Cornwall 18 • 19 • 20 • 21 • 23 • 24 • 29 • 30 • 31 • 35
Cumbria 36 • 37 • 40 • 41 • 43 • 44
Devon 59 • 63 • 65 • 66
Dorset 73 • 74 • 78
Durham 79
Essex 81
Gloucestershire 84 • 85 • 86 • 87 • 88
Herefordshire 101
Kent 108 • 109 • 110
London 112 • 113 • 114 • 115 • 116 • 117 • 118 • 119 • 120
Norfolk 123 • 124 • 125
Northumberland 133
Oxfordshire 136 • 140 • 141 • 142
Somerset 149 • 152 • 156 • 157
Suffolk 159 • 160 • 161
Sussex 168
Warwickshire 169 • 171
Yorkshire 176 • 181 • 182 • 186 • 188

Scotland
Dumfries & Galloway 204
Edinburgh & the Lothians 207 • 208 • 209
Glasgow 212 • 213 • 214
Highland 218 • 219
Orkney 234
Perth & Kinross 235 • 237 • 239

Wales
Cardiff 243 • 244
Carmarthenshire 246
Gwynedd 249
Pembrokeshire 253 • 254
Powys 257 • 258 • 259

Photo Quentin Craven

Fragile Earth series

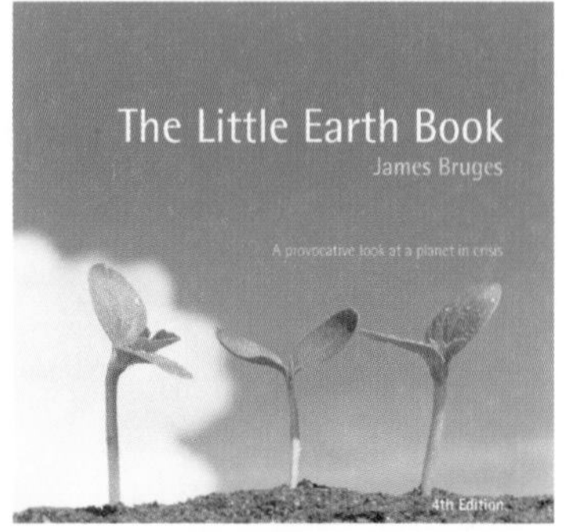

The Little Earth Book

Edition 4, £6.99

By James Bruges

A little book that has proved both hugely popular – and provocative. This new edition has chapters on Islam, Climate Change and The Tyranny of Corporations.

The Little Food Book

Edition 1, £6.99

By Craig Sams, Chairman of the Soil Association

An explosive account of the food we eat today. Never have we been at such risk - from our food. This book will help understand what's at stake.

The Little Money Book

Edition 1, £6.99

By David Boyle, an associate of the New Economics Foundation

This pithy, wry little guide will tell you where money comes from, what it means, what it's doing to the planet and what we might be able to do about it.

www.fragile-earth.com

Six Days

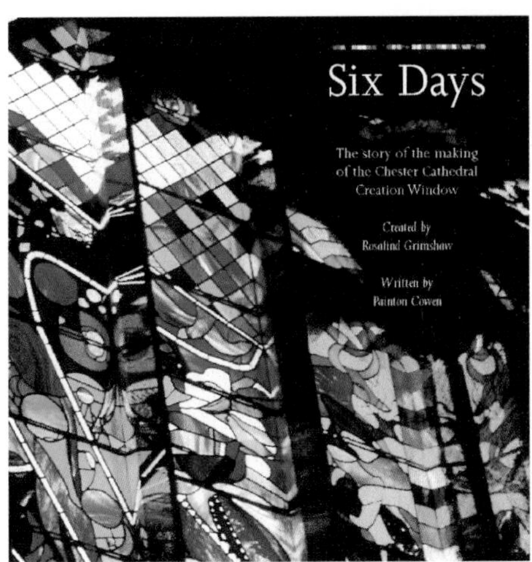

Celebrating the triumph of creativity over adversity.

An inspiring and heart-rending story of the making of the stained glass 'Creation' window at Chester Cathedral by a woman battling with debilitating Parkinson's disease.

"Within a few seconds, the tears were running down my cheeks. The window was one of the most beautiful things I had ever seen. It is a tour-de force, playing with light like no other window ..."
Anthropologist Hugh Brody

In 1983, Ros Grimshaw, a distinguished designer, artist and creator of stained glass windows, was diagnosed with Parkinson's disease. Refusing to allow her illness to prevent her from working, Ros became even more adept at her craft, and in 2000 won the commission to design and make the 'Creation' Stained Glass Window for Chester Cathedral.

Six Days traces the evolution of the window from the first sketches to its final, glorious completion as a rare and wonderful tribute to Life itself: for each of the six 'days' of Creation recounted in Genesis, there is a scene below that is relevant to the world of today and tomorrow.

Heart-rending extracts from Ros's diary capture the personal struggle involved. Superb photography captures the luminescence of the stunning stained glass, while the story weaves together essays, poems, and moving contributions from Ros's partner, Patrick Costeloe.

Available from Alastair Sawday Publishing £12.99

Order Form

All these books are available in major bookshops or you may order them direct. Post and packaging are FREE within the UK.

British Hotels, Inns & Other Places	£13.99
Bed & Breakfast for Garden Lovers	£14.99
British Holiday Homes	£9.99
Pubs & Inns of England & Wales	£13.99
London	£9.99
British Bed & Breakfast	£14.99
French Bed & Breakfast	£15.99
French Hotels, Châteaux & Inns	£13.99
French Holiday Homes	£11.99
Paris Hotels	£9.99
Ireland	£12.99
Spain	£13.99
Portugal	£8.99
Italy	£12.99
Mountains of Europe	£9.99
Europe with courses & activities	£12.99
India	£10.99
Morocco	£10.99
The Little Earth Book	£6.99
The Little Food Book	£6.99
The Little Money Book	£6.99
Six Days	£12.99

Please make cheques payable to Alastair Sawday Publishing. Total £ __________

Please send cheques to: Alastair Sawday Publishing, The Home Farm Stables, Barrow Gurney, Bristol BS48 3RW. For credit card orders call 01275 464891 or order directly from our web site www.specialplacestostay.com

Title First name Surname

Address

Postcode Tel

BH6

If you do not wish to receive mail from other like-minded companies, please tick here ☐
If you would prefer not to receive information about special offers on our books, please tick here ☐

Report Form

If you have any comments on entries in this guide, please let us have them. If you have a favourite house, hotel, inn or other new discovery, please let us know about it. You can e-mail info@sawdays.co.uk, too.

Existing entry:

Book title: ______________________________

Entry no: ______________ Edition no: ______________

New recommendation:

Country: ______________________________

Property name: ______________________________

Address: ______________________________

____

____

____

Tel: ______________________________

Comments: Report:

____

____

____

____

____

____

____

Your name: ______________________________

Address: ______________________________

____

____

Tel: ______________________________

Please send completed form to ASP, The Home Farm Stables, Barrow Gurney, Bristol BS48 3RW or go to www.specialplacestostay.com and click on 'contact'. Thank you.

www.special-escapes.co.uk

- New Maps
- Hotlists
- Extra pictures
- Extra links
- Extended searches
- Full write-ups
- Owner content

Discover your perfect self-catering escape in Britain...

We have launched a brand new self-catering web site covering England, Scotland and Wales. With the same punch and attitude as all our printed guides, www.special-escapes.co.uk celebrates only those places that we have visited and genuinely like – castles, cottages, bothies and more...

Special Escapes will be a shining beacon among the mass of bleak holiday cottage sites cluttering the search engine pages. Each place will be written about with the flair and style for which Alastair Sawday Publishing is so well known - and since it won't be published anywhere else, you'll be able to read the full entry, not just the first couple of lines.

Russell Wilkinson,
Web Site Manager
website@specialplacestostay.com

Quick reference indices

Wheelchair-accessible

These places have full and approved wheelchair facilities.

England

Scotland

Wales

Limited mobility

Need a ground-floor bedroom and bathroom? Try these.

England

Photo Sara Allan

Quick reference indices

Photo www.paulgroomphotography.com

Organic

Most ingredients are organically grown, home-grown or locally grown.

Under £100

These places offer a double room for under £100 a night

Photo www.paulgroomphotography.com

Special deals – weekends

Special deals available at weekends

Quick reference indices

Special deals – weekdays

These places offer weekday reductions

Photo Phillipa Gibbon

Gardens

These are the places for lazing on the lawn or gasping at the greenery

England

Bath & N.E. Somerset 2
Bristol 12
Cheshire 15
Cornwall 16 • 20 • 21 • 23 • 27 • 28 • 29
Cumbria 38 • 39 • 40 • 43 • 45
Derbyshire 46 • 47
Devon 48 • 50 • 54 • 55 • 56 • 57 • 58 • 59 • 61 • 65 • 66 • 68 • 71
Dorset 72 • 75
Durham 79
Gloucestershire 82 • 83 • 89 • 91 • 94
Hampshire 98
Herefordshire 100 • 101
Isle of Wight 105

Photo Jackie King

Kent 107 • 108
Manchester 122
Norfolk 126 • 128 • 129 • 130
Oxfordshire 137 • 140
Shropshire 146 • 148
Somerset 152 • 155 • 156
Suffolk 161
Sussex 166 • 167
Warwickshire 170 • 171
Wiltshire 172
Worcestershire 174
Yorkshire 176 • 177

Channel Islands

Jersey 191

Scotland

Aberdeenshire 193
Argyll & Bute 195 • 196 • 197 • 199
Dumfries & Galloway 205 • 206
Edinburgh & the Lothians 209
Highland 217 • 219 • 222 • 228
Moray 230
Perth & Kinross 237 • 238

Wales

Denbighshire 247
Gwynedd 249 • 250
Powys 256 • 257 • 259 • 262

Peace and quiet

These places are in particularly quiet & peaceful locations

England

Bath & N.E. Somerset 2 • 3
Bristol 12

Quick reference indices

Meeting room available.

Photo John Coe

Photo www.paulgroomphotography.com

Modem connections available here.

Channel Islands

Scotland

Wales

Photo above www.paulgroomphotography.com
Photo opposite Phillipa Gibbon

Index by property name

Index by property name

Index by property name

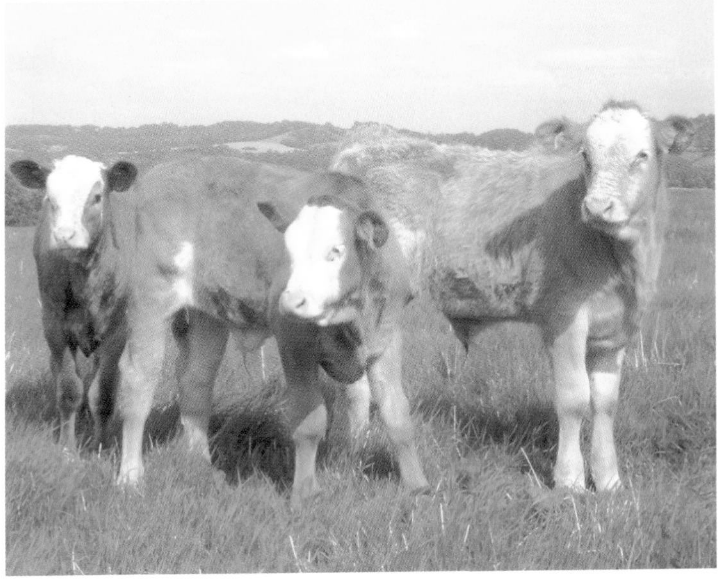

Photo Luke Hasell

Index by place name

Index by place name

Photo Phillipa Gibbon

How to use this book

1 Yorkshire

The Star Inn

Harome, Nr Helmsley, Yorkshire YO62 5JE

2 You know you've 'hit the jackpot' as soon as you walk into The Star – it ticks over with such modest ease and calm authority. Andrew and Jacquie arrived in 1996, baby daughters Daisy and Tilly not long after, and the Michelin star in 2002. It's been a formidable turnaround given this 14th-century inn had an iffy local reputation when they took over, yet there's no arrogance; the brochure simply says: "He cooks, and she looks after you"... and how! Andrew's food is rooted in Yorkshire tradition, refined with French flair and written in plain English on ever-changing menus: try dressed Whitby crab, beef from two miles away, Ryedale deer, or maybe Theakston ale cake. Fabulous bedrooms, all ultra-modern yet seriously rustic, are just a stroll away. Thatched and 15th-century, Black Eagle Cottage has three suites; the rest of the rooms are in Cross House Lodge, a breathtaking new barn conversion; the largest room has its own snooker table. There's also the Mousey Thompson bar, the roof mural, the deli and the Coffee Loft – just possibly the most enchanting attic in the world. Brilliant.

rooms	11: 6 doubles, 2 double/twins, 3 suites.	3
price	£120-£195.	4
meals	Lunch from £3.50. Dinner, à la carte, £25.	5
closed	Mondays inc Bank Holiday Mondays. Christmas Day.	6
directions	From Thirsk, A170 towards Scarborough. Through Helmsley, then right, signed Harome. Inn in village.	7

Inn 8

Andrew & Jacquie Pern
tel 01439 770397
fax 01439 771833
web www.thestaratharome.co.uk

Map 7 Entry 183 10

9

explanation

1 county

2 write up
Written by us.

3 rooms
Assume rooms are en suite; unless we state otherwise.

4 price
The price shown is for two people sharing a room. Half-board prices are per person. A price range incorporates room/seasonal differences.

5 meals
Prices are per person. If breakfast isn't included we give the price.

6 closed
When given in months, this means for the whole of the named months and the time in between.

7 directions
Use as a guide and travel with a good map.

8 type of place
Usually either a hotel, inn or restaurant with rooms.

9 symbols
see the last page of the book for a fuller explanation:

- wheelchair facilities
- easily accessible bedrooms
- all children welcome
- no smoking anywhere
- cash or cheque only
- good vegetarian dinner options
- guests' pets welcome
- owners' pets live here
- pool
- bikes on the premises
- tennis on the premises
- information on local walks

10 map & entry numbers

www.specialplacestostay.com

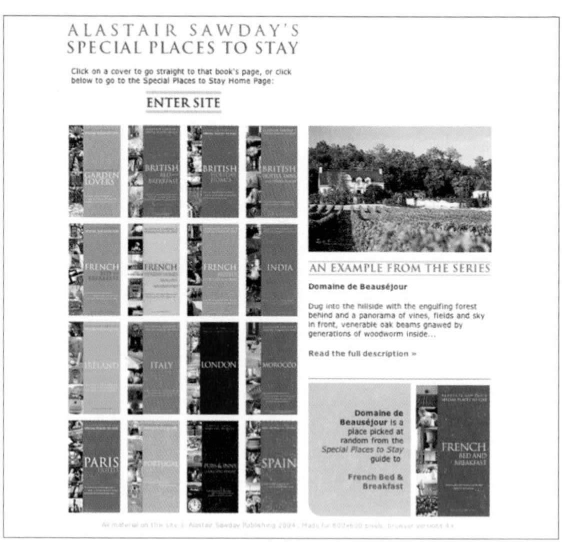

Britain • France • India • Ireland • Italy • Morocco • Portugal • Spain... all in one place!

On the unfathomable and often unnavigable sea of online accommodation pages, those who have discovered www.specialplacestostay.com have found it to be an island of reliability. Not only will you find a database full of trustworthy, up-to-date information about all of our Special Places to Stay, but also:

- Links to the web sites of all of the places in the series
- Colourful, clickable, interactive maps to help you find the right place
- The opportunity to make most bookings by e-mail – even if you don't have e-mail yourself
- Online purchasing of our books, securely and cheaply
- Regular, exclusive special offers on books
- The latest news about future editions and future titles
- Special offers and news from our owners

The site is constantly evolving and is frequently updated with news and special features that won't appear anywhere else but in our window on the worldwide web.

Russell Wilkinson, Web Site Manager
website@specialplacestostay.com

If you'd like to receive news and updates about our books by e-mail, send a message to newsletter@specialplacestostay.com